Although much significant material on the Italian Fascist party became available when the regime collapsed, scholars have not made extensive use of it until now. In this study, which is based on all the available sources, Professor Germino describes the functions of the party, explains how it was organized to perform its tasks, and discusses conflicts between the party and other power elements in the dictatorship. He reaches a conclusion contrary to that of most other scholars — that Fascist Italy was a full-fledged totalitarian state resembling Nazi Germany and Soviet Russia in political structure and ideological content.

The Italian Fascist Party in Power

THE ITALIAN
FASCIST PARTY
IN POWER

A Study in Totalitarian Rule

Dante L. Germino

UNIVERSITY OF MINNESOTA PRESS · MINNEAPOLIS

PRINTED IN THE UNITED STATES OF AMERICA AT THE JONES PRESS, INC., MINNEAPOLIS

3 2

Library of Congress Catalog Card Number: 59-10186

PUBLISHED IN GREAT BRITAIN, INDIA, AND PAKISTAN BY THE OXFORD UNIVERSITY PRESS, LONDON, BOMBAY, AND KARACHI AND IN CANADA BY THOMAS ALLEN, LTD., TORONTO

TO THE MEMORY OF MARGARET

Preface

THIS work is an analysis of a totalitarian single party in action. An attempt is made to describe the functions which the Italian Fascist party performed, how it was organized to fulfill these tasks effectively, and the kinds of conflicts that it had with other centers of power in the dictatorship as a result of its activities. Since the party is the core of any totalitarian dictatorship — and my reasons for adjudging Mussolini's empire to have been totalitarian are explained in the final chapter — it is reasonable to expect that a treatment of a given totalitarian party will also shed considerable light on the nature of the entire regime in which that institution is embedded. I believe that the time is overdue for a fresh look at the Italian Fascist regime, now that it has passed into history.

Although political scientists displayed great interest in Italian Fascism while it was in power, there has been almost no writing on this subject since the fall of the dictatorship. This situation compares most unfavorably with the feverish research which scholars have conducted on Nazi Germany. Lack of interest in Italy is difficult to understand, for since the destruction of the regime scholars have had access to a large quantity of significant new information, and they should now be able to see these painful twenty years of Italian history in more nearly accurate perspective.

With the notable exceptions of Gaetano Salvemini and Luigi Salvatorelli, reputable Italian scholars have preferred to forget what Mussolini sonorously proclaimed "The Fascist Era." One may respect their reasons for choosing this course, even though repression of the unpleasant may be considered as psychologically unhealthy and morally vitiating for nations as it is for individuals. The reticence of foreign political scientists and specialists in Italian studies to grapple with Fascism demands some other explanation. Part of the difficulty may be traced to the unavailability of certain documents. The confiscating, editing, and publishing of secret papers did not occur in Italy as it did in Germany, because Italy had no war crimes trials prosecuted by the Allies. The Italian government, for its own reasons, has not seen fit to allow scholars to consult any of the Fascist documents in the possession of the *Archivio di Stato*. It is probable that no one will be permitted to investigate the *Archivio*'s material relating to the party for fifty years. Despite this blackout of possibly valuable material, there is enough new information to justify further research on Fascist Italy at this time. Existing sources on the party are quite sufficient to enable the political scientist to sketch with accuracy the major contours of the subject.

The present volume does not essay to give a detailed history of the party, either as a whole or in particular provinces. Rather, the over-all role of the party and its central functions within the dictatorship are the foci of attention. I have based my research upon the many volumes of the printed "orders of the day" issued by the various divisions of the *Partito Nazionale Fascista*'s national office, the publications of provincial and local party organizations, the large amount of secondary material written by Fascists and non-Fascists on the party and the regime, and the copious memoirs of former Fascist leaders, writing in retrospect after the fall of Fascism. Most of the research was carried out in Italy, where I was a Fulbright scholar during the year 1954–1955. In addition to examining the sources listed above, I obtained aid in clarifying obscure points from interviews with Italian political scientists, historians, and former Fascist party officials. This is the first time that a scholarly study of the role of the Fascist party has been attempted, although a number of primarily juridical analyses were published while the regime was in existence.

A word should be added about the time limits which have been imposed. I have chosen to concentrate on the period from the abolition of opposition parties on January 3, 1925, to the beginning of World War II. The study will deal only briefly with the party before the March on Rome and its part in the three-year consolidation of the dictatorship because this is intended to be an analysis of why the party continued to exist and what function it served after it secured power for its leader. I have decided to exclude the period of World War II from primary consideration because during the war Italy became necesarily ever more subordinate to the commands of Nazi Germany. At least until 1937, and in fact until 1939, Fascist Italy, although influenced by Germany, maintained an independent existence. This book, which considers the operation of the internal political imperatives of a particular dictatorship, understandably seeks to eliminate as many extraneous factors as possible.

I have tried not to write about the party in static terms. The totalitarian single party was perpetually evolving. In contemplating its activities at any point in the history of the regime, I have sought to indicate which stage in its evolution the party had reached at that time. Institutions, however, do not merely change; they develop toward an end, a pattern. In order to understand a phenomenon it is well to know both the phases of its growth and its appearance when fully developed. The Fascist party began as a tiny seed, but it grew to be a noxious, poisonous plant. How it looked in full bloom is at least as interesting as a history of its growth. This is more a study of a party *in esse* than *in posse*.

To Professor Carl J. Friedrich, my teacher and friend, I owe the original suggestion that I undertake a study of the Fascist party. He encouraged and aided me at every step in the writing of this book and my debts to him cannot be sufficiently acknowledged. Professor Zbigniew K. Brzezinski also read the manuscript in one of its early forms and made helpful criticisms on the basis of his extensive knowledge of totalitarianism. My distinguished colleague at Wellesley, Professor Louise Overacker, read the manuscript and gave me needed encouragement at a critical point in its preparation. All students of Italian Fascism are indebted to Luigi Salvatorelli for his mammoth history of the regime; he was kind enough to receive me at his home and to discuss Fascism with me; the late Professor Gaetano Salvemini rendered me a similar courtesy. I am grateful to both of these astute observers of the Italian dictatorship.

Without the assistance of a Fulbright grant I would not have been able to study Fascism at first hand in Italy. Signorina Cipriana Scelba of the American Commission for Cultural Exchange with Italy was most obliging in every way, as were the other staff members of the commission. In the summer of 1957 Wellesley College awarded me a Huber Foundation grant, which enabled me to complete work on the manuscript. To all of these individuals and institutions, and to the person who prefers to go unnamed, my deep, if inadequately expressed, thanks.

Any errors in the general conception of the work or in such matters as translation from the Italian are, of course, exclusively my own.

D. L. G.

Wellesley, Massachusetts
December 1958

Contents

The Italian Fascist Party in Power

As man is the most noble of animals if he be perfect in virtue, so he is the lowest of all, if he be severed from law and justice.

Aristotle, *Politics*, 1253a

1

A New Tool for a New Despotism

ALTHOUGH it is safe to say that the Fascists were always wrong when they claimed that Mussolini was always right, few would deny that *il Duce* knew whereof he spoke when, in his famous and definitive article on Fascist doctrine, he intoned: "A party which governs a nation in a totalitarian manner is a new fact in history. Comparisons . . . are impossible."

Mussolini had on many occasions felt the power of his party. When he appeared with the party secretary on the balcony of the Palazzo Venezia in Rome he could be certain beforehand of what would follow. He would greet there no undisciplined mob, but a gigantic organized collectivity, responding as one man to the secretary's ritual shout and raised right arm. The words *Salutiamo il Duce, Fondatore dell'Impero* would reverberate through this vast and ancient *piazza*. The throng of tens of thousands of persons, led by the party delegations, militia units, and youth groups arranged before the dictator in precise formations, would whip itself into a frenzy of adulation and enthusiastic submission by the finish of its leader's oration. Mussolini was aware that, even as he spoke in Rome, his voice was being piped into the main square of every city, town, and village of Italy with nearly identical effect, thanks to the party's careful manipulation. When he had retired to his chambers, exhilarated and exhausted, he could with satisfaction ask himself whether there had been any previous dictator able thus to hold an entire nation in his grasp. He knew the answer: he had possession of something unique in history, a new tool with which to capture and dominate the masses in a new way.

Rome's own hallowed soil bore the prints of many great dictators.

All of them, from the Roman Emperors to Cola di Rienzo, the four-teenth-century mystic and adventurer who captured the city and during his brief rule dreamed of the resurrection of ancient Rome's imperial glory, appealed from time to time to the masses against various forms of "privilege," but they had no conception of an incessant, organized, and directed process for keeping the masses perpetually wedded to their cause.[1] The powerful Renaissance tyrants who won Machiavelli's admiration came no closer to the totalitarian dictator; they were in comparison but "lonely hero[es]," who lacked "the massive capability of a modern militant party."[2] Still more recent history failed to produce examples of despots who had at their disposal what we could call today a single mass party. The two Napoleons fall short in this respect, and the idea of a mass party would never even have occurred to the absolute monarchs of the Age of Enlightenment.

The single mass party was an institution unique in the history of dictatorships because the totalitarian dictatorship of the twentieth century was a new form of despotism demanding new techniques for the realization of its aims. Tyrannical, authoritarian, and autocratic regimes were as old as Western history. Plato and Aristotle wrote descriptions of the tyrant which are still unexcelled and which provide us with valuable insights into the latest manifestations of the despotic urge in man. But if these great mentors of the West had been able to return during the decade before World War II and to observe the political systems of Germany, Italy, and the Soviet Union, they would have conceded that here was a new kind of tyranny unforeseen in their original analyses.

The novelty of the three great twentieth-century despotisms[3] was evident both in their objectives and in the methods of control and manipulation which were available to them. One trait that would have astonished Plato and Aristotle was that the new dictator and his guardsmen were obviously not primarily interested in obtaining the traditional fruits of despotic power. Wealth, adulation, women, the headiness of power — these were not their main concern. Plato's masterly portrait of the totally unjust man,[4] whose soul is consumed by desire and who is beyond the control of reason, seems only partially to apply to these modern tyrants. For these were ascetic men, who were not merely seeking to retain power for their own personal advantage. We may call them "ideologists," for they did not regard the retention of power as an end in itself. The ideological dictator was content with nothing less than the perpetual expansion of his own system of political faith. He was impelled by that faith to conquer and to destroy — even at the risk of his own life. He thought of himself as the perfectly just man, who sought power only as a means with which to build a new, perfect society on earth.

Each of the new ruling cliques had a different vision of society. Hitler, Goebbels, and Himmler, the ideologists of Germany, rushed ruthlessly to create a racially pure *Volk*, and they saw the Third Reich as the culmination of history. Stalin, Molotov, and Khrushchev professed to labor to achieve the Marxist goal of a classless society, in which man would no longer be alienated from the means of production but would dominate and control them to his own advantage. Mussolini, Starace, and Farinacci envisaged the construction of a Third Rome, a universal political entity based on the principles of Fascism. Fascism promised to overcome the rootlessness of atomized democratic-liberal society by incorporating the individual into a rejuvenated Roman *civitas*. The New Rome, with its massive "corporative" structure into which every individual would be fitted and in the service of which every person could find fulfillment and the release of his vital energy, would perfectly reconcile the individual with the state.

Although the images of the three societies were different, the ideologies supporting them were similar in one respect. They were political religions, imbued with a startling messianic quality. All three ideologies looked to the establishment of a final, perfected realm, the chiliastic termination of history. This was what Professor Talmon has termed "political messianism." The ideologists attempted to build heaven on earth, or, as Nicholas Berdiaev aptly wrote, a "Kingdom of God without God."[5]

Faith in the illimitable capacity of man, or, better, of the right men, to perfect the world is a relatively recent development in Western intellectual history. This most extravagant of man's self-intoxications was related to the decline of belief in traditional religious restraints and to the remarkable advances in technology beginning in the nineteenth century.[6] The advent of modern means of production, transportation, and communication spawned in some Western minds the

5

hope of achieving a flawless world, characterized by social stability, individual happiness and security, and a high level of material prosperity. These were the ideas of the Age of Ideology, and the totalitarian dictators took Auguste Comte's vision of history's Third Stage seriously.

THE NEW DESPOTISM TRIUMPHS IN ITALY

Almost exactly five years after the first totalitarian regime in history had established itself in Russia, the Italian Fascists successfully conducted their March on Rome. The victory was swift and surprising even to the Fascists themselves; there is as yet no fully adequate explanation for the total collapse of liberal parliamentary democracy in Italy on October 28, 1922. There probably never will be, for the web of history is too complex for the mind of man to untangle. However, it is possible to isolate some of the strands.

Adverse historical, economic, and social factors made the task of the leaders of postwar Italian democracy an arduous one. The war which Italy had presumably won had brought her nothing but widespread unemployment, economic instability, and civil unrest. As a nation she could not even gain solace in substantial territorial gains. Fiume and Dalmatia had been withheld from her, and, rightly or wrongly, some groups of veterans were convinced that Italy had been betrayed at Versailles and at Rapallo. Feelings of disillusionment, rootlessness, and alienation were common among great numbers of persons unable to find a reasonably secure status in the rapidly shifting social structure of the times.

In addition to these "organic" factors making for chaos and disorder in the political realm, there was a lack of effective leaders among the proponents of Italian democracy. Except for the brief ministry of Ivanoe Bonomi, the premiership was occupied during the period 1919 to 1922 by three Italian liberals. Francesco Nitti, the first peacetime head of the government, was competent if unspectacular; however, he was unable quickly and energetically to halt the deterioration of the Italian economy during the immediate postwar period, when matters were at their worst. Nitti lost the confidence of Parliament in the spring of 1920; as his successor, the center parties called on the near-octogenarian Giovanni Giolitti. Giolitti, the dominant figure in Italian politics during the decade before the war, proved to be unequal to the task. Although Italy made some economic progress under this veteran politician, his leadership in many areas was unimaginative and indecisive. When the old master of shrewd parliamentary maneuvering finally stepped down because of the absence of a dependable majority early in the fateful year of 1922, his understudy, Luigi Facta, apparently an average man in every respect, was the only person on whom the democratic parties could agree. The choice was an unfortunate one, for he was so weak and vacillating as to be not really a leader at all.

During the year preceding Facta's investiture, Italy had become the preserve of private political armies. Law and order were a mockery in many regions. Although he pledged himself to restore the dignity and authority of the state, Facta actually did little or nothing to halt the building up of Fascist armed gangs. Nor was the Italian monarchy a rallying point for supporters of a constitutional regime; concerned above all with the preservation of his crown, the weak-willed Victor Emmanuel III, who later became the complete captive of Fascism, was a political force of negligible significance.

Into this vacuum in leadership came Benito Mussolini, an unscrupulous fanatic with a flair for propaganda, organization, political strategy, and mass agitation.

The man who was to rule all of Italy had had a checkered career before World War I. Born in the Romagna region, of lower middle class parents, Mussolini during his early adult life worked at occasional jobs both in his native country and in Switzerland. His thinking during this period was strongly anticlerical and tinged with romantic anarchism. After resettling in Italy he became active in the Socialist party and for several years edited the party's newspaper in Milan. In 1915 he dramatically repudiated the official Socialist position of neutrality, and came out for Italian intervention in the World War on the side of the Allies. For this action he was expelled from the party, along with a small band of other interventionist Socialists. During the war, he had a brief and undistinguished period of military service in the Italian army.

It was after the war that Mussolini decided to form his own political movement, and he took the leading role in founding the first *Fascio di Combattimento* (literally Bundle for Combat). The greater part of the fifty to one hundred persons who met in the hall of a building overlooking Milan's Piazza San Sepolcro on March 23, 1919, to pass on the *fascio*'s constitution were ex-Socialists who, like Mussolini, had split with that party in 1915 over the neutrality issue. At first the movement had only an amorphous ideological program; Fascism, it was announced, was a movement above political parties which had as its aim the fundamental renovation of the national life. Although there was a good deal of policy disagreement among the members, and contradictory statements may be found in its first program, there were certain ideas shared by the great majority of its adherents from its inception, the most significant being the exaltation of action and violence and the detestation of the liberal parliamentary regime. Much of what later came to be known as characteristic of Italian Fascism was taken over by Mussolini from the poet Gabriele d'Annunzio, with whose unlawful occupation of the city of Fiume from September 1919 to December 1920 the Fascists were in sympathy. The invocation of the greatness of imperial Rome, the concept of a corporativist society, the Fascist salute, the black shirt, the dialogue between leader and crowd, the use of the mass plebiscite — this agglomeration of symbols and ideas was borrowed by the Fascists from the little mad poet-dictator.

Within a matter of months after the historic meeting of March 1919 in Milan, Fascist organizations had been formed over the greater part of the Italian peninsula. The movement was strongest in northern and central cities such as Genoa, Cremona, Bergamo, Brescia, Trieste, Bologna, and Florence; but there were also well-organized *fasci* in Rome and Naples. Almost from the very beginning, the movement fed and thrived on violence. By 1920 the technique of the "punitive expedition," carried out by local "squads of action," had been developed. Under the direction of squad leaders like Roberto Farinacci, Italo Balbo, Giuseppe Bottai, Augusto Turati, and Achille Starace, these armed gangs burned Socialist newspaper buildings and meeting halls, and administered severe beatings to active members of the leftist parties. The public justification for these tactics was that Italy faced the danger of a Communist[7] revolution; because the liberal state was too weak and inept to deal with this menace, Fascism had no recourse but to take matters into its own hands and defend the populace against "antinationalist subversion."

It is now commonly accepted that the danger of a victorious proletarian revolution in Italy, if it had ever been grave, had passed by the

8

end of 1920. In the spring and summer of both 1919 and 1920 the revolutionary segments of the Socialist party had attempted to bring about the destruction of the state by means of general strikes, the occupation of factories and farms (especially in the cities of northern Italy and the agricultural regions of the Po valley), and other similar measures. Although these tactics compounded the economic and political woes of the liberal regime, they were not successful, and it was clear even to the Socialists themselves that their attempt to take over direct control of the state had failed.

Yet, in spite of the fact that the danger of overthrow of the government had passed and that the control of the Italian labor movement by extremist Socialists was growing weaker rather than stronger after the summer of 1920, the Fascists chose in the winter and spring of 1921 to commence a great intensification of their terroristic expeditions against Socialist and Communist organizations, rallies, strikes, and so on. As the crusade of the Blacks against the Reds gathered momentum, support came to the Fascists from certain industrialists and wealthy landowners, who viewed Fascism as the last bulwark against Communism. Not a few liberals were content, also, for the state to sit back and let the Fascists teach left-wing radicals a lesson. The success of the Fascist punitive expeditions increased the prestige of the Fascist movement and swelled its ranks with new members. Indeed, the first noteworthy showing made by the Fascists in an Italian general election came in May 1921, as the campaign of terror increased in tempo.

By the spring of 1922, the strength of the Fascist movement had grown enormously, as mass demonstrations at Milan, Bologna, and elsewhere attested. Emboldened by these gains, Mussolini, head of the Fascist parliamentary delegation and indisputable *Duce* — leader — of his party, began to call for new elections and to threaten the seizure of power by his own forces if his demands were not granted, which they were not. In early October of the same year, Mussolini moved to centralize the command of the various squads and to prepare them for possible direct action by appointing a Quadrumvirate to draw up plans for a *coup d'état*.[8] His party was received with considerable popular acclaim when it staged its national congress at Naples later in the month. It was now clear to all observers that Fascism had vastly increased its following since the elections of May 1921.

With the resignation of the Facta government in late October, Mussolini and his cohorts determined on action. The Quadrumvirate "seized" the Umbrian town of Perugia, within striking distance of Rome, on October 27 as a preliminary to the conquest of the capital city. It was announced that squads all over the country were mobilized, and that many officers of the regular army were ready to cooperate with the Fascist storm troopers. In the face of the Fascist threat both Facta and the king vacillated; a proclamation of a state of siege which had been voted by the caretaker cabinet was refused the royal signature at the last moment, perhaps on the advice of Facta himself. During the evening of October 28 thousands of Blackshirts converged on Rome unmolested by the army or the police, and Victor Emmanuel, after attempting unsuccessfully to persuade Mussolini to serve in a government headed by Antonio Salandra, a conservative, called the Duce to Rome from Milan to assume the premiership. Thus, liberal democracy in Italy surrendered without so much as a shot being fired.

It is possible now to look back over the history of Fascism from its accession to power in 1922 until the outbreak of World War II in 1940 and discern five phases in its development. The first phase, which lasted from October 28, 1922, until January 3, 1925, was a period during which Mussolini, while he steadily consolidated his power, maintained at least the pretense of constitutional legality. Opposition parties, their strength greatly reduced by new elections, were permitted representation in the Chamber of Deputies. Mussolini governed with a coalition cabinet composed of Fascist, Nationalist, Liberal, and Catholic (Popular) deputies who were willing to cooperate with his regime. However, freedom of the press and other civil liberties were greatly curtailed, and Fascist party squads were permitted to roam the country almost at will harassing and humiliating those who voiced opposition.

The murder of the Socialist deputy Giacomo Matteotti by Fascist thugs in the summer of 1924 produced the first major crisis of the regime. For several months, Mussolini wavered in the face of popular indignation over the episode; apparently he even seriously considered resigning from his post.[9] The most serious threat to his continued rule occurred when a large number of non-Fascist members walked out of the Chamber of Deputies to meet secretly in various places in Rome, hoping by this dramatic gesture to bring about Mussolini's fall. This

10

group called themselves the Aventine Secession, a name drawn from
an episode in the history of the ancient Roman Republic when the
leaders of the plebs are reputed to have seceded from the city to the
Aventine hill. Urged on by the Fascist party leadership, Mussolini
decided finally to resolve the crisis in a manner most tragic for the future history of his country: in the famous "intransigent" speech to the
Chamber of Deputies on January 3, 1925, he announced that Italy was
thenceforth a totalitarian state, that all opposition parties were disbanded, and that all the force of the state would be employed to crush
dissenting elements. After this date, Parliament (including the Senate), the courts, and the monarchy became the rubber stamps of the
one-party state.

Thus began the second phase in the development of Fascism,
marked by the vigorous and unscrupulous use of force and terror to
establish absolute power; it continued until the end of 1926, when
Mussolini, content that his rule was now secure, decreed a "normalization" of affairs. The next period, from 1927 to 1930, was characterized by a relaxation of terror and tension at home, by a more dignified and reasonable conduct of Italy's foreign relations, and by the
historic Concordat with the Vatican. Fascism began to seem respectable in the eyes of democratic leaders of other countries.

But, beginning with the campaign against the adult and youth organizations of the Catholic Church in 1931, the Fascist regime made
it quite clear that it would stop at nothing less than the totalitarian
absorption and control of all areas of national life. Its foreign policy
became more belligerent as increasingly greater emphasis was placed
on the "call of Rome" as the central concept of its ideology. Italians
were told that they could not dwell in peace, that their country was
destined to rule Western civilization again just as it had in the days
of Roman imperial greatness, that they must discipline themselves for
the conquest of a new empire in the days ahead. Mussolini even went
so far as to envision all of Europe as an organization of Fascist states
under the hegemony of the new Rome, the totalitarian and Fascist
Rome. The ideology called for conquest; it also insisted on the absolute, monolithic hierarchical organization of the whole people into
a disciplined "army" which would be capable of achieving this conquest. The state and the party became ever more centralized and
autocratic in internal organization. The political police, during this

11

period from 1931 to 1935, the fourth phase of Fascist history, became more instead of less powerful, in spite of the fact that overt resistance to Fascist rule had never been more feeble.

The most extreme phase of Italian Fascist totalitarianism can be dated from the brutal conquest of Ethiopia in 1935 to the joining of destiny with the Nazis in war in 1940. It was during this period that the grim results of all the years of ideological indoctrination and the perfecting of totalitarian institutions became evident to all mankind. On both the domestic and the international scene, Fascist Italy reached the zenith of its evolution. Albania followed Ethiopia into the Fascist empire, and it was announced that Nice, Corsica, and Tunisia would be next. The people of Italy had never been so regimented as when the regime embarked on a "reform of custom" campaign with the purpose of eradicating the more civilized and gracious manners and traditions of the Italian people and replacing them with hard, efficient, ruthless, and militaristic habits of talking, acting, and thinking. For the first time anti-Semitism became the official policy of the Italian state. Totalitarianism had emerged in the very seat of Western civilization.

Professor Herman Finer asks himself at one point in his book on Italian Fascism whether the rise of totalitarianism in Italy was inevitable: "It looks as though it were the product of an unbroken deterministic chain: economic contradictions, political confusion, parliamentary weakness . . . Yet Fascism seems to me to have been avoidable if Mussolini had not functioned as he did, to aggravate the economic tension, to make political confusion worse confounded, to enter Parliament only to decide to overthrow it. His will to power, and the ruthlessness in its realization, alone made Fascism *inevitable*, even as it now continues to make it possible."[10] This statement was written in 1935. From what we know now, we can say with assurance that Finer was incorrect in stressing so strongly the personality of Mussolini as the key to the triumph of Fascism and its continuation in power. For Mussolini did not rule alone: he also had the monolithic single party. An understanding of this unique institution is essential for a proper appreciation, not only of how Fascism first acquired power, but also of how Italy was transformed into a totalitarian state, into a despotism qualitatively different from ordinary political tyrannies.

12

STEPS IN THE PARTY'S DEVELOPMENT

The single party was nowhere forged in a lightning moment, least of all in Italy. The Italian Fascist party — *Partito Nazionale Fascista* (PNF) — only gradually developed into a completely totalitarian institution, organized "in a strictly hierarchical, oligarchical manner . . . under a single leader . . . and superior to . . . the bureaucratic governmental organization."[11] There is no evidence that Mussolini consciously planned to set up an institution along these lines, once he had attained power, although it is true that he and party leaders like Roberto Farinacci did study the Soviet party structure with interest. In Italy the movement evolved into a totalitarian party in response to the imperatives of totalitarian rule, as the next chapter will show.

The formation of the first fascio in 1919 hardly marked the creation of a political party in any full sense of the term. It is true that the Milan body had a governing *giunta*, or council, with undefined powers, as well as a newspaper, of which Mussolini was the editor. But the *giunta* did not impose its control on groups outside Milan. To organize a Fascist group in another city was a simple affair; the only requirements for a new fascio to be in good standing were that it award a membership card to each member and that it hold regular meetings. In July 1919 Mussolini wrote that "the fasci are not, do not wish to be, and cannot become a party . . . Fascism . . . has neither statutes nor rules." And a year later he re-emphasized that Fascism was anti-party, as well as anti-parliamentarian. Fascism was also anti-dogmatic; therefore, unlike regular parties, it insisted on no concrete program. However, Mussolini did evince concern about the "vastness and complexity" of the growing movement and the need for greater discipline and order within its ranks.[12] During the following months a central committee composed of representatives of the various autonomous fasci was set up to survey problems of the movement as a whole.

As a matter of strategy, the majority of the leaders of the various provincial organizations decided that the movement's rise to power would be hastened if it sought seats in the Parliament it despised in order to carry on there tactics of legal obstructionism, which would supplement the subversive activities of its armed gangs. Accordingly, in the general elections of May 1921 the Fascist so-called "anti-party" offered its own list of candidates, which succeeded in winning thirty-five seats in the Chamber of Deputies. From his position as head of this parliamentary delegation, Mussolini was able to reverse the original tendency toward a loose organizational structure in the movement and to transform it into a party subject to his leadership. A special national congress, called at the suggestion of the Fascist parliamentary group, met in November 1921 and enacted a party statute carefully setting forth lines of authority and responsibility. A national party directorate was established with the power to "impose on the members the strict observance of the political program outlined . . . by the congress . . ." The independence of the local and provincial squads of action was curbed by the appointment of an inspector general to coordinate their activities. The congress also established a permanent national party bureaucracy, headed by a secretary, three vice-secretaries, and one administrative secretary,[13] who at first were subordinate to the directorate. Without the restriction on the autonomy of local fasci, the strengthening of discipline, and the creation of a kind of high command over the squads, it is difficult to see how Fascism could have attained power in the fall of 1922. However, not every party *ras* (a term, borrowed from Ethiopian usage, employed by the Fascists in referring to a powerful local or provincial "boss") was immediately brought under firm control by the national headquarters; during the first years following the conquest of power, a number of provincial leaders, impatient with what they considered to be Mussolini's slowness in establishing a complete dictatorship, tended to reassert their autonomy.

When Mussolini, following the murder of Matteotti, announced his intention to forge a fully totalitarian state, he decided at the same time once and for all to put an end to unauthorized actions on the part of some of his followers in the party. Accordingly, the party was reorganized along the lines of an army. The local and provincial fasci were denied the privilege of electing their own officers, and the national secretary of the PNF was placed in full command with the power to appoint and remove all leaders at the lower levels. Roberto Farinacci, who had been secretary of the Fascist party of Cremona and who had stood by Mussolini as his stanchest and most militant supporter during the darkest days of the Matteotti crisis, was the first to exercise these vast powers. He was appointed national secretary by the Duce in early 1925. By the end of his tenure of office in 1926, the Fascist party had emerged as the sole legal party of the state; its rigid hierarchical structure was due in large measure to the organizational efforts of the tough leader from Cremona.

Almost as soon as the PNF had been established as the single legal party (*partito unico*) of the state, opposition to it arose within the Fascist ranks. Despite an imposing façade of unity, totalitarian dictatorships always breed factions among the ruling elite, and Italian Fascism was no exception. In Italy a group which one might call the "moderates" (in contrast to the party "extremists") gradually came into existence after the victory of 1922. Some members of the moderate faction were former Nationalist party men like minister of the interior Luigi Federzoni and minister of education Francesco Ercole, who wanted to make Fascism "respectable," and who deplored unnecessary violence, illegality, and repressive measures. They were joined by some "reformed" ex-squadrist leaders like Italo Balbo, Dino Grandi, and Giuseppe Bottai, and by the philosopher Giovanni Gentile. The moderates sought to minimize the police-state characteristics of the regime. They frankly saw no need for the continued existence of the monolithic, powerful, armed single party, with a select and narrow membership, now that all opposition to Fascism had been overcome and the whole nation was loyally Fascist.[14] They would have transformed the party into a decentralized system of discussion clubs, with voluntary membership and uncontrolled speech. It was their hope that this organ of constructive criticism would attract the most promising young minds in the service of the Fascist cause.

Augusto Turati, Farinacci's successor as secretary, rejected these arguments,[15] and, what is more important, so did Mussolini. In the years ahead the party retained and reinforced its military structure and brought everyone in the country into the grasp of its numerous associated organizations. Some observers writing in the late twenties predicted that the Fascist party would disappear,[16] but instead it dramatically expanded its power during the following decade.[17]

Under Giovanni Giuriati, who became PNF chief in 1930, the party led Fascism's bitter struggle with Catholic Action, the Church's largest and most powerful organization of Italian laymen, which dared to challenge the dictatorship's claim to have a monopoly in youth activities. Giuriati resigned a year later and was followed by Achille Starace, who remained at the helm until shortly before World War II began. Starace, more than any other single party leader, left his imprint upon the party. Under this relentless and efficient zealot, Fascism entered its most totalitarian phase. The tentacles of the party reached into every corner. Youth and propaganda activities were greatly intensified. This was the period of the reform of custom and the racial campaign, both pet projects of the secretary. Under his persistent direction, the party concerned itself with the most minute regulation of the personal habits and thoughts of the citizenry.

By the late thirties the party had made its presence felt everywhere, to such an extent that even the Fascist secretary of the interior expressed his fear of "the dangerous hegemony of the party in all sectors of national life."[18] The single mass party had become an inseparable and essential part of the Fascist system; in fact, it had become the very core of the dictatorship. The party's steady expansion and monolithic development were inexorable, given the totalitarian animus which came to permeate Mussolini's regime.

THE PARTY AND THE PARTIES

In an effort to emphasize the unique quality of the single mass party, numerous writers have suggested that the institution be designated by other terminology, to differentiate it from the political parties of constitutional democracies. The labels "order," "church," and "army" have been proffered as substitutes for the word "party."[19]

It is undeniably true that, when it had fully developed, the single party in Italy did resemble all three of these institutions in certain respects. Like a religious order, the party demanded the unwavering allegiance of the individual — body, mind, and spirit. The party was to be revered as a sacred institution which would last beyond the lives of its members, just as a church endures despite the death of its martyrs. The PNF had its own sanctuaries, saints, hymns,[20] sacred writings, prayers, solemn ceremonies, and even marriage services.[21] As the PNF was in part order and church, so could it also be compared to an army. Possessing its own arsenal of weapons and its own militia, it was organized from top to bottom in military fashion.

Fundamentally, however, this novel totalitarian instrument, which we shall continue to call the party (although on occasion one of the other terms will be peculiarly appropriate), was neither order, church, nor army. The party was a pseudo-religious institution, but it served a *political* religion. To include the Fascist party and the Franciscans

16

in the same category would tell us little about the Fascist party and everything grotesquely wrong about the Franciscans. If in structure the party resembled an army, the ends which it pursued were not military, but political. Others could win battles with guns and tanks; the field on which the party fought was far more vast. The aim of the PNF was more basic: the inculcation of an ideology.

Although the totalitarian party was a new institution, it grew out of something older, the democratic multiparty system. Political parties appeared in profusion in Western democracies during the nineteenth century, mainly as a consequence of the widening of the suffrage. In each of the three countries where it ultimately proved victorious, the totalitarian party at first appeared as simply one of a number of parties. After attaining power, it preserved the essential characteristics of a party. Totalitarian regimes were born in a democratic setting; the idea of party was taken over from the democratic past. Konrad Heiden has summed up the matter succinctly: "A despotism [of the old order] ignores the will of the people; but these new states . . . take the will of the people so seriously that they create it and shape it themselves . . . For this they use methods which they have preserved from the democratic surroundings of their origins. Although all other parties have been destroyed, the concept of party has remained." [22]

A noted political scientist has defined the political party as a "group of human beings, stably organized, with the objective of securing or maintaining for its leaders the control of a government, and with the further objective of giving to members of the party, ideal and material benefits and advantages." [23] Both the totalitarian single party and the parties in a constitutional democracy fit this definition. More than a church, an order, or an army, the militant supporters of the new despotisms constituted a party: they were a stably organized group of men whose objective was essentially *political.*

In stressing the fact that totalitarian and democratic parties possess enough common traits to justify the application of the term "party" to both institutions, the historically unique nature of the totalitarian single party is not thereby denied. The single mass party was not merely an old instrument put to unprecedented uses; the old instrument was refashioned into a new tool. Between the totalitarian and democratic parties there is all the difference that similarly exists between a sword and a plowshare.

2

The Indispensable Party

Aᴠᴛᴇʀ 1925, the Fascist regime had every opportunity to reduce the party to merely ornamental status. Once the dictatorship had consolidated its power and eliminated all overt opposition, the party seemed to some to have lost its *raison d'être*. To a moderate like Giuseppe Bottai, who frequently fought the party from his post as minister of corporations, the monolithic single party served no useful purpose; on the contrary, it positively hindered the effort to reinforce the regime's power with the voluntary consent of the people.[1] The party had been needed only as midwife to the birth of the Fascist state; it should now be sent on its way, since its task was successfully completed. The moderates argued that, if retained, a strong single party would inevitably emerge as a counter-state. Fascist ideology, they insisted, could not countenance such a development, for, in contrast to both Nazi and Soviet thought, Fascist political theory exalted the state and required that the party and all other organs of the regime be subordinated to the governmental organization.[2]

But the regime did not evolve in the direction preferred by its more temperate supporters. If in the late twenties it appeared that the party and its extremist leadership were on the way out and that the dictatorship was being "liberalized," events of the following decade were to present a different picture. As time passed, the party, far from withering away, steadily expanded, and came to wield extensive power that was independent of the governmental machinery.

Mussolini made it plain in numerous speeches that he regarded the party as the mainstay of his regime. He declared in 1929: "It is not a question of whether the party ought to exist or not, because if the party did not exist I would invent it, and I would invent it exactly as the Partito Nazionale Fascista is now constituted: numerous, disciplined, ardent, and with a rigidly hierarchical structure." Five years later he saluted the party as "the formidable . . . instrument which admits the people into . . . the life of the state." "The more the Revolution unfolds and grows, the more the existence of the party is shown to be necessary," Mussolini affirmed. In 1939 he praised the party as the "creator of the Revolution, the backbone of the Regime, the motor organ of national activity."

Fascist theorists found a powerful single party to be perfectly compatible with the strong state required by the ideology. Party and state were not opposed, but united; both constituted "the state in the ethico-political sense of the term." The party was the "dynamic, political, anti-bureaucratic" element of the state; without its vitality, the state would perish.[3]

Once the leaders had determined to forge a totalitarian state, the party logically attained a commanding position in the Fascist system. The regime found the party to be literally indispensable in the achievement of its unprecedented objectives, for the party rendered certain essential services which it alone among the institutions of the totalitarian state was capable of performing.

THE PARTY PROPS THE REGIME

Each despotism must find methods of self-preservation. The tyrannies with which Aristotle was familiar sought to ensure themselves against overthrow by pursuing three policies — preventing mutual trust from arising among their subjects, rendering the citizenry incapable of action, and breaking the spirit of the populace.[4] Totalitarian dictators worked toward these same ends, although they used more refined techniques. Tyrannies of the past employed a kind of secret police, but the primitive system of paid informers could not in any way compare with the highly organized machine of terror developed by the new despotisms. Furthermore, the totalitarian dictatorship does not stop with one organization of spies. In addition to the relatively small police network it has the massive apparatus of the party as a bulwark of defense against attack from within. The PNF, "civil militia of the Fascist state," was the dictator's personal army, constituting through its strength "a support as solid as granite."[5] When the regime appeared to be tottering during the Matteotti crisis, the party rallied behind the Duce and fiercely combated his enemies. Had a coup been attempted, the party would have been vigilant in his defense.

The Fascist dictatorship was concerned not only with active opposition. The party and police wished to create conditions under which revolt would not even be thought of. The party helped to accomplish this through compulsory organization of the populace into one network of party-controlled associations and through close surveillance of the Fascist ruling class itself. By suppressing all spontaneous, voluntary associations and replacing a society of pluralistic corporate groupings with the monolithic corporative state, Italian Fascism was able to prevent its subjects from forming any conflicting loyalties. Free trade unions, religious youth groups, professional and business associations, cultural societies, and athletic organizations were all disbanded. Aristotle noted that the tyrannies of ancient Greece also prohibited "societies for cultural purposes, and any gathering of a similar character" in order to "make every subject as much of a stranger as is possible to every other."[6]

The party was able to observe the activities of people in all parts of the country and to wipe out any centers of potential resistance. But the chief value of the party in maintaining the regime lay in its system of control over persons in responsible governmental positions.[7] Party informers were planted throughout the bureaucracy, the army, the police, and even the party itself.[8] Members of the party elite, the ideological purists, were regarded as the most dependable and least corruptible supporters of the dictator. Consequently, they were given the duty of exercising "a political control over all organizations of the regime and over the assignment of offices and responsibilities . . . to Fascists."[9]

Even a person belonging to the governing class and outwardly professing loyalty was not exempt from the party's constant scrutiny. The rulers were ruled and the informers informed upon. A network of spies upon spies enabled the totalitarian dictatorship to survive any attempt at internal revolution. Montesquieu observed that despotisms are based on fear; the new despotisms were based on fear compounded into terror.

20

THE PARTY PROMOTES THE REGIME

Unlike ancient forms of tyranny the new despotisms were not content merely to enjoy the acquiescence of their subjects and to be secure in the knowledge that the citizenry would not overthrow them. The masses could not simply endure the regime; they had also to sing its praises. As Luigi Salvatorelli has perceptively written: "One difference . . . between the old absolutist and the recent totalitarian regimes is that the latter do not content themselves with the passive obedience of government officials and of citizens, but wish to mold these people according to the ideas of the party . . . Formerly it was a question of juridical obedience, exterior in nature, [but the more recent despotisms demand] the allegiance of the conscience . . ."[10]

The single party performed the essential tasks of inculcating the ideology in the people and of evoking continuous affirmations of approval from them for specific policies. Democracy had made the masses politically alive; totalitarianism channeled this energy into the service of its ideology. The new despotisms therefore claimed to be democratic, because through the party, the "capillary organization of the regime," the state was able to reach and be in constant communication with the people. "More than exercising an authority, [the party] exercises an apostolate in the midst of the people. Through the defense and propagation of Fascist principles [and] the political and social education of the people . . . it gives to the authority of the state the voluntary consent . . . of the popular masses."[11]

In actuality, the party brought the people into close contact with the state not in order that the masses might gain control, but in order that the regime might mold them. Robert Ley, chief of the Nazi Labor Front, accurately compared the single party to an octopus which gripped with its tentacles every person in the society. "Nobody can escape us . . . The Party penetrates into every house, every factory, every farm, and every workshop." Only if a person were "dead or asleep" could he elude the party.[12] Instead of serving as an organ for the registration of mass sentiment, the single party in Fascist Italy was, as one leader in the youth organizations said, an instrument for the "continual conquest of the masses."[13] As the only political party in Italy the PNF had a complete monopoly over what political ideas might circulate.

In order to fulfill its objective of converting the entire populace into militant Fascists, the party instituted an extensive indoctrination program which was perpetually in operation. The great plebiscites, which, until 1939, were held every five years, were used by the party for its most intensive indoctrination campaigns. For weeks in advance of "election day" every wall was covered, every newspaper crowded, and every radio hour occupied with party propaganda and lectures on Fascist ideology.[14] Other party propaganda activities proceeded year in and year out. A series of "Conversations on Fascist Culture" was annually offered to older youths. The Conversations[15] lasted three months and were taught by party officials and youth leaders. Four meetings were on the history of the Fascist revolution, five on the political and economic institutions of Fascism, and three on war, imperialism, and Italian foreign policy. The courses attracted several million students each year that they were held.[16]

The party had propaganda programs designed to reach every element of the population. A set of lectures designed especially for women was given at regular intervals under the auspices of the *Fasci Femminili*, the women's group affiliated with the PNF.[17] For the working classes, the party sponsored through the *Dopolavoro*, the dictatorship's "leisure-time" organization, an annual course on the Revolution, party organization, the Fascist syndicates, and the youth organizations.[18] The Institute of Fascist Culture directed its activities toward the professional classes. Similar programs were held in the rural areas.[19] In the unlikely event that anyone had escaped these indoctrination sessions, the party held Sunday afternoon rallies in the town squares.[20] Those who had anticipated a pleasant afternoon walk found themselves constrained to listen to the harangues of a party orator.

These propaganda campaigns were nationally directed; in the provinces and local communities zealous party organizations were free to devise their own supplementary programs, apparently on the theory that too much indoctrination was just enough. In some provinces the party sent around mobile theater groups to present Fascist "morality" plays, usually followed by commentaries from local party leaders. Specially prepared films were shown from time to time.[21] The active party organization of Milan presented what it called the *Lectura Ducis*, arrogantly modeled after the *Lectura Dantis*, a famous series of lectures on the poetry of Dante Alighieri, given by renowned scholars in the Orsammichele of Florence. In the *Lectura Ducis* a party leader read one of Mussolini's speeches and commented on its relation to the Duce's thought as a whole.[22]

The party used its capillary structure for special propaganda campaigns as well as for general ideological indoctrination. When the dictatorship decided on a new policy, the party went into action to ensure enthusiastic acceptance of the new line by the masses. Thus, in 1926, when the regime embarked on a deflationary economic policy, the party held nationwide rallies to persuade workingmen of the soundness of a policy for lowering wages. Or, if there was a shift in foreign policy, the entire party machinery worked overtime to manufacture popular support for the change. When, for example, Mussolini determined to gamble on the invasion of Ethiopia, the PNF organized gigantic assemblies all over Italy. From 3:30 P.M. until 7:30 P.M. on October 2, 1935, party leaders in every Italian commune prepared the people to receive Mussolini's announcement of his intention to defy the League of Nations. The rallies included Fascist songs, cheers, band music, the noise of sirens, and short, fiery speeches by local and provincial party leaders. An estimated twenty million persons were on hand to hear the Duce's voice boom over the loudspeaker: "To economic sanctions we will oppose our discipline, our sobriety, our spirit of sacrifice. To military sanctions we will respond with military measures. To acts of war we will answer with acts of war. We have no thought of yielding without first having fought to the last." All over Italy crowds screamed delirious approval of the speech. The party had successfully stimulated the violent impulses of the masses; PNF leaders hailed the rallies as a national plebiscite in favor of war. On the next day Italian troops invaded Ethiopia without a declaration of war.[23]

At Mussolini's specific direction, less dramatic foreign policy decisions were also accompanied by party campaigns to attract popular support. The diaries of Count Galeazzo Ciano, Mussolini's son-in-law and the foreign secretary of Italy from 1936 until 1943, have revealed Mussolini's interest in manipulating public opinion in favor of his latest diplomatic move.[24] Frequently, the party was instructed to arouse national sentiment on a given question even before governmental policy was announced, in order that the Duce could lay claim to "following" the will of the people.

The racial campaign of 1938 affords one of the best examples of the party's role as propagandist for newly adopted Fascist schemes. Once again, the party prepared the nation before the new policy was publicly revealed by governmental authorities. Party secretary Starace had for months been grinding out anti-Semitic statements for the press, and the party had encouraged the publication of a new journal, *La Difesa della Razza*. Several weeks before the Grand Council — the supreme organ of the Fascist state, composed, as it was, of the top officials of the party and state — enacted the ban on intermarriage between Italians and Jews, the PNF inaugurated special lectures for members of its women's organization and youth groups on such topics as "Preserving Racial Integrity" and "The Danger of Mixed Marriages."[25] Later, well-known party leaders made speeches on the new racial doctrine to the general populace. Sample subjects were "Purity of the Race from Roman Times," "Liberation from Zionism," "The Jew and Modern Culture," and "Race and the Problems of Civilization." The lectures received thorough newspaper and radio coverage, and the most important of them were published in book form for use in the schools.[26]

One of the party's principal tasks, then, was to make every individual conscious of Fascist principles, and to transform him from a lukewarm, perhaps opportunistic supporter into a zealot who believed wholeheartedly in the regime and in the truth of its ideology. Unlike the Hobbesian Leviathan, which sought only to control men's bodies, the Fascist dictatorship demanded its subjects' minds as well. The regime used the party not only to gain and keep power, but also to spread "truth." As Albert Camus has written, in totalitarian dictatorships there exists "no organ of conciliation or mediation . . . between the leader and the people . . . [except] the party which is the emanation of the leader and the tool of his will to oppress."[27]

THE PARTY PRODS THE REGIME

The totalitarian single party is a strange beast; it is able to assume various shapes at the same time. Paradoxically, it is both guard and vanguard of the dictatorship, both the first line of defense and the shock troops of attack. For the party elite, to remain in power is not enough. The regime must remain in power without compromising the demands of the ideology. Hence, in one of its forms the PNF was the intransigent band which fought those within the regime who sought

24

to "corrupt" the purity of the ideology, who were more interested in survival than in the victory of Fascist principles. The party militants opposed the temptations to opulence, laziness, and compromise which inevitably beset any men of entrenched power. These militants were the extremists of the regime; there was a sense in which they were more Fascist than the Duce.

Most of the party leaders had participated in the glorious March on Rome, and they were determined that Fascism's pristine "revolutionary" fervor should not be dissipated now that its leadership had gained control of the state. To the party, the Revolution was a continuous event; no sooner had one goal been achieved than another had to be pursued. The demands of totalitarian ideology were insatiable: new disciplines had to be imposed upon the masses, new imperial conquests had to be made, and ever greater pressure had to be exerted on each member of the governing class to guarantee his devotion to the Cause. As one Fascist author expressed it: "The party has the permanent task of creating . . . in today's generations the spirit of imperialism and expansion. Italy cannot consider herself 'arrived.' . . . 'He who stops is lost': this is the party's commandment."[28]

Mussolini was not always willing to go as far and as fast as his party leadership advocated. At times he saw fit to give the more moderate members of the ruling clique their day.[29] In order to consolidate his power, he moved far more slowly during the early years than party extremists wished. Also, following the resolution of the Matteotti crisis there ensued, as indicated earlier, an interval of quiet and "normality." During this period, from 1926 until early 1930, Fascist Italy behaved cautiously both at home and abroad. A Concordat was signed with the Church, and the dictatorship seemed less rigid and more respectable in the eyes of the outside world. But the party shock troops were in reserve, ready for the occasion when their leader would call them forth. In the thirties the party found its opportunity, first in the struggle with Catholic Action, and later in the reform of custom and the racial campaign.

The period following the Ethiopian War vividly illustrates the party's role as vanguard of the regime. With popular enthusiasm for Fascism at its zenith as a result of the victory in Africa, there was considerable sentiment within the ruling elite for liberalization of the dictatorship.[30] But to the party leadership the Ethiopian conquest was only the first stone in the new imperial edifice. His totalitarian appetite whetted, Mussolini directed the party to transform the Italians into an "imperial people."

Under Starace's orders, the PNF began in 1937 the celebrated Fascist reform of custom. Each month the party secretary issued directives on what constituted proper Fascist behavior. These rules were mandatory for all government and party personnel, and, so far as enforcement was possible, for the whole citizenry.[31] The objective of the directives on Fascist "style" was to make the Italians less likable and more ruthless. *L'uomo nuovo, il Fascista*, was to be the inverse of the traditional Italian stereotype: he was to be serious, efficient, hard, and militaristic.

The two most enforced, resisted, and famous of the reforms of custom were the "Roman salute" in place of the handshake, and the use of *voi* instead of *lei* as a form of address. Actually, the handshake had been forbidden among party members since 1933, when Starace had denounced it as "unaesthetic, time-consuming, and . . . a cause of uneasiness because of the inevitable exclusions resulting from it."[32] Only in 1937 was the Fascist salute established as the required form of greeting for the masses. Like other reforms of custom, this one was meant to test a person's capacity to "rid himself of old usages," and to prove the intensity of his Fascist faith.[33] In early 1938 the party further intruded itself into the everyday life of the average Italian by ordering that the polite form of address, *lei,* be dropped from the language. It was discovered that *lei* had been forced on the Italians during the Spanish occupation in the eighteenth century. *Voi*, the native form, became mandatory for both speech and writing. Failure to observe the change cast suspicion on one's loyalty to the regime.[34]

The regulations on Fascist style contained a variety of prohibitions. In addition to refraining from using the handshake or *lei*, the true Fascist would not wear formal dress attire, be deferential and over-polite in manner, tip his hat, have tea late in the afternoon, sympathize with the Jews, go on holidays in the country, or drink excessive quantities of coffee.[35] The Fascist would be known by his terse and abrupt manner of speaking and writing; he would have no time for garrulity.

The extent to which totalitarian societies were able to interfere with the private lives of their subjects was unprecedented. The Fascist party was bent on nothing less than making the Italian citizen over into a new man, a man who thought, acted, and believed according to the dictates of the ruling ideology. Italy during the "Era Starace" resembled a huge barracks; civil servants were even required to wear military uniforms while working. But actually the Italians were worse off than soldiers, for no army had ever demanded the unconditional and total submission that the Fascist dictatorship required of those unfortunate enough to be caught under its massive thumb.

One of the most dismal chapters in the history of Fascism was the racial campaign, which commenced in October of 1938. The decision to adopt racism as official doctrine was a striking departure from traditional Fascist policy. In his talks with the historian Emil Ludwig in 1932, Mussolini had denied any biological basis for ideas of racial superiority and had called them "95% sentiment." The Duce had then affirmed that racist doctrines would "never succeed" among the Italians.[36] And as late as February 17, 1938, in a note published in *Informazione diplomatica*, the Italian government had denied that the "Jewish problem" was of any significance in Italy.[37]

But times had changed. At some point during the spring of 1938, Mussolini, with the vigorous support of the party leadership, determined to make racism an issue. The reasons the Fascists may have had for adopting such a policy are many, but the most valid explanation is that racism fitted neatly into Starace's reform of custom. To assure the Italians that they were members of the master Aryan race was regarded as indispensable to the party's campaign for converting the Italians into a people of warriors and conquerors.[38] If the Italians could be imbued with a "racial conscience," then "the sediment of the old Italy" could be scraped away from the souls of the people.[39]

The adoption of racism as dogma by the Italian Fascists has been attributed by more than one scholar to Nazi influence.[40] Although Nazi pressures on the Fascist regime were strong, it is probable that even without them Italian Fascism would have arrived at some form of racial doctrine. As Italy acquired colonies for its new empire, the Fascist regime found racism a convenient aid in its campaign against Italian fraternization with subject peoples. In addition, racism — specifically anti-Semitism — provided the regime with an opportunity to heighten terroristic activities within Italy. The new reign of terror increased anxiety throughout the country; an anxious, nervous people was an energetic people, far more useful in the building of empires than a complacent and satisfied citizenry could be. It is more nearly true to call Fascist racism a result of the inner workings of the Fascist system — and of the development of Fascist ideology — than an imitation of totally foreign developments.[41]

The racial doctrine became official policy in Italy only after prolonged and intense struggle within the ruling clique. Once again, it was the party leadership which advocated the new policy, and the moderate group in the government which opposed it. To Starace and his associates racism offered simply one more opportunity for the extension of Fascism's totalitarian ideology. Those who demurred were standpatters and compromisers.[42]

The party began preparing the country to accept a racial philosophy as early as July 1938, when the secretary appointed a committee of "scholars" (*studiosi*) to report to him on problems of race. The committee's conclusions were that race was a biological, and not simply a cultural, fact; that the Italians were pure Aryans; that the Italians must not corrupt their racial purity, which had remained unsullied for one thousand years, by mixing with Africans and Orientals; and that the Jews were racially as inferior as Africans and Orientals.[43] The report of the *studiosi* sparked the party's fight to get the Grand Council to enact harsh racial legislation. According to Ciano, the participating chronicler, it was the party secretary who laid before the Council the first draft of the proposed legislation at the meeting of July 26.[44] From then until October, party extremists and government moderates thrashed out the issue in long nocturnal sessions of the Council. Finally, at the meeting of October 6, 1938, the Council accepted the party-sponsored legislation, in spite of the continued opposition of three of its members: Luigi Federzoni, Italo Balbo, and Emilio De Bono. (Balbo and De Bono had been appointed to high positions in the air force and army respectively; Federzoni, a former minister of the interior, was then president of the Senate.) The racial law forbade intermarriage of Italians with "non-Aryans." Jews were prohibited from heading businesses employing more than one hundred "Aryans," and from holding more than a small amount of property. Jews could not serve in the government or armed forces; nor could they teach in the schools.

Following the enactment of this legislation, the lot of Jewish persons in Italy became steadily more difficult. In some areas, squads of party men assaulted Jewish people and "Aryans" suspected of aiding Jews. Particularly in the Turin and Trieste areas, synagogues were burned to the ground.[45]

THE PARTY PERPETUATES THE REGIME

In addition to serving the regime in the present, the single party was a necessary element in a totalitarian dictatorship because it was the one institution which looked to the future. A distinguishing trait of totalitarian dictatorships is that they are obsessed with desire to see their regimes become immortal. One of the party's major tasks was to select the most promising of the younger generation and to give this elite group especially intense training. Thereby, the Fascist ruling class of tomorrow would come into being.

The party was the means by which the old guard's authority was passed on to new hands. In Italy, as in both Nazi Germany and the Soviet Union, an elaborate system of party leadership schools, extending from the provinces to a national school in Rome, was created in order to ensure that the future ruling clique would be thoroughly grounded in the principles of Fascist ideology.[46] The party conceived of this leadership sequence as a kind of apostolic succession, which would bind the present regime to an infinite number of future Fascist generations. The party was determined that time would not extinguish the torch of truth, and that the dictatorship would live on long after its founder had perished.[47]

THE PARTY: INDISPENSABLE SUPPORT OF THE DUCE

Without the powerful single party as an organic component of its make-up, the totalitarian monster would have fewer claws with which to ward off attack, no tentacles with which to gather in and hold its subjects, no goading passion to shake it from contented slumber, and no organs of reproduction. In short, without the party, it would no longer be the same frightening monster. This is what is meant in calling the single party "indispensable" to a totalitarian dictatorship. The party is needed; therefore it appears, and therefore it does not wither away.

Actually, it would be possible for a dictatorship to remain in power without depending upon the party. For it is also the job of the secret police and the army to preserve the regime from overthrow. However, totalitarian regimes have found that the surest method for guaranteeing the loyalty of the army and the police is to place them both under the surveillance of a third force, the party. And the other three services which a single party performs for a totalitarian dictatorship could not be rendered by any other agency. Only the party has the ideological passion to train the regime's successors and to goad them into perpetual action on behalf of unrealized objectives. Only the party has the structure through which the dictatorship can lay hold on the bodies and capture the minds of its subjects.

In Italy, the single party at times had difficulty in combining its several roles. It is apparent why this should have been a problem, for there was an inherent tension between the requirements for survival and the demands of the ideology. Party members pledged themselves to shed the last drop of their blood, if necessary, to keep the regime in power; however, in unremittingly pushing the regime to new acts of imperialistic aggression and more violent waves of internal terror, the party leadership tended to make unrealistic judgments of the potential power available to the dictatorship. Thus, in the end, the party vanguard brought the regime to destruction by insisting on the rapid and complete implementation of the goals envisioned in Fascism's totalitarian ideology. Unwilling to pause and be satisfied with the power already in their grasp, the party leaders ultimately carried the regime to ruin because they could not slake their lust for total domination.

Fascist Italy's fatal error, was, of course, the decision to become involved in aggressive total war on the side of Nazi Germany. After the victory in Ethiopia the extremists of the party were able to win over Mussolini to the idea of steadily increasing Fascist power both at home and abroad. The conquest of Albania, the anti-Semitic legislation, and the reform of custom had only been leading up to the big prize — world domination in cooperation with Italy's brother regime, Nazi Germany. Mussolini's moderate counselors told him to keep out of the war; Italy was not militarily prepared, they said, and even if the Axis won, Italy would have to be subordinated to Nazi Germany in any new world order. But to the men of the party the stakes were too great: total power was within their reach. They insisted that it would be weakness to vacillate or stop, that "40 million Italians were ready to give their lives for the Duce," and that Italy should join Germany in this last and greatest historical enterprise.[48]

The party could not have forced Mussolini to follow the extremist course advocated by its leadership. That he eventually did so was his own decision. During the first years of his reign, the Duce was a cautious, calculating ruler, who seemed unlikely to take the dark path toward the totalitarian state. But his basically totalitarian temperament was revealed in the late twenties when he decided to maintain the party in a position of great strength in the dictatorship. From that point on the party was present, to be used whenever he thought the moment was propitious. The party did not, on its own initiative, push Italy over the brink of totalitarianism; but, by offering its constant support to the most radical policies the Duce could contrive, the party made it possible for Mussolini to create a totalitarian society when, after 1935, he chose to do so.

If the powerful single party had not existed, it is unlikely that Mussolini could have overcome the moderate clique's opposition to adopting totalitarian policies after the Ethiopian victory had been secured. With the abetment of a strong, military party it was possible for him to create a totalitarian Italy; without the party, the Duce never could have achieved his objective. The party demonstrated itself to be an indispensable weapon in the arsenal of the would-be totalitarian dictator.

3

The Flexible Structure

IN ORDER to discharge the party's responsibilities effectively, a complicated structure was gradually erected by the leadership. In one respect the party administration was a model of simplicity. Its nucleus was a perfectly integrated hierarchy, with lines of responsibility sharply drawn. From another perspective, however, the party appeared to be a sprawling assortment of overlapping agencies.

Roberto Michels has appropriately compared the Fascist party to an accordion, which now swelled "excessively up to the point of embracing nearly the whole nation," and then suddenly contracted to a relatively small band of militant Fascists.[1] The metaphor is instructive in that it stresses the flexibility of a modern totalitarian party. Necessarily, the Fascist party's structure was adaptable. The different kinds of services the PNF was called upon to perform simultaneously meant that the party had to possess a variety of organizational forms. It was both a mass organization and an elite corps. When indoctrinating the citizenry, the PNF took on a much enlarged appearance; it encompassed millions of people and dozens of institutions. But the party's hard core of ideological fanatics, bound together by discipline and loyalty, comprised only a few hundred thousand men. The one party had many shapes; all of them taken together constitute the strange apparition known as the monolithic party.

THE PARTY APPARAT

The heart of the party structure was the *apparat*. This select group was composed of men who spent the major part of their time in party administration. They had made the party their career, and they manned the thousands of leadership positions which a totalitarian party creates. The apparat directed all the party's organizations. As in Orwell's *Nineteen Eighty-Four,* a man of the "inner party" had no spare time; in contrast to the rank-and-file party member, whose regular occupation was elsewhere, the member of the apparat gave all his waking hours to party activities.

The party's inner organization was operated on the principle of strict subordination. Nothing was done on initiative from below. Everything had to be cleared through the office of the national secretary. The party chief had absolute powers of appointment, removal, and policy-making; any power that lesser officials in the provinces might possess came only as a result of delegation from his mighty hand.

The Fascist party did not assume power with a centralized, hierarchical structure. When first organized, the party was little more than a federation of autonomous local fasci, each of which was free to choose its own delegates to the national congress. There was a national secretary, but he was a weak figure, "subordinate to the central committee and the directorate."[2] Many of the provincial party bosses possessed their power independently of Mussolini. In contrast, Hitler had won full power to appoint and remove all the regional leaders of the *Nationalsozialistische deutsche Arbeiterpartei* (NSDAP) several years before his conquest of government power.[3]

After the March on Rome, the party began to emerge as a more disciplined unit. Early in 1923 the original party statute was drastically altered, and the Grand Council was established as the supreme governing authority of the PNF. The party leadership was chosen by the Council, not elected by the national congress of fasci.[4] The Council quickly voted harsh penalties for those in the provinces who violated party discipline. The party was still far from unified, however. Many provincial *ras* retained considerable independence. The national party machinery was in a state of disorganization and confusion. No one person was clearly in charge; instead, a kind of collective leadership attempted to administer the party's affairs. The nominal secretary, Michele Bianchi, had to share power with a number of other key figures, among them Giuseppe Bastianini, Giovanni Marinelli, Nicola Sansanelli, and Roberto Farinacci.

Farinacci, made PNF leader in 1925, was the first in the line of

33

autocratic party secretaries. He moved quickly to crush any vestiges of *rasism* which remained in the provincial party organizations. Under the new party constitution of 1926 local and provincial fasci were no longer permitted to elect their own secretaries; their officers were appointed by the national secretary, with the approval of the Grand Council. This is how the apparat originated. From 1926 onwards, the party leaders at every level were almost without exception the national secretary's men. Party decisions were made at the top; the job of the men at the lower levels was simply to carry out orders with military efficiency.

The secretary in theory remained subordinate to the Grand Council until the party statute of 1932 was enacted. This statute recognized the transformation of the Grand Council from a party institution to the highest governing authority in the Fascist state — after the Duce, of course. It had expanded its membership to include the highest officials of the government, and it had ceased to concern itself with purely party affairs. In 1932 party affairs became officially the exclusive domain of the secretary, who now was chosen by and responsible to the Duce alone and who could now select his own directorate. The latter body served as his cabinet, but in the American not in the British sense. He could appoint and remove its members, as well as all other subordinates, at will. All final decisions were made by the secretary alone, the directorate merely assisting him in carrying the enormous burdens of his office.[5]

What was true at the highest level applied also in the provincial and local party organizations, wherein the secretaries were given absolute power and responsibility, and the directorates and other advisory groups became mere appendages. The PNF, like the totalitarian parties of Germany and the Soviet Union, was administered according to what C. J. Friedrich has termed the "radical monocratic" principle. At each stage of the apparatus, one official alone was in charge. No person in the chain of command had any authority other than that entrusted to him from above.

The rigidly hierarchical structure of the PNF was discussed in an article written by one of Bottai's followers in the mid-thirties. The writer, disgruntled by the total absence of any effort on the part of the leadership to encourage initiative and imagination in the rank-and-file party member, described a typical meeting of a local fascio: "Who asks to speak? No one. Who makes ideas circulate? No one. Who criticizes? No one. And precisely because there is little one is allowed to criticize." The meeting was for the sole purpose of receiving orders from the secretary; no party member could raise substantive questions or enlarge on his own political views.[6]

Party disciplinary machinery was gradually perfected, so that by the time Starace became secretary in 1932 an elaborate system of party "courts" had been set up. In each of the ninety-two provinces there was a seven-member Commission of Discipline, presided over by one of the vice-secretaries of the province. The Central Court of Discipline in Rome had as its chairman none other than the national secretary, assisted by five other members. The great majority of the cases handled by the Central Court involved expulsion. No provincial court could inflict expulsion; this power was reserved by the national secretary. It was a considerable power to possess, for in Fascist Italy dismissal from the party meant certain political death and was often followed by imprisonment and persecution. The party tribunals dispensed or recommended six degrees of punishment: reprimand; suspension for a definite time, from one month to one year; suspension for an indefinite time; retraction of the membership card; "cancellation" from the rolls; and expulsion.[7] Members of the party were indeed "doubly disciplined," as Mussolini was fond of saying. Offenses were many and varied, ranging from violations against Fascist style to treasonable utterances, disobedience, and the misuse of party funds. What constituted an offense often depended on the passing whim of the secretary. The arbitrary nature of the punishment system kept the apparat on its toes.

On both the national and provincial levels party personnel were supervised by a group of inspectors appointed by the national secretary and responsible directly to him. Starace was the party chief who used surprise inspections of provincial and local party organizations most efficiently. Employing about fifteen aides, he was able to have many geographically separated party organizations inspected simultaneously on selected days.[8]

The national secretary had other remedies than expulsion or removal from office at his disposal to counteract any tendency toward autonomy in the provinces. As a routine matter, no party head was allowed to remain in one province long enough to develop a separate

35

base of power. Every few years, and sometimes more frequently, provincial secretaries were transferred, a process known as "change of the guard." At times many provincial secretaries were "promoted" to other, chiefly honorary, jobs. This happened in 1934, when forty-four of the ninety-two provincial secretaries were given seats in the powerless Chamber of Deputies to make way for a group of Starace's hand-picked stooges.[9] The monolithic party demanded that its lower officials be shrewd and competent flunkies rather than imaginative and provocative leaders.[10]

Thus, in the most advanced stage of its structural development the PNF assumed a pyramidal shape. At its pinnacle was the Duce himself. He held party membership card number one, and was by law *Capo del Partito*.[11] The national secretary was next in line. He was the dictator's personally appointed representative, who possessed plenary powers to make all decisions concerning party organization and activity. To execute the secretary's commands there was an extensive bureaucracy, officially entitled the political and administrative secretariat. Two national advisory bodies were set up to aid the secretary in the efficient discharge of his duties. The directorate, which included three vice-secretaries, the administrative secretary, and eight members, served as executive council to the party chief. Customarily the directorate met weekly with the secretary. The national council was a less significant body, convening only annually or semiannually. Council membership was large, including, along with the directorate and the national inspectors, the ninety-two provincial secretaries. The main purpose of such a gathering was to impress on provincial leaders the unity of the entire party and to give them a view of problems common to the party as a whole.

The party provincial organizations were similar in structure to the national office. The provincial secretary, referred to as the "federal" secretary, was fully in command as the personal emissary of the national secretary. He was advised by a federal directorate, composed of a vice-secretary and seven members, all appointed by him with the approval of the party's national office. There were provincial inspectors to keep tabs on the local fasci. A political and administrative secretariat did the necessary work of keeping records on finances and party membership.[12]

Within the ninety-two provinces each commune had its fascio. These local fasci, the base of the PNF hierarchy, showed the typical party organization in microcosm: there was a local secretary, appointed by the federal party chief, with full delegated authority, a directorate, and a political and administrative secretariat.

The size of the fasci in some of the larger cities like Milan made further local subdivisions desirable for efficient administration. Wards, sectors, nuclei, and sections were the partitions used. Ward units *(gruppi rionali)* might include several thousand members. As of 1937 the city of Milan, for instance, had twenty-eight party ward organizations, each with a large, well-equipped headquarters.[13] Sectors included as many as five hundred members, nuclei up to one hundred, and sections up to twenty-five.[14] The monocratic principle of command was followed down to the smallest subdivision of the party. Persons assigned by the secretary of the fascio to lead the ward organizations were known as *fiduciarii*, while those who headed the smaller units were called *capi*. The smallest unit of the PNF was comparable in size to a Communist party cell. But the sections of the Fascist party were organized on a geographical basis; usually they comprised all the party members living in the same apartment building. Communist cells, on the other hand, are composed of members having a common economic status. The subdivisions of the PNF corresponded more closely to those of the NSDAP, which also adhered to the territorial principle of organization.[15]

On paper the apparatus of the PNF was a monolithic marvel, governed according to the Fascist administrative theory of *gerarchia* (hierarchy). The national party chief had only to press a button and the entire machinery of the PNF, from the central office in Rome down to the tiniest sector in the cities and the smallest fascio in the countryside, would automatically execute his command. This was planned as a smoothly running mechanism; no friction was to impede its efficient operation. The skeptical observer naturally asks whether the Fascist party in fact ran this way. The surprising answer is that here, at least, is one point at which Fascist theory and practice to a large degree coincided. After 1926, the PNF apparatus was a hierarchically structured, disciplined organization. If in some instances the orders of the national secretary were not carried out, the fault lay not in hostile resistance at the lower level, but in the laziness and incompetence of some minor officials.

There were a few broken links in the rigid chain of vertical relationships, however, and these bear mentioning precisely because they were exceptional. Within the national office, for example, the administrative secretary, Giovanni Marinelli, was able for many years to retain considerable authority that was independent of the national secretary. Marinelli had been one of the original associates of Mussolini in forming the first fascio of Milan in 1919. He became the party's administrative secretary in 1921, and he remained in that office while many party chiefs came and went. He was especially close to Mussolini and occasionally succeeded in convincing the dictator to override the advice of the party secretary.[16] Marinelli's powerful position was demonstrated in 1931 when Mussolini was confronted with Giuriati's demand that Marinelli be fired, for the dictator chose instead to dismiss the chief of the party.[17] Starace appears to have been more successful in subordinating the administrative secretary to his will; at least, no open conflicts between the two seem to have occurred. Starace probably dealt more lightly with Marinelli than with some of his other associates because the administrative secretary, with his unequaled experience, presumably knew more about details of party organization than any other single person.

After the mid-twenties the central party leadership had only occasional difficulty with provincial secretaries who threatened to attain positions of entrenched and independent power. Mario Giampaoli, party secretary and virtual dictator of Milan, became a law unto himself during Turati's administration, but he was removed from office and expelled from the party in the celebrated purge of 1929. When Starace ascended to the national leadership in 1931, *rasism* was finally and completely entombed. Haughty in demeanor and ruthless in revenge, Starace exacted from the provincial party leaders an almost oriental obeisance. He replaced nearly half the federal secretaries with persons of his own choosing; it has been said, with more truth than blasphemy, that Starace created a new class of officials in his own image.[18]

Even under Starace's careful reign, however, there were a very few party leaders from the provinces who had independent access to Mussolini and were consequently not mere parrots of the secretary.[19] The most outstanding of this select group was Roberto Farinacci, who stepped down from national party leadership in 1926 but remained federal secretary of the Fascist party in the northern industrial city of Cremona throughout the life of the dictatorship. No national secretary, not even the heavy-handed Starace, was able to discipline or liquidate Farinacci. The boss of Cremona always enjoyed the protection of Mussolini, who was grateful to Farinacci to the end for his firm support of the regime during its most critical period. The brutish, coarse, and unprincipled Farinacci, one of Fascism's most colorful and most cruel personalities, exercised a leading voice in party councils. He was always popular with the party old guard throughout Italy, and, although technically only a party leader in a medium-sized province, he held membership on the Grand Council for many years. His newspaper, *Regime Fascista,* had a wide national circulation and was comparatively free of government and party supervision.

A less notable example of a provincial party secretary who was able to acquire a certain amount of independent power was Alessandro Pavolini, secretary of the PNF in Florence. Pavolini was adept enough to go over the head of Starace and gain Mussolini's confidence. The Duce was so impressed with the Florentine party chief that, in time, he appointed him minister of popular culture, a position corresponding in power to that of Goebbels in Nazi Germany.[20]

There were, then, a few chinks in the party's monolithic armor. But on the whole the actual power relationships within the party followed the lines drawn on the official organization charts. Focal point of the party structure was the national secretary. At his direction the party gathered itself for action; without his orders the meticulously organized apparatus was immobile.

Mussolini, of course, was theoretically chief of the PNF. But like Hitler and unlike Stalin,[21] he rarely took a direct hand in party affairs. He received the secretary daily in order to give instructions and to learn of the general condition of the party,[22] but his span of attention was limited, for he was a man and not a god, and this prevented his giving special notice to the detailed operation of the party apparatus. As long as the secretary retained the Duce's trust and did not seem to become so powerful as to upset the delicate balance of forces on which every totalitarian dictatorship uneasily rests, he was given free rein. The secretary was absolute lord over the party's vast domain.

39

The Italian Fascist Party in Power

THE EXPANDED PARTY

If this were a study of a democratic party or even of a totalitarian party lacking uncontested control of the state, a description of the structure of the apparat would outline the entire party organization. But in a totalitarian dictatorship, the single party does not remain simply a party; it fattens itself, adding flesh to its organizational skeleton. To secure the victory of the ideology's extreme demands, the party is driven to acquire ever increasing political power. The single party manages to gain control of one institution after another, until finally it outwardly resembles a bureaucratic state more than a political party.

The similarity between the party and the state is only superficial, however; for at the center of the party the apparat is still intact, giving a revolutionary, nonbureaucratic impulse to the sprawling party machinery. The party structure contains two institutions standing side by side, the apparat and the expanded party. General Rodolfo Graziani, viceroy of conquered Ethiopia and until the very end of the regime one of Mussolini's closest military advisers, was only partially right when he judged the Fascist party to be "an enormous bureaucracy . . . which was an end in itself."[23] For, if the party's bureaucratic outer layer had been peeled off, the efficient, disciplined, cohesive, militant apparat would have been visible beneath. To the extent that the PNF could be called a bureaucracy, it was expansive and aggressive, constantly colliding with the tradition-bound officials of the government.

The spread of party activities and institutions is indicated by a survey of the positions held by the national secretary. According to the party statute of 1938, the secretary, besides being chief of the party apparat, was secretary of state in the Council of Ministers, secretary of the Grand Council, commanding general of the youth organization, president of the associations for civil servants and teachers and of the leisure-time organization for workers, and a member of the Defense Council, the National Council of Corporations, the Central Corporative Committee, and the Council of Education. Unofficially, this jack-of-all-trades had other powers as well. He controlled the syndicates, in which every worker was compulsorily enrolled, and directed the party militia, the women's organizations of the regime, the national sport association, and two nationwide charitable institutions.

40

In order to administer these and other activities which accrued to the party, departments were created within the national office to handle each undertaking. Every department was headed by a member of the party directorate; these high party officials actually ran what were termed its "dependent" organizations. The secretary could only supervise his deputies in a general way, for it was patently impossible for one man to carry out personally all these responsibilities.

Within the national office there were, in addition to the political and administrative secretariat, the following administrative offices: press and propaganda, syndical affairs, economic policy, inspection and control of the dependent associations, youth, university students, women's affairs, leisure-time activity, sport, university faculty, social assistance, party organization in the colonies, and cultural activities.[24] Liaison with the militia was maintained through a coordinating agency in the political secretariat.[25] With the exception of the division for party activities in the colonies, each of these offices was duplicated in the provincial and local party administrations.

Among the most important dependent party organizations were the five large associations of government employees and teachers, the militia, and the youth groups. Millions of Italians were enrolled in these organizations. Through its control of them the party often conflicted bitterly with the governmental bureaucracy, the regular army, and the state school system. Separate chapters have been set aside for a more extended discussion of the operation and influence of these party-dominated organizations.[26]

One of the most notable dependent organizations was the *Opera Nazionale Dopolavoro* (OND), which, like the Nazi *Kraft durch Freude*, aimed at monopolizing the workingman's leisure time on behalf of the regime. The OND was established in the spring of 1925 as one of the first organs of the new totalitarian state. In the beginning the state, and not the party, controlled it; however, the party had staked out an early claim in the labor area. Before the March on Rome the PNF had organized a Confederation of Fascist Syndicates to compete with the Communist, Socialist, and Catholic trade unions. Between 1922 and 1925, when all unions other than those of the Fascist party were suppressed first in fact and then in law,[27] the Fascist syndicates swelled their membership many times. In April 1926, the Charter of Labor, the fundamental statute of the corporative state, in effect made membership in the Fascist syndical organizations mandatory for all workers. From that time forward the working population of Italy was "represented" in collective bargaining by leaders appointed by the Fascist party. The party continued to control the syndicates throughout the regime's duration, and the PNF was thereby enabled both to suppress the workers' discontent over low wages and to utilize syndical meetings for Fascist propaganda. Given the party's control over the trade union structure, it is not surprising that the PNF eventually took the leisure-time organization under its authority. Since the party regulated the worker on the job, this supervision was easily extended to the employee's private life. Accordingly, the OND was transferred from the state to the party three years after its inception.[28]

As stated in its 1931 statute, the OND had as its primary purpose "the development of the moral, physical, and intellectual capacities of the worker in the spiritual climate of the Fascist Revolution."[29] To implement this commission the organization had an extensive national office headed by a director general, chosen by the party secretary, and two general secretaries, one for administrative and another for political affairs. There were bureaus for athletic events, excursions, education, art, and social assistance.[30]

The headquarters of the local Dopolavoro sought to supervise and control for political purposes all organized leisure activities for workingmen. Even amateur symphony orchestras and theatrical companies came under its scrutiny. During vacation seasons, the OND provided special trains at reduced fares for its members. The Dopolavoro buildings were equipped with recreation facilities and lecture rooms for political and cultural talks. The party made every effort to induce workingmen to spend their free time at the local OND *casa*.

Although membership in the syndicates was compulsory, the Fascist dictatorship did not require participation in the OND. This policy was quite different from that pursued in Nazi Germany, where all persons incorporated in the Labor Front had to take out membership in *Kraft durch Freude*.[31] As a consequence the total membership of Dopolavoro, although considerable, was never as great as that of the comparable organization in Germany (see Table 1).

The party's reach into the economic sphere extended beyond the control of the employees' associations. Under the terms of the corporative legislation, management also was organized into one network

42

Table 1. Membership in the Dopolavoro

Year	Number	Year	Number
1926	280,548	1932	1,775,570
1927	538,337	1936	2,809,985
1928	882,589	1937	3,180,693
1929	1,445,226	1938	3,566,813
1930	1,662,140	1939	3,832,248
1931	1,772,085	1940	4,612,294

Sources: Achille Starace, *L'Opera Nazionale Dopolavoro*, p. 89; *Fogli d'ordini* nos. 167, 185, and 244; *Regime Fascista*, October 28, 1938, p. 1; and Attilio Tamaro, *Venti anni di storia, 1922–1943*, III, 444.

of authorized economic bodies, officially supervised by the government's Ministry of Corporations, but actually coordinated by the party's intersyndical committees. The intersyndical committees, composed of the leaders of the Fascist syndicates and the representatives of the employers' associations, were presided over in each province by the federal secretary of the PNF, or by his deputy. These bodies, which came into existence in 1928, formulated general wage and price policies for the entire area within their jurisdiction. Such agencies were vital to the Fascist economy because free collective bargaining and strikes were illegal. At the national level the PNF created a central committee for economic activity to give general direction to the provincial committees. A member of the national directorate represented the secretary as head of the central committee. Under Starace, this position was held by Dino Giardini, his economic expert.[32]

After the outbreak of the Ethiopian War, the PNF intensified its price control activities by forming a new special committee. Inflation was a serious problem for the dictatorship, and the new committee undertook to regulate minutely the prices of food and other basic commodities. Heavy legal sanctions were invoked against merchants who disobeyed the party's price directives, and an inspection system was set up to detect and apprehend violators. The directors of the party's ward units appointed teams of spies, euphemistically called *corrispondenti*, to check in the stores on owners' compliance with orders and to report discrepancies to the intersyndical committee for appropriate action.[33]

After the Ethiopian victory the Fascist dictatorship embarked on a full-scale war economy when the decision was made to pursue a policy of economic autarky. A supreme commission, on which the party had a predominant influence, was established to implement this objective. The commission assumed the power of regulating industrial expansion and of allocating priorities on raw materials. The party's central committee for economic activity took the lead in demanding full realization of the autarkic goals; in directives to the supreme commission, it pressed for the development of new domestic industries through protective tariffs, tax subsidies, and legislation obliging merchants to buy a certain quota of the new industries' production. The state, said the committee, should build the concerns directly if private industry proved unwilling. The party was determined to replace "classical" with Fascist economics; autarky was interpreted as the economic policy logically deducible from the regime's ideological goal of founding a new Roman empire.[34] The party's role in the economic arena is an excellent example of its "prodding" function in the regime.

The PNF intruded not only in the areas of labor and economics; it entered the cultural field as well. *L'Istituto Nazionale Fascista di Cultura*, created in 1925, was yet another organization subsidiary to the Fascist party. Its function was to recruit Italian intellectuals into the service of the dictatorship. It had chapters throughout Italy and a membership of approximately one hundred thousand. The chapters were inspected and supervised by the provincial party headquarters in their areas. In addition to sponsoring lectures and publishing Fascist political theory, the institute conducted seminars and issued reports on political topics assigned for investigation by the party secretary.

The PNF also ran two large charitable concerns, the *Opera Nazionale Maternità ed Infanzia* and the *Ente Opere Assistenziali* (EOA). The former gave money, medical care, and food to poor and unwed mothers and found homes for abandoned children. Lest it be thought that the party had suddenly turned humanitarian, it should be pointed out that here, as always, the party was acting in accordance with its interpretation of the ideology. The regime's campaign to increase Italy's surplus population in order to have more cannon fodder for future imperial wars was behind the party's concern. Similarly, the EOA distributed bread and fuel to needy large families and issued loans at low interest rates to encourage marriages and births.[35]

The PNF found its vast network of subsidiary organizations highly useful for transmitting propaganda. And at every level of the apparat and within every organ of the extended party from the youth groups to the civil service associations and the Dopolavori, the masses were perpetually indoctrinated. An *Ufficio Propaganda del Partito* at the center of the apparat administered and coordinated all the party's propaganda. The PNF utilized its capillary structure primarily to implant correct ideas in the masses, but the party could also sound out public opinion through it. Requests for secret information on popular reactions to certain of the regime's policies were sent out sporadically from national headquarters.[36]

The single party in Fascist Italy assumed the form and features necessary to perform its assigned roles. The first phase in the PNF's structural evolution was concerned with the welding of a tightly disciplined apparat, or inner core, so essential for the defense of the regime and the consolidation of all power in the hands of the dictator. The party could afford to remain relatively small at that point, but, as it added new functions, an expansion of its framework was requisite. To pursue the never-ending campaign for mass conversion through indoctrination a ubiquitous capillary structure had to be built across Italian society. To ensure the regime's continuation, a gigantic youth organization had to be created. Finally, as Chapters 6 and 7 will show in greater detail, in order to be certain that ideological intransigence would overpower temporizing weakness in the high councils of the state, the party erected a powerful counter-state, administered by a huge bureaucracy, but governed by the party elite. As Fascist Italy became increasingly totalitarian the party permeated more and more of the state organization. The PNF added organizations which interfered with the state in one area after another. To its enemies, the party was a giant that had torn down the edifice of the state and from the wreckage was building and expanding its own dwelling.

4

Leaders and Followers

As the party grew in power it also increased in size. The most astounding accretions to the strength of the PNF came from the new subsidiary organizations created by it. The majority of Italy's population eventually was enrolled in some institution dominated by the single party. What is even more interesting is that in time the sacred portals of the temple itself were opened and hordes of new faithful were permitted to enter. Party membership, which at first had been severely restricted to those who had joined before the conquest of power, was greatly expanded. In the fateful autumn of 1922 the followers of Fascism had numbered between four and five hundred thousand men; after fifteen years of Fascist rule that contingent had swelled to claim over two million adherents.

The augmented membership posed a serious problem for the party. With so many new followers, how could the militants be separated from the opportunists? How could the fidelity of the apparat be guaranteed? Many observers reasoned that the party would inevitably lose its revolutionary *élan* and its political vigor as a result of too indiscriminate an admissions policy. That this never happened was due to the careful preservation and renewal of the original apparat. Through all the outward changes in the party's make-up, the old-guard "Fascists from the first hour" continued to exercise the positions of authority within the apparat. They constituted a party within the party, and persons who finally succeeded in breaking through the wall between the party and the populace to become party members themselves faced another barrier more ominous than the first. The new adherents were in, but not of, the party.

THE INNER CIRCLE

Those who held the places of leadership and influence in the PNF were selected from three groups. In order to penetrate the party's inner circle, a person must have been an active member of the party before the March on Rome, or have joined and worked diligently for the party during the Matteotti crisis, or — among aspirants from the new generation — have been graduated with an excellent record from the youth organizations and the leadership schools. Leadership posts in the apparat were reserved exclusively for those who could meet one of these three tests.[1] Length of party membership was of crucial importance, and all card-holders were carefully ranked according to seniority.

The leadership cadres were composed primarily of veterans of the March on Rome. Positions of the first rank were occupied by the men who had founded and led the most prominent provincial fasci before 1922. In that year, Farinacci had been party chief of Cremona, Renato Ricci had been PNF leader in Carrara, Starace headed the Trent organization, and Augusto Turati was the key man in Brescia. Farinacci, Turati, and Starace later took turns serving as national secretary, and Ricci headed the youth organization for many years. Other old-guard party organizers to assume high governmental posts after 1922 were Leandro Arpinati of Bologna and Cesare Maria De Vecchi of Turin, the former heading the Department of the Interior and the latter handling major responsibilities in the Foreign Office.

A goodly portion of the old-guard leaders were as violent, fanatical, and ruthless a collection of men as one could expect to encounter anywhere, even in a study of totalitarian regimes. Some of them, like Starace and Farinacci, possessed the storm trooper mentality, and balked at nothing. No weapon of terror was too deadly and no amount of slaughter excessive if the cause of Fascism was furthered. Fascist ideology extolled fierce combat as the highest and most heroic form of human activity; these men gloried in such barbarism. They learned to use violence and cruelty against their political opponents in the turbulent Italy of 1919–1922, when the Fascist squads utilized merciless beatings, bombing of Socialist and Communist party headquarters, and even the murder of prominent political enemies as the normal methods of political warfare. Many of the early party leaders were brutal men, consumed with an implacable hatred of all opposition, and

47

determined to liquidate those who refused to accept Fascist ideology and the authority of the party. These traits, deeply ingrained in the character of Fascist man, were not passing behavioral aberrations; they continued to manifest themselves in the personalities of the most notable Fascist leaders until the regime was destroyed. Totalitarian man is far more terrible to behold than the despotic or oligarchic man described by Plato.

Because Starace was the archetype of the party militant, his career as a Fascist organizer provides a pattern for that of other veteran Fascist leaders. Starace joined the party as a young man, first working for the Trent fascio. He led squadrist action in Venezia Tridentina. He next dedicated his talents to smashing the Red organization in Puglie. Immediately preceding the March on Rome he worked in Milan, leading assaults on the Socialist party and directing the work of the militia. Although still a young man, he was elected one of the first PNF vice-secretaries in November 1921. Having shown his prowess at the provincial level, he was graduated to the national leadership, where he worked steadily up to the top post.[2]

Like Starace the other party leaders of the first rank were tested on the field of violent action during Fascism's struggling years; those found too squeamish to do the work required of a Fascist party leader were weeded out. The ones who rose to the summit were, with a few exceptions, cruel men, possessed of relentless ambition.[3] In any other type of society the worst of them would have been branded criminals; in the Fascist dictatorship they were appointed to the highest councils in the land. And they were the models for the young leaders the party was attempting to create through the educational process of the new youth organizations.

Almost all major and minor positions within the apparat were at first manned by pre-1922 members of the party. This situation changed somewhat in later years as certain graduates of the youth organization were given jobs as party officials, replacing a few of the old guard who had been put out to pasture. But as late as 1934, at least two thirds of the provincial party organizations were headed by members of the old guard.[4] The extensive change of the guard that occurred among the provincial secretaries in 1934 only replaced men advanced in age with younger party veterans. In spite of the influx of graduates from the new party leadership schools, the most important positions in the apparat continued to be held by veteran Blackshirts throughout the party's history.[5]

The old guard of several hundred thousand men constituted the backbone of the party. The party veterans supplied both the party's officers and its most reliable and dedicated supporters. Men who had been in the party before the fall of 1922 and who had participated in the Revolution were given special certificates, called *brevetti della Marcia su Roma*. Party veterans had *squadrista* stamped on their membership cards, and in many fasci they had their own special units apart from the rest of the party organization. In 1939 a national rally was held in Rome to commemorate the twentieth anniversary of the founding of the first fascio, and party veterans gathered from all over Italy, wearing special squadrist insignia on their uniforms. The NSDAP also went to great pains to give special status to its veteran adherents who had joined during the darkest days before the conquest of power.

Although no precise statistics are available, it is possible to infer that the party inner circle was drawn chiefly from the middle and lower middle classes. The peasant and industrial working classes were only slightly represented in the ranks of the leadership; even the rank-and-file members were overwhelmingly middle class. In this the Italian Fascist party was different from both the Nazi and Soviet political aggregations. The NSDAP at one time claimed that one third of its supporters were from the working class, while the Russian Communists, with perhaps a broader scheme of classification, announced that two thirds of the men in their ranks were proletarians.[6]

Fascism, then, appears to have attracted its converts and militant fanatics from the anxiety-ridden, status-conscious Italian middle classes. The inner circle of the PNF was composed primarily of men with a fair amount of talent and education, who were determined to make a mark in the world and who harbored deep resentments against the previous society for having withheld from them the recognition they believed their due. Within the party thousands of these people found careers in the apparat; the others gained relief from the monotony and anonymity of their daily lives through participating in party meetings, campaigns, and ceremonies. They earned great satisfaction from their squadrist past; because of that status, they were persons of distinction and influence in local party organizations.

49

As young men were graduated from the youth organizations and older veterans began to die off, the problem of replenishing the ranks of the inner circle became important to the leadership. Not much was accomplished until Starace became secretary, when a system of party leadership schools was founded. Boys whom youth organization leaders judged outstanding in ability and Fascist conviction were encouraged to attend the schools, where they received intensive ideological training, often coupled with an apprenticeship at some party job.[7] Upon successful completion of the prescribed courses, the budding party leaders were given minor positions in the apparat or in one of the party's many subsidiary institutions. In the Milanese fascio, for example, graduates of the party schools began by serving as officers in the youth organizations, assistants to provincial inspectors, directors of Dopolavoro units, or aides to the *fiduciarii* of the ward organizations.[8]

It is not possible to gauge how effectively the party trained selected members of the rising generation to take the places of the old guard. Before World War II began, very few major positions had been turned over to youthful aspirants. And, with the approach of war, young party members were sent into the armed forces. Fascism did not survive long enough to test its system for perpetuating the party elite. There is every reason to believe, however, that the system would have worked perfectly well had the regime not been destroyed in the war.

THE RANK AND FILE

In contrast to constitutional political organizations, totalitarian parties do not permit anyone to join who wishes to do so. In Max Weber's involved terminology, totalitarian parties are not characterized by "formally free recruiting." Even during the period before the seizure of power, such parties make no effort to acquire the greatest possible number of adherents, for they do not need mass membership to achieve their ends: they have no scruples about using subversion and revolution to gain control of the government. Indeed, totalitarian parties oppose too large an influx of members, fearing a commensurate loss in revolutionary energy. Party membership to a Fascist or a Nazi was a serious thing; it required a total, almost religious, commitment on the part of the initiate. Partial adhesion for non-ideological reasons was intolerable.

50

Consequently, totalitarian parties come to power with a relatively small group of militant members. When the party becomes the only road to political influence — when it emerges as the single party — millions of persons, a few with genuine and many with spurious motives, clamor to be added to the ranks of the party faithful. The old guard naturally is suspicious of these new converts. The veterans have nothing but contempt for opportunistic latecomers, who merely want to share in the spoils of power. They reason that if the party is filled with place-hunters the organization will become corrupt and lazy. Instead of a revolutionary army perpetually fighting to make the dreams of the ideology a living reality, the party will degenerate into a privileged caste, a loathsome and degrading spectacle.

Initially all the totalitarian regimes resolved to admit no new members into the party save the younger people whose minds had been tempered and emotions molded by the youth organizations. Gradually, for various reasons, this prohibition was removed, and in each system a selected number of adults who had not possessed the prescience to join before the triumph of the new despotism were given the honor of party membership.

Each dictatorship handled membership procedures in its own way. In the Nazi case, since the handwriting on the wall had for perhaps two years before the event foretold the victory of the NSDAP over the faltering Weimar government, a relatively large number of Germans sought, and gained, party membership in the early period. Furthermore, the NSDAP did not close the doors to new adult entrants until three months after Hitler had been appointed chancellor. As a result, the Nazi party had nearly three million members at the outset of the dictatorship. This figure is six times the following claimed by the PNF in the early days of the Fascist regime. Except for recruits passed on from the *Hitler-Jugend*, the NSDAP did not admit any new members until 1937, when it permitted a flood of older citizens, mainly civil servants, to come in.[9]

The Communist party in Russia did not completely ban new adult memberships after 1917, but it subjected both youths coming up through the *Komsomol* ranks and older applicants to a much more rigorous screening than either the Nazis or the Fascists required of their applicants. Would-be Communists had to secure recommendations from members in good standing, and after passing the first examination they served an apprenticeship of from one to two years. The Communist party has always remained a relatively small organization, never including more than 3 per cent of the Russian people (see Table 2). In both Italy and Germany, however, from 5 to 8 per cent of the population were enrolled in the party.[10]

Because the Nazi party, like the PNF, pursued a comparatively lax admissions policy, it became necessary for the Germans to distinguish sharply within party ranks between the militants and those who were subsequently allowed to get on the bandwagon. Like the Fascists, the Nazi party had its inner circle. By legislation of May 9, 1933, party

Table 2. Membership in the Communist Party of the Soviet Union*

Year	Number	Year	Number
1917	23,600	1932	2,203,951
1918	115,000	1934	1,826,756
1919	251,000	1935	1,489,907
1920	431,400	1938	1,405,879
1925	440,365	1940	1,982,743
1926	639,652	1945	3,965,530
1928	914,307	1952	6,013,259
1929	1,090,508	1956	6,795,896

Sources: Merle Fainsod, *How Russia Is Ruled*, p. 212; and Gwendolyn M. Carter, John H. Herz, and John C. Ranney, *Major Foreign Powers*, p. 582.
* These figures do not include candidate members.

Table 3. Membership in the Partito Nazionale Fascista*

Date	Number	Date	Number
Summer 1919	17,000	June 9, 1933	1,099,626
Summer 1920	100,000	October 28, 1933	1,415,407
September 1921	300,000	October 28, 1934	1,851,777
Summer 1922	477,000	October 28, 1936	2,027,400
September 1925	700,000	October 28, 1937	2,152,240
October 15, 1926	937,967	October 28, 1938	2,430,352
September 6, 1927	1,000,052	October 28, 1939	2,633,514
October 25, 1928	1,027,010	October 28, 1940	3,619,846
February 28, 1930	1,040,588	June 10, 1943	4,770,770

Sources: *Fogli d'ordini* nos. 11, 34, 51, 167, 185, 244; *Atti del P. N. F.*, III (1934), 31, 312; Vincenzo Sinagra, *Profilo storico del Partito Nazionale Fascista*, I; Roberto Farinacci, *Un periodo aureo del Partito Nazionale Fascista*, p. 14; *Regime Fascista*, March 1, 1930, and October 28, 1938; Luigi Salvatorelli and Giovanni Mira, *Storia del fascismo*, p. 937; Attilio Tamaro, *Venti anni di storia, 1922–1943*, III, 400; and Carl T. Schmidt, *The Corporate State in Action*, p. 43 (the figures for 1919, 1920, and 1922).
* The statistics beginning with 1933 are more nearly accurate than the earlier ones. Of the enormous 1943 enrollment, 1,600,140 persons were in the armed forces.

veterans were given special status in the party organization; these included the three hundred thousand party members who had been first to join and all persons who belonged to the *Sturmabteilung* (SA) and the *Schutzstaffel* (SS).

In Italy, party membership increased steadily over the years (see Table 3). There were periods when persons from the older age groups were allowed to join. In other years the doors remained tightly sealed to all except those admitted by way of the youth groups. The party ranks were open to new recruits for several months after the March on Rome, but only a fraction of those requesting membership were satisfied at that time, and on April 24, 1923, the newly created Grand Council decreed a halt to the acceptance of new members. Some influential persons were still able to obtain party cards because the provincial secretaries possessed the power to grant honorary membership to a few "outstanding" individuals. This custom was abolished in 1924.

With the outbreak of the Matteotti crisis, when the regime was in sore need of convinced supporters, the lists were reopened. Those who joined between the summer of 1924 and the first months of 1925 were later accorded a place in the party second only to the veterans of the March on Rome. As the regime gained strength and power, the party once again tightened its requirements. Provincial organizations were enjoined to be strict about taking in new members. The PNF, which had come to power with fewer than five hundred thousand names on its rolls, numbered almost one million men in the fall of 1926. Almost all of these additional members were "tardy" Fascists, for the youth groups had not been in operation long enough to produce a sizable crop of graduates. Accordingly, from November 1926 until November 1932, the gates were again barred to new adult members.[11]

Augusto Turati, the national secretary during those years, explained to party leaders that the restrictive admissions policy was necessary in order that the party might always remain a revolutionary elite. "At first, when there were only a few of you," he told his fellow Fascists, "many laughed and found you ridiculous . . . But, once victory had been achieved, everyone crowded the doors asking to enter into the Fascist ranks."[12] The party should remain a select group, in order to preserve the distinction between "those who made the revolution, and those who did not . . ."

The year 1932 marked a fundamental reversal of party membership policy. As a "gift" commemorating the regime's tenth anniversary, the 1926 ban on new admissions was lifted. Beginning on November 5, 1932, the PNF received applications for membership until August 1, 1933, when the lists were closed again. What is unique about this recruitment period is that civil servants, schoolteachers, police officers, and most army officers were *forced* to take out party cards if they wanted to keep their jobs. Fascist Italy was the only one of the three major totalitarian states to make party membership a precondition for employment by the state.[13] The 1933 invitation to join the party was not extended to the general population; it was addressed only to certain categories of people, and the persons who received it had no option but to accept if they wished to remain in public life.

The recruits of 1932 were on the whole regarded contemptuously by party militants as political neutrals. The leadership was under no illusion that it was adding hundreds of thousands of devout, fanatical Fascists. These latecomers had previously either missed their opportunity to become members of the true party, the inner circle, or had been denied admission to that charmed company because they were deemed to lack the qualities of crudity, simple-mindedness, and blind devotion to the ideology so essential to the party militant. The party's objective in forcing the so-called neutrals to enter its outer ranks was to obtain greater control over their minds and acts than it had formerly been able to exercise. As party members they were directly under the secretary's authority — required to obey his commands, subject to his discipline, and scrutinized by his inspectors. To the ordinary bureaucrat, his newly acquired membership was hardly a privilege; it was the latest and most burdensome of the chains with which the dictatorship had shackled him.

To ascertain the precise number of adults admitted during the 1932–1933 campaign is a difficult matter. An aproximate idea of the number can be deduced, however. The official membership statistics (given here in Table 3) show an increase of 752,151 members during the seventeen-month period from June 9, 1933, until October 28, 1934. It took many months to process all the new applications; the probability is that the greater part of the increment came from the newly recruited neutrals. The party did not reveal how many of the new members were graduates of the youth groups; nor is there any way of determining the number of persons who died or were expelled during this interval, although the number expelled is known to be slight. All in all, it appears likely that the PNF secured within its 1932–1933 open period from five to six hundred thousand adults formerly outside the pale. Such an augmentation of the rank and file was a political fact of major importance.[14]

Although it would have been impossible for the party to conduct a thorough examination of the record of every candidate for admission, the PNF leadership did undertake what amounted to a vast loyalty check of as many of the new applicants as feasible. Candidates were required to secure the recommendations of two party members, and, in cases where there was doubt in the minds of party officials, every facet of the person's life was investigated. For this purpose the party had access to secret police records.[15] Persons who were denied admission either were placed under close police surveillance or lost their jobs.

A prospective member was required to apply for admission through the party headquarters in the locality where he resided. Some fasci were more strict about rejecting applicants than others, but everywhere only a few were turned down. Only 3 per cent of the candidates in the Turin area were refused; Milan had an unusually large group of rejections, but even there they amounted to only one tenth of the total applicants.[16] The national office warned that the provincial and local organizations should not take "sickly" persons into the party, lest they injure the health of the entire body. Careful investigations, said the national leaders, should be made of all applicants. These regulations were complied with as closely as was possible, considering the hundreds of thousands of applications which had to be processed in a short time.[17]

Some scholars, among them Maurice Duverger, have suggested that the rather lax admissions standards of the PNF brought decadence to the party. This overlooks one fact: the distinction between the inner and outer party was meticulously preserved. The new members were awarded no positions in the apparat; they were given no opportunity to exert any real influence on party policy or administration. Since they were inducted in order to be more easily manipulated and controlled by the party within the party, the driving force of the PNF, only in a formal sense were they party members.

Most veteran members referred to the 1932 recruits derisively as *fascisti del pane* and said they had joined the party *per necessità familiare.*[18] Indeed, so much abuse was heaped on the novices that the national secretary found it necessary to issue a stern warning to party veterans to refrain from making "inopportune comments" about the new members.[19]

Between 1933 and 1939 one further exception was made to the normal policy of granting no new adult memberships. In November 1936 persons who had volunteered for service in the Ethiopian War or who had distinguished themselves with exceptionally brave actions were permitted to request admission to the PNF. As the statistics in Table 3 indicate, this did not cause a sharp rise in party membership between 1936 and 1937. The large increases for 1938 (over 275,000) and 1939 (more than 200,000) were derived mainly from the progressively greater number of graduates from the youth organizations. In 1940 by order of Starace's successor, Ettore Muti, the lists were opened once more. This time it was decreed that all who served in the armed forces could have the privilege of joining. As a bonus, their seniority was to date from March 3, 1925. That accounted for the last major jump in party adherents. Significantly enough, when the party was reconstituted in 1943 under the Social Republic, these gratuitous memberships were not honored. The party was officially reduced to what it had always been in fact: only the inner party veterans and militant youngsters remained members of the PNF.[20]

THE PARTY PURGES ITSELF

If the party added to its rank and file periodically, it also developed the habit of throwing sizable numbers of persons out from time to time. The party gave; it also took away. The policy on expulsion was by no means as carefully thought out as the admissions program, however. The Fascist party in Italy never developed the purge into a scientific technique, as the Communists in the Soviet Union were able to do during the thirties. Extensive purges were not conducted with precise regularity; their frequency and intensity depended largely upon the whim of the secretary in charge. The Fascist purges generally did not involve whole categories of people who were convicted on purely trumped-up charges. The courts of the PNF usually arraigned only isolated individuals or cliques in a given locality on indictments of corruption, disobedience, or treason. There were no open trials and public confessions. The Nazis were at one with the Fascists in disdaining Russian methods in this area.

The change of the guard was the Fascist regime's only technique for perpetually reinvigorating its leadership cadres. This was a pale substitute for the Soviet purge, however; it might succeed in breaking up independent centers of power within the state or party machinery, but the lax, the unenthusiastic, the corrupt, and the cynical were simply transferred to other, sometimes more influential, positions.

Although by comparison with the Russians the Fascists were amateurs at the purging art, the PNF's power to expel aroused great trepidation in the rank and file. The Fascist expulsion policy was arbitrary, erratic, and unpredictable. It struck down a relatively small number of Fascists, but no member could be sure that the lightning would not strike him. As a result, the average member was suspicious and alert. He guarded his speech and actions and carefully conformed to the requirements for "Fascist behavior." From the leaders' point of view, the purge policy was successful, for they believed control of the actions of the body was the surest path to power over the will of the soul.

The first purge conducted by the PNF occurred in the spring of 1923, only a few months after its political victory. Tens of thousands of persons had sought and gained membership in the PNF following the October triumph. In April the Grand Council decreed that many thousands be dropped from the rolls; some provincial fasci had been far too charitable in admitting these latecomers to share in the privileges of power.[21] There is no way of determining precisely how many were axed in the following months. Some years later, Mussolini informed Emil Ludwig that during his first year in office he had to "get rid" of 150,000 Fascists.[22] Most likely, the Duce was exaggerating, as dictators are in the habit of doing. At that time the PNF was too disorganized and in too chaotic a condition to conduct such an enormous purge. But it is undeniable that large numbers were expelled; most of these were the tardy ones who had joined after October, but some were dissident members of the original Blackshirt formations.

When Farinacci became secretary, he tried to root out those who had wavered in their loyalties during the Matteotti crisis or who were unwilling to conform to centralized party discipline. "Expulsions," stated the secretary in a speech to the party's national council in October of 1925, "must be courageously carried out by a revolutionary party if it wishes to progress and truly march forward." He cited approvingly the harsh position on expulsion taken by the Russian Communists.[23]

One student of Italian Fascism has put the number of party members expelled by Farinacci at eight thousand. As might have been expected in this stage of the party's structural evolution, the new party chief had great difficulty with some provincial organizations, most notably those of Turin, Genoa, and Trieste. In each of these provinces the party chief was threatening to usurp the power of the governmentally appointed prefect and to institute a reign of terror; these provincial rebellions were undertaken contrary to the instructions from the national office. Accordingly, special commissions were sent from the Roman headquarters to purge the party groups responsible.[24]

The years under Augusto Turati were peaceful, so far as internal party politics were concerned. Judging from the lists of expellees, for the first and only time reprinted in the party's official publication, the *Fogli d'ordini*, there were only two or three thousand members ejected from the PNF during Turati's four years of tenure. In fact, the secretary warned provincial leaders in one circular that they should exercise greater caution in recommending "the grave penalty of expulsion."[25] Even during this calm period there occasionally were expulsions involving groups. In early 1928, for instance, a number of members were dismissed from the party because they refused to pay the heavier dues levied on them as a result of their greater wealth.[26]

Probably the largest purge in party history was that led by Giovanni Giuriati, Turati's successor, during the years 1929–1931. In his first order of the day, dated October 29, 1930, the new secretary indicated that discipline would be tightened. He curtly announced that the Duce had given him "the task of eliminating dead wood from the party." Giuriati's primary objective was to dispose of Fascists who had used their positions of influence in the PNF to embezzle funds or to carry on a variety of illegal activities under cover of their privileged status. In his unpublished memoirs, the former party chief claims to have either expelled or inflicted serious penalties upon no fewer than a hundred and twenty thousand members. This purifying operation aroused tremendous enmity in certain party circles. Mussolini himself eventually became appalled over the extent of the purge, and, in a moment of anger, forced Giuriati to resign.[27]

Like his predecessors, Giuriati had his problems of internal discipline. Giampaoli, one of the leaders of the March on Rome and party boss of Milan, had by the late twenties become virtual dictator of this northern metropolis. Giampaoli had stirred dissension within party ranks and had managed to incur the bitter hatred of Arnaldo Mussolini, the Duce's brother. Giuriati gave Starace, then one of his vice-secretaries, special powers to investigate the Milanese *federazione* and to take such action as seemed necessary. Starace's remedy was drastic: he removed from office and expelled Giampaoli and from eight to nine thousand of his Milanese supporters.[28] This event went down in party histories as the *epurazione milanese*.

After Giuriati's crusade against insubordination and the Italian version of honest graft had spent its fury, there ensued a period when harsh disciplinary procedures were eased. A halt was called to further mass expulsions, and the party demonstrated its capacity to forgive as well as to chasten by granting an amnesty to all members who had received penalties less severe than expulsion. No expulsions were rescinded, but those who had been suspended or who had suffered the retraction of their cards were pardoned. Like the decision to admit new members, the amnesty of 1932 was widely heralded as a proof of the regime's generosity on the occasion of its tenth anniversary.[29]

Notwithstanding the general relaxation of party discipline at the end of 1932, a few famous trials were held during this interval which resulted in the expulsion of persons highly situated in Fascist circles. Some of the cases involved government officials,[30] but others implicated former members of the party high command. The case attracting the most notoriety involved no less a personage than Augusto Turati, the former national secretary. Turati had become editor of Turin's powerful newspaper *La Stampa* following his resignation as PNF leader. On November 30, 1932, Starace's office revealed that Turati had been "indefinitely suspended" from the party on the grounds that he had used "deplorable and inadmissible expressions" about certain Fascist leaders in personal letters which had fallen into the hands of party spies. Turati lost his editorship, and for the remainder of his life he was kept under careful watch. He never again held a position of responsibility under Fascism.[31]

Turati's sad fate provides an interesting lesson in the politics of totalitarianism. Even the watchers were watched, and no one, save the

Duce himself, managed to escape scrutiny of the omnipresent spy system. It is likely that Starace feared Turati's power; as soon as he had a pretext for destroying him, he quickly proceeded to do so. The episode was a grim reminder both to the ruling elite and to the rank and file that the party was always watching and waiting.

Throughout his tenure in office Starace directed the purging machinery at key figures who he feared might threaten his own security. No mass expulsions of the rank and file à la Giuriati occurred while Starace was party chief. Official statistics for this period are scanty, but an indication of how few persons were expelled in the thirties was given in a report of the Milan organization. From 1933 to 1937 there were only 525 expulsions or membership revocations in the Milan federation, a far cry from the eight to nine thousand ejected in a single year under Giuriati.[32] Starace did crack down on party officials who defied his stringent discipline or who attempted to circumvent his office in order to gain favors for themselves. In 1934 he expelled a number of provincial leaders who had intrigued to get seats in the Chamber of Deputies.

One possible exception to the statement that no great waves of expulsions of ordinary members took place under Starace is the Jewish purge of 1938. All members declared by the new racial laws to be Jewish were expelled from the party in the autumn of 1938. There are no available statistics on the number of Jews who had been enrolled in the party, but since there were about fifty thousand persons of Hebraic descent in Italy at the time, it is possible that this purge involved several thousand members.

This review of party disciplinary machinery in action indicates that the purge was an effective instrument for keeping both the apparat and the rank and file in line. Expulsion is a potent weapon for a totalitarian single party to wield. If a man was thrown out of the Fascist party in Italy, not only was his status in the party affected, but his position in the community as well. He was banned from public life, often suffering imprisonment by the state, or bodily injury at the hands of party toughs. His existence became hardly bearable.

As indicated earlier, the Italian Fascists never perfected the purge to the extent that their Russian brethren were able to do under Stalin. The PNF did not "purify" itself at regular intervals by expelling for its own sake, by ejecting great hordes of members known *not* to be guilty. But the PNF was all the same a disciplined party, well worthy of the respect of the totalitarian mind. The Fascist party denied all but its most hardened militants positions of influence as members of the inner circle; and even this chosen elite felt the breath of the inspectors on their necks and the sting of the party whip.

The Molding of Youth

ALL totalitarian dictatorships display an extraordinary interest in the younger generation. This concern with reaching the juvenile mind is a characteristic peculiar to recent despotisms. In the past, autocratic rulers were at the most careful to see that no clearly subversive ideas were spread through the educational systems of their societies; they lacked the zeal with which the totalitarian leader endeavors to empty susceptible young minds of old ideas and to substitute his own *Weltanschauung* for the outmoded morality of the old order.

Enthusiasm for winning over the youth cannot be traced solely to the desire of the regime to retain power. Rather, totalitarian leaders believe that, since their ideology contains the truth that will save the nation and ultimately the world, they have a mission to spread that doctrine to every segment of the population. No one may be left without the redeeming word. And not only must the new political religion be made known to the world today; it must be made secure for future generations as well. The leaders will pass away, but the truth must stand forever. The only way to perpetuate that truth is to raise up new prophets who understand it, receive it as a precious legacy, and are willing to fight and die for its triumph in the world. Out of the millions of younger subjects a new guardian class must be selected. Hence, the ideology, the new dispensation, demands that all the youth be courted, organized, trained, entertained, and indoctrinated, and that the few most worthy be chosen.

The single party was the logical body to undertake the task of molding youth. The party was the elite of the older generation; its leaders best understood and most faithfully worked to realize the new ideology and were best suited to choose the new elite. It possessed the kind of structure that would make the total incorporation of the younger people a simple matter. Accordingly, in all three major dictatorships of the twentieth century, the party controlled the process of indoctrinating the youth.

FROM THE ONB TO THE GIL

Totalitarian parties are preoccupied with winning the loyalty of youth even before achieving power. The PNF organized Italian Fascism's first youth groups many months before the March on Rome. By June of 1922 the party had three youth formations for the age groups eight to fourteen, fourteen to eighteen, and twenty-one to twenty-eight. The unit for small children was named after a legendary boy hero, Balilla, who in the eighteenth century inspired nationalist demonstrations throughout Italy by slinging a rock at some Austrian policemen.[1] When, in 1926, the regime made the combined party youth organizations into a legal institution of the state, Balilla was further immortalized by the Fascists, for the official youth organization of the Fascist state was named *Opera Nazionale Balilla* (ONB).

Technically speaking, the party lost control of its youth groups when they became an agency of the government. In 1929 the ONB was placed under the authority of the Ministry of National Education, thereby removing it even further from party control so far as the law was concerned. Actually, the change was only for the sake of appearance. The dictatorship's purpose was to dramatize its determination to monopolize the entire education of youth. The regime was eager to combat the claim of the Roman Catholic Church to any rights in the area of education. From the ONB and the state schools Italian youth would receive their "military, physical, professional, technical, spiritual, and cultural" training. The ONB would preserve the youth of the nation uncorrupted in an atmosphere of "discipline and service to the nation."[2] The same development occurred in Nazi Germany: the Hitler-Jugend eventually was made an agency of the Reich, although the NSDAP retained effective management of Jugend activities.[3]

Despite the changes in the legal status of the ONB, the same person remained in charge. Renato Ricci was a prominent member of the party directorate; as ONB president he had the authority to appoint all provincial, and to approve all local, officials of the organization.

Although tension later developed between Ricci and others in the PNF leadership, in any number of ways the ties between party and ONB remained close and intimate — the party apparat supplied the leaders for the ONB; the older boys' divisions were always present at PNF ceremonies and parades; and party inspectors often included ONB headquarters in their rounds of checking on party establishments.

The major turning point in the development of the Fascist youth groups was the struggle with *Azione Cattolica* (AC). Within a year after the establishment of the ONB as the state-sponsored youth organization, the dictatorship had begun to challenge the existence of Catholic youth groups. When the Catholic boy scouts, the *Esploratori Cattolici*, were disbanded by the papacy in 1927 because of the ignominious conditions attached by the government to their continuation,[4] the Fascists scored an important victory, because the scouts had been the only remaining rival to the ONB in camping and athletics. Catholic Action, a large organization of young Catholic laymen interested in applying Catholic principles to political and social life, was permitted to survive for the time being. Under its auspices a number of religious youth groups had been organized for boys and girls from elementary school to university age levels. Several hundred thousand young people were enrolled in these youth auxiliaries.

In the spring of 1928 the regime threatened, for tactical reasons, to abolish the AC, but the order was rescinded shortly after it was issued. The Lateran negotiations were then in a most delicate state; the power to dissolve Catholic Action was a useful bartering tool for Mussolini in his effort to procure a Concordat with the Church, thereby ending the sixty-year-old *dissidio* between the papacy and the Italian state. Article 43 of the Concordat of 1929 recognized the Catholic Action groups so far as they pursued "activities disassociated from any political party." The Fascist leadership had accused the AC of attempting to reconstitute the defunct Popular party, and Article 43 was designed to check any direct political activity on the part of the Church.[5]

No sooner had the ink dried on the Concordat than an anonymous book was issued by a publishing house controlled by the PNF attacking the AC as an "opposition political party."[6] The volume, which was widely read and circulated, insisted that all matters concerning the education of Italian youth were properly under state jurisdiction, and that the Church should withdraw completely from this area. Alarmed by these statements, Pius XI released the encyclical *Rappresentante in terra* at the end of 1929. The letter asserted that the Church had the minimal right to decide what kind of education was contrary to Christian truth or harmful to morality, and it attacked the ONB for its excessive emphasis on violence in training exercises and its attempt to monopolize all the free time of members. Three weeks later the party took up the battle of words, and the leaders of the PNF issued what, with all its pretentiousness, sounded like a counter-encyclical. The national secretary ominously declared: "The Regime intends to prepare spiritually all Italian youth, from whom by a process of . . . selection must emerge the future ruling class of Fascist Italy. The Fascist Revolution requires the totalitarian principle of youth education . . . in order to realize its intention of enduring into the future."[7]

During 1930 the skirmish between the party and Catholic Action continued, but for the most part it was not conducted in the open. The PNF did loudly protest the formation of a special division of the AC concerned with the improvement of working conditions. In 1931, with Giuriati at the helm as new party chief, the campaign was intensified, and party leaders made widely publicized speeches all over the country attacking the Church and Catholic Action. Finally, on May 30, 1931, Mussolini decreed the dissolution of the youth groups of Catholic Action. The party announced that it possessed documentary evidence that anti-Fascism flourished in AC ranks, and all local and provincial fasci were alerted to aid in the execution of the May 30 order.

A month later the Pope responded with the eloquent encyclical *Non abbiamo bisogno*, which termed the proposal to organize, to the exclusion of all other groups, the entire youth of the nation, from earliest childhood to adulthood, "pagan statolatry." The pontiff deplored the use of violence by party squadrists, who had attacked the leaders and damaged the buildings of the religious organization. He reaffirmed the Church's "natural rights" to supervise and conduct the education of youth, and he condemned the oath required of all members of the party and its youth organizations. To the words "I swear to execute without discussion the orders of the Duce and to serve with all my strength, and if necessary with my blood, the cause of the Fascist Revolution," Pius XI advised Catholics to add the mental reservation that they would do nothing contrary to the laws of God and the

Church. The issue was joined, and the Roman Church, which for hundreds of years had fought the excessive political pretensions of countless regimes, locked horns with the most ferocious enemy of all, the totalitarian state.

In July the party leadership, taking notice of the intolerable statements in *Non abbiamo bisogno,* announced the incompatibility of joint membership in the party and Catholic Action. As for the Pope's suggested mental reservation for Catholics confronted with the necessity of taking the party oath in order to continue to work and earn their daily bread, Giuriati issued a special circular denouncing the papal counsel. "We reject absolutely any reservation whatsoever," ran his belligerent notice. Fascist squadrism, revived during the next six weeks, lent force to the party's words.

Faced with such unrelenting opposition, the papacy gave in and accepted the surrender terms set by the Fascists. *Non abbiamo bisogno* had branded as false all the allegations leveled against the AC by the party, which had charged that the Catholic organization pursued political activities and harbored known anti-Fascists in its leadership. In the accord reached on September 2, 1931, however, the Church implicitly recognized the validity of many of the Fascist accusations.

According to the terms of the settlement the AC was again recognized by the government, but in an exclusively "diocesan" form. The leaders could not be chosen from "those who belong to parties which are the enemies of the regime." This provision, directed mainly against leaders of the AC who had formerly been active in the Popular party, in effect gave the regime the power to veto any nominations for official positions in the organization. This control was facilitated by another provision in the accord which canceled the right of the Catholic laymen to elect their own leaders. From that time on the bishop in each diocese was to appoint the group's officers. Catholic Action, continued the agreement, was not to concern itself with "political matters." Its syndical and professional groups were disbanded. The youth circles were prohibited from wearing any uniforms or insignia of their own and were required to display the tricolor at all meetings. The youth units were under no circumstance to participate in athletic or political activities of any kind; they were to serve exclusively as religious discussion groups. A few days after the settlement the party directorate rescinded its ban against simultaneous membership in the party and

Catholic Action. The Pope did not renew his objections to the oath. As Salvatorelli observed, "The battle of ideas . . . was abandoned by the papacy."[8]

A. C. Jemolo has called the September 2 settlement "a peace of compromise, without conquerors or conquered: a dignified peace, which the Church was able to conclude with tranquillity . . . "[9] And even so unbiased and perceptive a writer as Hannah Arendt, in speaking of the conciliatory policy of the Church toward Italian Fascism, has applauded the "wisdom of the Church, which very sagely recognized that Fascism was neither anti-Christian nor totalitarian in principle . . ." and so permitted "a separation of Church and State" to be effected by the Fascists.[10]

In actuality the September 2, 1931, agreement was a dangerous defeat for the Church. Limited and cramped in its activities, the residual shell of Catholic Action could offer far less to youth, naturally fascinated with the Fascist athletic and political programs, than the party-state organizations. Even more important, the accord and the withdrawal of the objections to the Fascist oath in effect gave the Church's blessing to the Fascist youth groups. In so doing the Church, in this area at least, allowed itself to be used as that *instrumentum regni* which Fascism wished religion to be. After 1931 the priests who before had accepted positions as chaplains to the youth organizations could fulfill their office in true earnest, many of them consenting to perpetuate such horrors as the "Fascistized masses" without an apparent twinge of conscience.

Once the conflict with Catholic Action had been resolved, Fascist youth organizations developed rapidly. In 1931 the party formed a new youth group, the *Fasci Giovanili di Combattimento,* for non-university men from the age of eighteen to twenty-one. Upon reaching their eighteenth birthday ONB graduates were to pass automatically to the Fasci Giovanili,[11] which was meant to serve as a proving ground for youth worthy of party membership. The organization quickly mushroomed in size, until by 1936 it included over a million and a quarter men in its ranks. The PNF chose to retain direct control of the Fasci Giovanili, as well as of the university students' group (the GUF, or *Gruppi Universitari Fascisti*). Thus, in legal status at least, part of the Fascist youth organizations were under state supervision and part were managed by the party.

As head of the ONB, Ricci had not been pleased with the party secretary's decision to keep the older youth units separated from his own ONB. Although the party and the ONB continued to work closely in harness, by the late thirties the personal feud between Starace and Ricci had become so intense that the administration of the youth program was beginning to suffer. The problem was resolved in the fall of 1937 when Starace managed to jettison the ONB president and to bring the entire youth machinery under the party's complete control. Some of the undercover stratagems employed to achieve this objective have been revealed by Ciano. Starace succeeded in winning over the opportunistic foreign secretary on this issue, so that on September 5, 1937, Ciano recorded in his diary: "The youth should depend exclusively on the party. I have said so to the Duce, who has thought so even before now."[12] Finally, on September 17, 1937, Mussolini made the decision to eliminate Ricci and the ONB and to create a new all-inclusive youth group directly dependent on the national party leadership: the *Gioventù Italiana del Littorio* (GIL).[13]

The statute of the GIL was published on October 27, 1937. Article One contrasts sharply with the milder language of the original 1926 statute creating the ONB. The GIL is described as the "unitary and totalitarian organization of the youth of the Fascist regime . . . instituted in the very heart of the party."[14] In each province and commune the party secretary was to be "general commander" of the GIL, while to one of the vice-secretaries was delegated the task of guiding the organization's detailed operations. At the lower territorial levels, the GIL administration was divided into three sections: *Giovani Fascisti*, for men from eighteen to twenty-one; *Balilla* and *Avanguardisti*, for boys from six to seventeen; and the youth groups for girls. Each section was subdivided into a number of agencies dealing with propaganda, sport, discipline, premilitary training, and comparable matters.[15]

After the formation of the GIL, no further modifications were made in the general organization of the Fascist youth groups, although the GIL was expanded to include units in the growing empire. An Albanian GIL, for example, was established shortly after the Italian victory in 1939 for the purpose of winning the "Aryan" youth of that country to Fascism.

The only youth group to remain outside the GIL was the university students' organization, the GUF. Exactly why this exception was made is not clear. Although the GUF was kept under party control, as it had been from its origin, nevertheless, especially in places like Rome, the band possessed a degree of autonomy. On the national level, the GUF was headed by a member of the party directorate. According to its statute of 1937, in the provinces the groups were run by a *fiduciario* appointed by the provincial secretary. Each provincial organization of the GUF was divided into six sections: organization; culture, art, and the press; courses of political preparation; sport; assistance; relations with foreign students. All the larger university organizations published a newspaper, the contents of which were supervised by the national office; the latter also directed special subjects for each paper to explore. Nationally, the organization published the periodical *Libro e Moschetto* (*Book and Rifle*). In addition the national GUF office directed the "School of Fascist Mysticism" at Milan, one of the party's principal leadership schools.[16]

The activities pursued by the youth groups were many and varied. Great emphasis was placed on thorough ideological training; after the GIL was formed in 1937, even more attention was given to this aspect of the youth program. But Fascism, as its adherents never tired of reminding the world, was not only faith, but also action. Consequently, the youth organization's function was not merely to teach the young a way of thinking, but to train them in the Fascist "style" of life. All gentleness, compassion, and charity were to be driven from them, and a pagan exaltation of violence and military vigor was to replace the soft and degenerate mores of the pre-Fascist generations. Thus, fifteen thousand Avanguardisti gathered at the annual *Campo Dux* outside Rome were exhorted by the party secretary to "love arms wildly, to love them and to know how to manage them so that tomorrow you may fight victoriously with them."[17] The model young Fascist was one who "tempers all enthusiasm with iron discipline . . . despises fear, loves the hard life, and serves with faith, passion, and happiness the Cause of Fascism."[18]

The major part of the activities of the youth organization were directed toward arousing in the young the desired warlike temperament. Athletic activities — including hiking, skiing, bicycle racing, track events, gymnastic training, and camping — and programs of military training were administered in such large doses as to interfere seriously with normal schoolwork. The entire Saturday of each week was devoted to these youth organization activities, as were many afternoons and evenings during the week. In the older boys' units, the Giovani Fascisti, military training was stressed exclusively. Rifle and machine-gun practice was held frequently, courses on military science and strategy were given by officers from the party militia, and the young men were allowed to participate in maneuvers held by the militia and regular army. Roman military terminology was used in naming the divisions within the youth organization. Each provincial group of Giovani Fascisti was broken down into legions, cohorts, centuries, and squads. The leader of the organization was called the commander, and he was advised by a general staff (*Stato Maggiore*).[19]

At frequent parades, rallies, and ceremonies, Italy's rifle-carrying youth were enjoined to be worthy servants of the Third Rome, to offer up their entire selves to the State. Fascism was in a sense a reversion to the pagan idolatry of the *polis,* and at its ceremonies the GIL attempted to arouse in its members a sense of awe and religious reverence for the regime. The annual *Leva Fascista,* the occasion on which the members moved up from a younger unit to one designed for their new age group, was accompanied by all the ritual one would expect to find at the initiation ceremonies of a mystery cult in ancient Rome.[20]

In spite of the papal opposition to this Fascist statolatry, some priests lamentably allowed Catholicism to be utilized by the Fascist leaders as a reinforcing civil religion. Thus, the youth organization succeeded in politicizing the Mass itself. A Mass held at the 1938 *Campo Dux* commenced with the singing of "Giovinezza" and an invocation to the Divine Being to aid Mussolini in the quest for empire. The camp's chief chaplain then began saying Mass, with the party secretary serving at the altar. At the elevation of the Host fifteen thousand youths drew their bayonets from their sheaths and pointed them toward the sky. The service was concluded with a prayer to the Duce and the singing of the GIL anthem.[21] In the Fascist inversion of values even the religion of Christ was interpreted as sanctioning conquest, violence, and hatred. Christian virtue was replaced by Machiavellian *virtù.*

Beginning in 1938, the Fascist youth organization adopted an official catechism summarizing the principles of the new morality. This volume[22] confirms that the goal of Fascism was to teach the youth "a new ethic, a Mussolinian and Fascist ethic." According to the cate-

chism, the youth should serve the Fascist state with passionate devotion, because the state "embraces the life of the nation in all its aspects: political, economic, spiritual, and moral." As Friedrich and
Brzezinski have commented on the efforts of the Nazi and Fascist
youth organizations to arouse the more savage aspects of human nature: "It is a melancholy thought that much of the idealism and love
of adventure which is perhaps the best part of boyhood was thus
channeled by these organizations into activities which stimulated the
lower instincts. The free organizations of the democratic countries,
whether boy scouts or religious or artistic groups, and even those con-
nected with political parties, though at times outwardly resembling
these youth organizations, are yet very different; even when the
slogans they use are similar, when they stress character and sports
and the benefits of outdoor life, the purpose is individual improvement
and a finer personality rather than the brute objectives of war and
conquest."[23]

MEMBERSHIP GROWTH: ASPIRATION AND FACT

When the ONB was originally established, the Fascist leaders did
not yet have clearly in mind the total incorporation of Italian youth
as an objective. There were voices in the inner circles urging that the
youth organization should remain an elite corps of militant Fascists
instead of expanding into a gigantic mass institution. These views
were subsequently suppressed, and in the thirties the regime embarked
upon a program to enroll every youngster in the appropriate group.

The Balilla enjoyed a period of rapid growth after Catholic Action
was rendered impotent in 1931. Between 1930 and 1937, membership
almost quadrupled (see Table 4). Notwithstanding these impressive
gains, the party leadership was dissatisfied that such a large percentage of the youth still remained outside the ONB. Perhaps the primary
purpose of creating the new GIL in 1937 was to expand the youth
organization to include virtually every young person in Italy. At its
meeting of October 6, 1938, the Grand Council of Fascism issued a
communiqué granting the party secretary a "mandate" to "reach in
the shortest possible time" the objective of the "totalitarian incorporation of all members of the new generation."[24] The youth were to be
morally, physically, and politically equipped to fulfill the "historic
mission of the revived Roman Empire." The October 1938 directive
was only the prelude to compulsory membership in the youth organi-

Table 4. Membership in the Opera Nazionale Balilla, 1924–1937

Date and Group	Number	Date and Group	Number
January 1924*	60,941	July 1, 1932	3,141,325
Balilla	7,120	Balilla	1,427,318
Avanguardisti	53,829	Avanguardisti	410,239
September 1925*	160,000	Piccole Italiane	1,184,424
Balilla	70,000	Giovani Italiane	119,344
Avanguardisti	90,000	July 1, 1933	3,454,069
October 15, 1926	480,355	Balilla	1,562,651
Balilla	269,166	Avanguardisti	443,278
Avanguardisti	211,189	Piccole Italiane	1,322,228
July 1, 1927	1,236,201	Giovani Italiane	125,912
Balilla	812,242	July 1, 1934	4,327,231
Avanguardisti	423,959	Balilla	1,952,597
July 1, 1928	1,268,368	Avanguardisti	535,974
Balilla	903,324	Piccole Italiane	1,637,689
Avanguardisti	365,044	Giovani Italiane	200,971
July 1, 1929	1,257,782	July 1, 1935	4,900,358
Balilla	933,178	Balilla	2,121,003
Avanguardisti	324,604	Avanguardisti	677,920
July 1, 1930†	1,687,478	Piccole Italiane	1,802,549
Balilla	742,933	Giovani Italiane	298,836
Avanguardisti	303,727	July 1, 1936	5,510,815
Piccole Italiane	550,252	Balilla	2,332,284
Giovani Italiane	90,566	Avanguardisti	788,896
July 1, 1931	2,126,166	Piccole Italiane	2,007,710
Balilla	947,340	Giovani Italiane	381,925
Avanguardisti	335,269	July 1, 1937	6,052,581
Piccole Italiane	755,810	Balilla	2,478,768
Giovani Italiane	87,747	Avanguardisti	960,118
		Piccole Italiane	2,130,530
		Giovani Italiane	483,145

Sources: 1924 and 1925 figures from Roberto Farinacci, *Un periodo aureo del Partito Nazionale Fascista*, pp. 156, 242; 1926 figures from *Fogli d'ordini* no. 11; 1927–1937 figures from *Gazzetta Ufficiale, Bollettino Mensile di Statistica*, 1933–1937.

* This was before the ONB was created a state institution.

† Before 1930 the Piccole Italiane and the Giovani Italiane had been included in the Fasci Femminili.

zations of the regime. Under Article Two of the *Carta della Scuola*, promulgated on February 10, 1939, all youths from the age of six to twenty-one were required to belong to the GIL, except university students, who were compelled to join the GUF. The subdivisions for age and sex are shown in the list on page 74.

This decision to make GIL membership compulsory caused the party to conduct an exhaustive survey of exactly what percentages of eligible youths were enrolled in the GIL as of May 31, 1939. Figures for all ninety-two provinces were obtained. (Table 5 supplies these

Table 5. Number and Percentage of Eligible Youths Inscribed in the GIL in Nine Provinces as of May 31, 1939

Province	Balilla	Piccole Italiane	Avanguardisti	Giovani Italiane	Giovani Fascisti	Giovani Fasciste	Total	%
Turin								
Eligible	40,634	48,022	36,346	26,095	33,496	37,297	221,890	
In GIL	35,280	37,692	21,788	12,730	19,208	14,425	141,123	64
Milan								
Eligible	84,956	102,476	72,992	57,228	69,589	81,241	468,482	
In GIL	75,654	81,734	43,359	27,766	28,809	20,799	278,121	59
Bologna								
Eligible	33,536	39,355	28,539	20,907	26,786	26,336	175,459	
In GIL	24,509	23,359	12,804	5,609	16,718	6,382	89,381	51
Florence								
Eligible	36,927	43,305	32,253	23,851	28,013	28,633	189,982	
In GIL	27,293	25,727	14,190	6,019	9,817	5,578	88,624	47
Rome								
Eligible	74,037	87,724	58,555	44,970	55,224	63,156	383,666	
In GIL	51,632	54,446	27,006	12,955	20,092	9,948	176,079	46
Perugia								
Eligible	30,477	35,624	24,262	17,049	21,112	18,611	147,135	
In GIL	19,593	16,207	8,166	4,119	9,840	4,838	62,763	43
Cagliari (Sardinia)								
Eligible	27,902	31,647	20,104	14,331	20,243	18,145	132,372	
In GIL	16,833	16,553	6,270	3,342	6,482	3,663	53,143	40
Venice								
Eligible	36,468	42,884	26,989	19,346	23,826	22,690	172,203	
In GIL	23,100	19,907	7,030	4,757	5,125	4,947	64,866	38
Naples								
Eligible	123,717	143,471	81,004	66,078	87,244	86,114	587,628	
In GIL	62,615	54,260	25,618	7,113	23,551	7,273	180,430	31

Source: *Fogli d'ordini*, May–December 1939.

73

Male	Female	Age
Figli della Lupa*	Figlie della Lupa*	6–8
Balilla	Piccole Italiane	8–14
Avanguardisti	Giovani Italiane	14–18
Giovani Fascisti	Giovani Fasciste	18–21
Gruppi Universitari Fascisti		18–28

statistics for nine provinces. The membership figures for the GUF are given in Table 6.) They reveal in what areas of Italy the youth were most highly organized, and within each province, which age group and sex contributed the most members. Unfortunately, no distinctions

Table 6. Membership in the Gruppi Universitari Fascisti

Date	Number
February 28, 1930	41,680
October 29, 1936	75,436
October 28, 1937	82,004
October 28, 1938*	93,175

Sources: 1930 figures from *Regime Fascista*, March 1, 1930; 1936 and 1937 figures from *Fogli d'ordini* nos. 167 and 185; 1938 figures from *Regime Fascista*, October 28, 1938.

 * The GUF was the only group to remain outside the GIL after 1937. However, it continued under the direct control of the party.

were made between rural and urban areas, or between large and small cities within each province. There is no question that participation was much heavier in the larger urban centers than even the highest percentage given for any province indicates.

The party divided the provinces into nine groups. The first, with from 64 to 71 per cent of the youth inscribed in the GIL, included primarily north central, middle-sized industrial areas where Fascism first demonstrated its strength. Novara, Cremona, and Bergamo are in this category. The second and third classes, with from 51 to 64 per cent participation, comprised large and medium-sized urban areas principally in the north, Tuscany, and the Romagna. Genoa, Milan, Bologna, Trieste, and Brescia are representative cities in these provinces. In the fourth category were Rome, Florence, and certain smaller localities in Tuscany and the Romagna, where from 45 to 51 per cent

* Usually combined with Balilla and Piccole Italiane in the statistics.

of those eligible had joined the youth groups. The remaining five levels included, with very few exceptions, exclusively provinces in the south.

Low participation in the *Mezzogiorno* does not imply that the youth of southern Italy were less enthusiastically Fascist than were their northern compatriots. A visit to southern Italy today will convince the traveler that nowhere was Fascism more popular than in these provinces, and it is no surprise that the neo-Fascist movement has thus far made its greatest gains in the south. The main reason for low GIL enrollment in the predominantly rural south was that a much lower percentage of children attended school beyond the first few grades than was general in the north. Also, youths still in school were often needed on the holidays for farm work and could not be spared for party parades, camps, military maneuvers, and so forth.[25] There can be no doubt that the urban community was more adaptable to the techniques of a modern mass party than was the agrarian sector.

The writer H. Stuart Hughes has contended that the Fascist youth organization attracted mainly upper and middle class children, and that "the working class and peasantry were frankly uninterested" in having their children join.[26] Although the party released no statistics enabling one to check this observation precisely, it appears to be true only within limits. A greater percentage of middle and upper class youths did join and *remain in* the GIL than did the children of workers and peasants. The basis for this phenomenon is quite apparent: membership did not bring the same tangible benefits for children of the lower classes. The parents of middle and upper class children took pains to enroll and keep their children in the youth organizations because GIL membership was an absolute prerequisite for eventual admission into the party. And party membership became steadily more essential for any kind of remunerative and pleasant employment in Italy. The class distinctions which Hughes delineates are important only where young people over fourteen years old are considered, however. His generalization does not take into account a significant trend caught in the 1939 youth census: the far greater percentage of youths in the GIL between the ages of six and fourteen than for the later age groups (see the sample figures in Table 5). In the northern and central provinces from 70 to 90 per cent of the children of both sexes were enrolled in the Balilla and Piccole Italiane. Even in the rural and mountainous southern areas, membership in the younger subdivisions of the

GIL was from 50 to 60 per cent. These figures must mean that a great many more youths than the middle and upper classes alone could produce were inscribed in the Fascist organizations between the ages of six and fourteen, perhaps the most crucial period for purposes of indoctrination. It is reasonable to assume that, up until the compulsory membership requirement of 1939, those who remained in the youth organization beyond the age of fourteen were most likely to be either ideological militants or prudent conformists who regarded continued membership as necessary for the advancement of their careers. (The objective of the youth organization, of course, was to convert the conformists into militants.) Upper and middle class youth made up the greater part of these two types.

Finally, it should be observed that, especially after the age of fourteen, the groups for older girls, *Giovani Italiane* and *Giovani Fasciste,* dropped in numbers much more drastically than did the boys' units, thereby lowering the total percentage of young people enrolled in the GIL considerably. Since membership of older girls is not a fact of major political significance for the study of Fascism, this reduction should be taken into account in evaluating the statistics.

The Fascist youth organization never achieved its goal of total incorporation of the younger generation. The advent of World War II directed the energies of the regime into other channels.[27]

THE PARTY LEADERSHIP SCHOOLS

The totalitarian party undertakes not only to train the mass of youth to adopt a novel way of thinking and acting; it also attempts to ferret out the elite of the younger generation for especially intense indoctrination. In both Nazi Germany and Fascist Italy special leadership schools were established for the purpose of providing the regime with a select group worthy to receive the mantle of authority from the old guard. As Hitler once remarked, the party is able to follow the lives of the youth from infancy, to observe "all their being," and finally "to choose those who seem best . . . and enroll them in the ranks of the old guard."[28] The charisma, or mystical leadership qualities, of the original elite would thereby be transmitted to selected persons in the rising generations. But it would be a highly regularized and carefully manipulated, rather than a spontaneous and creative, charisma that would be bequeathed to them.

76

The rulers of Fascist Italy wanted to raise up soldiers instead of leaders. All the tests conducted in the youth organizations from the early ages through the schools for older youth were designed to measure the individual's ability to follow orders without questioning them. In the same manner, the Nazis employed the term *Gefolgschaft* (followership) to designate the proper attitude they wished to inculcate in the new elite. As Ignazio Silone has written in *The School for Dictators*: "In spite of their pompous names . . . [the Nazi and Fascist schools for political preparation] are not schools for political leaders, but schools for obedient underlings . . . Their purpose is to train youths in docility and devotion." It is appropriately revealing that one Fascist writer, in searching for the correct phrase with which to describe the new kind of aristocracy Fascism was creating, could express himself only in military terminology. He labeled the Fascist ruling elite an *aristocrazia guerriera*. Fascist leaders were not chosen for intelligence, wealth, or heredity, but for the extent to which they displayed "warlike" characteristics.[29]

From their very first year in the Fascist youth organization, children were carefully watched by their supervisors. As they passed from Balilla to Avanguardisti to Giovani Fascisti, youths judged to be outstanding were called *scelti* (chosen). They were given special instruction by their provincial organizations, and they served as unit leaders. Many boys in the scelti category were sent to the National Training Camp outside Rome for two months in the summer, where they were subjected to an astonishingly heavy dose of ideology.[30]

The most important and far-reaching program of party training for youthful aspirants to leadership was initiated by decision of the national directorate on September 28, 1934. Beginning at the first of the year courses of political preparation were to be held in all the larger provinces. Youths from twenty-three to twenty-eight years of age "who possess the requisite intelligence, will, and character, and who have demonstrated these qualities in the party's organizations" were to be admitted. Depending on the size of the province, from fifty to one hundred persons were to be recruited each year. The courses were to last for two years, during which time the students would "put themselves at the disposal of the various fasci" in order to gain practical experience. At the termination of the courses the provincial secretary

77

would recommend those with the best records to party and state authorities for employment.

Subsequent directives defined more fully the nature and content of the courses. On February 9, 1935, the national secretary ordered that the schools be held in the evening hours so that they would be open to employed youths as well as to university students. The secretary insisted: "The deciding criteria for admission to the courses must be political passion and organizing ability . . . As a consequence, youths not frequenting the universities should also be admitted, because, if the political passion and organizing ability is present, then the youths will of necessity know how to arrive at an adequate cultural preparation." By combining theoretical training with practical experience, the courses would give the student a preparation "which the regular school cannot supply." These new courses, concluded Starace, crowned the "selective process" begun in the ONB and continued in the Fasci Giovanili di Combattimento. In the latter organization, the members passed through three screenings, one at the end of each year in the organization. Finally, the best of these would enter the courses of political preparation, the most successful ones passing to active service in the party and governmental machinery. "The existence of such a process," the directive concluded, "is of fundamental importance: it demonstrates how the Revolution gradually constructs a system for supplying a perennial ruling class of prepared and selected persons . . ."[31]

At about the same time a circular was issued outlining the examinations to be given at the end of the first year of the course. Students had to pass these examinations in order to be admitted for the second year, and only those who had attended at least two thirds of the lectures could qualify to take the tests. There were three written and four oral examinations. Some idea of the kind of material for which the students were responsible may be gathered from the oral tests, three of which covered the political and economic history of Italy from the Risorgimento to Fascism, Fascist doctrine, the history of the party, the organization of the Fascist state; the foreign and colonial policy of Italy; and public administration, corporative organization, social legislation, the press, problems of transportation, the army under Fascism, and the economic and demographic policy of Fascism. The final oral test was an interrogation on the candidate's written statement listing his activities in behalf of Fascism and the party during the past year.[32]

The party claimed that this new kind of educational experience would give the youth a more "integral preparation," developing "a complex of habits and skills which the particularistic character" of ordinary schools made impossible.[33] The party schools were of a new genre. Michels and other political scientists have described leadership schools set up by modern democratic parties, but these schools were limited to training students in certain technical operations, while the Fascist party schools claimed to create *l'uomo nuovo, il Fascista.* Another contrast between the schools of the *partito unico* and those of democratic parties is that the Fascists trained youths for state as well as for party positions.

The provincial courses were apparently regarded by the party as successful, for in the spring of 1939, on the fifth anniversary of their foundation, the party secretary announced that they would be continued for five more years. Further rules on admission and curriculum were issued, placing greater emphasis on selectivity at the end of the first year.[34] A subsequent directive concerned the more careful choice of teachers. Greater stress was to be placed on youthfulness through the utilization of GUF leaders and outstanding graduates of the courses as teachers.[35]

The party's network of schools in the provinces was capped on January 30, 1939, with the creation of a national Center of Political Preparation for Youth, to be located in Rome. According to its charter, the center was instituted to choose those who, "generation after generation," demonstrate the "greatest capacity for command," and to infuse them with the "spirit of the Revolution." Any party or GUF member between the ages of twenty-one and twenty-eight [36] was eligible to take the entrance examinations if he could fulfill at least one of the following requirements: to have passed a provincial course of political preparation; to have won a prize in the party's *Littoriali*, the essay contests for university students; to have been active in the organizations of the party; to have been graduated from one of the GIL's military or naval academies. The entrance examinations were intended to be difficult. They consisted of a written essay on a selected political theme, an oral examination "without specific limits as to subject matter," a "test of a military nature," and an athletic competition.

The course at the Center of Political Preparation was to last two years, including summers which were to be spent in travel. All students were required to live on the premises. The program for the first year was of a general nature and consisted of lectures and tours of government and party offices. The second year's training was to prepare the student "specifically and practically" for the job to which he was to be summoned upon graduation. The curriculum was divided into three parts: (1) the writings of Mussolini, Fascist doctrine and the history of the Revolution, party organization, military science, foreign languages, and political geography (these were to cover both years); (2) the history of revolutions and of political parties, colonial history, and the history of journalism (specifically for the first year); and (3) corporative economy, international relations, and "racial politics" (for the second year only). Each student at the center was required during the second year to write something resembling a thesis in order to be graduated. No final examinations were held. Instead, the students were closely observed at all times and careful reports were made at the end of each semester. The national center's governing board, presided over by the party secretary, decided on graduations and ratings.[37]

Only the educational curriculum of Plato's ideal Republic matches these schools in scope and thoroughness. This was education for the whole man. But the resemblance ends there. Where Plato intended to employ moral training to free the spirit from enslavement to the baser passions, the totalitarians were bent on destroying the spirit and evoking the dionysian elements in human nature. The Platonic curriculum for the guardians was centered on metaphysics; the Fascists taught their elite to despise wisdom and to glory in brute violence. Plato sought to develop the just man. The Fascists worked to mold the tyrannical man.

In July 1939, the screening of the first class for the center began at the provincial level. At the same time, the national secretary announced the establishment of a number of fellowships for youths unable to afford its tuition. On December 1, 1939, the center's first faculty of fifteen persons, all members of the party's old guard and including the race-baiting extremist Paolo Orano, was announced, and on December 30 the names of the first class of students — thirty-six in all — were revealed. The center began its first semester on January 3, 1940.

Table 7. Membership in the Soviet Youth Organization (Komsomol)*

Year	Number	Year	Number
1918	22,100	1927	2,000,000
1919	96,000	1931	3,000,000
1920	480,000	1936	4,000,000
1922	247,000	1945	15,000,000
1925	1,000,000	1954	18,825,327

Sources: 1918–1945 figures from Merle Fainsod, *How Russia Is Ruled,* pp. 243–246; 1954 figure from C. J. Friedrich and Z. K. Brzezinski, *Totalitarian Dictatorship and Autocracy,* p. 46.

* The Komsomol includes youth between the ages of fourteen and twenty-six. The 1945 figure represents 50 per cent of the eligible age group as incorporated in the Komsomol. The Young Pioneers and Little Octobrists, established after 1922 for the younger children, today have virtually all the younger Russian children in their ranks (the Pioneers have a membership of nineteen million — Fainsod, p. 249). The Komsomol is designed to be more exclusive and to take only the elite of the youth, the prospective party members.

Table 8. Membership in the Hitler-Jugend*

Year	Number	Year	Number
1932	107,956	1936	5,437,601
1933	2,292,041	1939	7,728,259

Source: *Nazi Conspiracy and Aggression,* I, 318.

* Hitler-Jugend covered the age groups from eight to twenty-one. The figures are for the end of the year. By 1942 the Jugend had more than ten million members, according to C. J. Friedrich and Z. K. Brzezinski, *Totalitarian Dictatorship and Autocracy,* p. 41.

Table 9. Membership in the Gioventù Italiana del Littorio

Year and Unit	Number
October 28, 1938	7,577,381
October 28, 1939	7,891,547
Figli della lupa	1,546,389
Balilla	1,746,560
Piccole Italiane	1,622,766
Avanguardisti	906,785
Giovani Italiane	441,254
Giovani Fascisti	1,176,798
Giovani Fasciste	450,995
October 28, 1940	8,495,929

Sources: 1938 figures from *Regime Fascista,* October 28, 1938; 1939 figures from *Foglio di disposizioni* no. 1449, October 29, 1939; 1940 figures from Attilio Tamaro, *Venti anni di storia, 1922–1943,* III, 400.

THE POLITICAL EFFECTIVENESS OF THE
FASCIST YOUTH ORGANIZATION

Although the goal of total incorporation of Italian youth into the GIL was not achieved, nevertheless Fascist attainments in this area were impressive. In terms of actual numbers of persons recruited proportionate to the total population, the Italians did very well indeed, as a glance at the membership statistics of the Komsomol (Table 7) and the Hitler-Jugend (Table 8) will indicate. In 1939, for example, the GIL actually had a larger following than did its sister organization in Germany (see Table 9). Most competent observers with whom one talks in Italy today agree that the youth emerging from these groups in the thirties were enthusiastically Fascist, and that the younger generation was one of the bulwarks of Fascist strength. Four men who spent their youth under Fascism have published interesting autobiographies describing their experiences in the youth organization.[38] According to these reports, even in the rural areas and the small provincial schools and colleges the long arm of the party youth organization intruded. Especially after the Ethiopian War, the pattern of GIL activities was imposed upon the youth in even the smallest and most remote villages. A constant round of political indoctrination sessions, rallies, military drills, parades, and athletic events was forced upon the student. The occasional youngster who was hostile to Fascism felt himself to be utterly isolated.[39]

It is of major significance that through the party youth organization, Fascism succeeded in monopolizing the indoctrination of the youth. Following the victory over Catholic Action, the Fascists possessed a total monopoly in Italian education. No less a student of totalitarianism than Adolf Hitler has judged Italian Fascism's handling of the youth problem worthy of his highest praise.[40] And well he might, for the Nazis borrowed many of their ideas on youth organization from their Italian precursors.

6

Internecine Struggles

T HE relationships between the single party and the other institutions of a totalitarian dictatorship form a fascinating pattern. Outwardly, the totalitarian state is a beautiful, harmoniously operating piece of machinery. But an examination of the inner mechanism reveals that in reality the parts are in constant friction with each other. The force which prevents the whole system from flying apart is the dictator. He exploits the differences within the regime, for he finds that the surest way of remaining in control and accomplishing his ideological objectives is to keep the various centers of power upon which his rule rests in balance, thereby preventing any one of them from overwhelming the others.

There were four pillars supporting the Italian Fascist dictatorship: the party, the governmental administration, the army, and the police. The weight of Mussolini's power was not distributed so as to rest equally on each of the Fascist caryatids. The center of totalitarian power was constantly shifting, now favoring one institution, later another. The party believed the other supports of the state were weak. Its eventual goal was, so far as possible, to supplant them all and to emerge as the sole bastion of totalitarian might. It would appear to be an imperative of totalitarian rule that, as the regime develops toward its ghastly *telos*, the party encroaches more and more on the original prerogatives of the other organs of the dictatorship. In the Nazi and Fascist states, a kind of "dual state"[1] finally appeared, in which the party duplicated all the traditional organs of government within its own organization. This substitute structure was available whenever the governmental institutions failed to meet the demands of the dictator. In the Soviet Union the process went still further; the party completely absorbed the state bureaucracy. Here was a full-fledged party-state.

Even in the Soviet Union, however, the army, the police, and certain government departments have been able to maintain a degree of autonomy. It is possible to put party men in non-party jobs, but experience indicates that they are as susceptible to the temptation of seeking their own independent bases of power as leaders in other governmental systems. Furthermore, a cabinet official in the state bureaucracy, or an army general, or a chief of the secret police sees problems from a somewhat different administrative perspective than do party leaders.

Although the party can predominate over the other centers of power, then, it cannot eliminate them entirely even in the most mature form of totalitarian dictatorship. In order to survive the regime needs other qualities besides ideological zeal; rationality, administrative regularity, and efficient military planning are also requirements of successful totalitarian rule. The Germans found that they could not subsist solely on the ideological passion of Himmler and Bormann; they also had to rely upon the precise, expert mind of Speer. Wherever there is totalitarian dictatorship there will also be internal strife among the single party, the government, the police, and the army. Each dictatorship reveals its distinctive pattern of tension, and each resolves these conflicts somewhat differently.

THE PARTY AND THE BUREAUCRACY CLASH

From the first, the leaders of the PNF apparat regarded the state bureaucracy as an obstacle to the complete triumph of the Revolution. They did not think that the great majority of civil servants, who were holdovers from pre-Fascist governments, were disloyal to the dictatorship; Franz Neumann has perceptively written that bureaucracy "always marches with the strongest army."[2] What aroused the opposition of the men of the party was the bureaucratic mentality, the tendency to look at matters in terms of rules, precedents, and orderly procedure. The party always viewed the state bureaucracy as a great boulder in the path of the revolutionary armies. The rock would eventually give way, but only after enormous exertion by the men who wished to pass it. Party and state were natural enemies. The victory of the ideology could be secured only by reducing the state to the position of servant of the party's will.

Several techniques were employed in the party's campaign to subjugate the state. At the highest level of policy formulation, the party succeeded in by-passing the cabinet and placing the Grand Council at the top of the political structure. The PNF leaders also were authorized to conduct a loyalty check of the civil servants. As a rule, those who were declared anti-Fascist were dismissed, frequently to be replaced by persons of the party's own choosing. Even top-ranking cabinet officials were ruined as a result of censure by the party. As time went on, the party developed other methods in its silent war with the government. It drafted all state officeholders first into its associations, later into the party itself. The party also expanded its structure, creating new subsidiary organizations that interfered with or duplicated activities formerly reserved exclusively to the government.[3]

Ruling circles in the party considered the recognition of the Grand Council as a more authoritative body than the cabinet a signal victory in its effort to maintain a position at least on a par with the state machinery. Through the meetings of the Council, the PNF exerted its influence on top policy decisions of the regime,[4] frequently succeeding in making extremist views prevail, as was the case, for example, with the racial campaign of 1938. The party used the Council as the appropriate place for airing charges against any important state officials who had been unfortunate enough to incur its suspicion.

The Grand Council legally became the "supreme organ that coordinates and integrates all the regime's activities"[5] in 1928. This statute merely confirmed in law what had existed in fact at least since 1925. Farinacci expressed the sentiments of the entire party elite on the enactment of the 1928 law when he exulted editorially that the "state and the party have in the Grand Council . . . their unifying center, through which the antithesis between party and government . . . is rendered no longer possible."[6]

The Council brought together the top leaders in the party and the government. Apparently Mussolini fancied himself to be copying Plato's idea (in the *Laws*) of the nocturnal council, for the meetings never began before midnight and often lasted until dawn. They commenced and ended with solemn ritual, the members rising to give the salute to the Duce upon the dictator's entrance and departure. Mussolini presided over the meetings, remaining in his chair for the entire session and refusing to take advantage of the coffee and cigarette breaks he allowed his less indefatigable colleagues.[7] In the event of the Duce's absence, inability to attend, or death, the chief of the party, who was also Council secretary, was empowered to serve as presiding officer. This could have given the secretary of the PNF an important advantage over other aspirants among the palace guard for the number one position, if the problem of succession to Mussolini had ever arisen, for the Council was the authority designated to decide who would fall heir to the Duce's toga.

There were three classes of members on the Council, totaling some twenty persons. In the first category, with life membership, was the Quadrumvirate of the March on Rome. The second group was composed of persons holding certain key offices in the regime, including the principal cabinet ministers, the chief of police and the president of the Special Tribunal, the party secretary, vice-secretaries, and selected other members of the directorate, the commanding general of the party militia, the president of the Institute of Fascist Culture, and, until 1937, the head of the ONB. In the third category were a limited number of special members appointed for a three-year term and chosen from men of the government, former secretaries of the party, and other "eminent men of the Revolution."

Party leaders were not satisfied with merely indirect influence on the governmental bureaucracy through their powerful positions on the Grand Council. They claimed for the party the right to determine the loyalty of every government employee, and through a system of informers they kept themselves apprised of the affairs within every ministry. The party was not strong enough to carry out vast purges of the bureaucracy in the years immediately following the March on Rome, but during the tense period after the Matteotti incident a large number of civil servants were fired as a result of intensified party surveillance.

Farinacci, as secretary, spoke belligerently about the condition of the civil service on many occasions, making no secret of the fact that the party intended to cleanse the government of all persons not acceptable to the party. "The work of the Fascist government has been truly marvelous," he declared in one of his first speeches as party leader, "but it has encountered one grave obstacle in the bureaucracy, where there still are men appointed by governments which our Revolution has buried forever . . . We have always maintained that the bureaucracy ought always to be a docile instrument in the hands of the regime for the actualization of its program."[8]

According to the memoirs of the secretary of the interior at that time, Luigi Federzoni, Farinacci maintained unusually direct control over that department. The party secretary dispatched two of his chief aides, Dino Grandi and Attilio Teruzzi, to the ministry to keep track of Federzoni's activities. They apparently succeeded in making life miserable for the minister and his associates, for whenever he resisted party pressure to remove certain officials, Teruzzi and Farinacci publicly vilified the culprits.[9] Federzoni continued to have difficulties with the party until he was hounded out of office. As a former member of the right-wing Nationalist party which had collaborated with the Fascists but had refused to merge with them until forced to do so by law, he was regarded with suspicion by party extremists, who thought him a conservative "man of order" rather than a Fascist totalitarian.

On December 24, 1925, the Chamber of Deputies enacted a law (No. 2693) giving responsible government officials the power and the duty to fire employees who, either on or off the job, "did not appear to give full guarantee of the faithful exercise of their duties," or who in speaking or writing expressed themselves "in a manner incompatible with the general political directives of the government."

About this time, the ministers of the interior, corporations, and communications (after 1937, "popular culture") met for monthly sessions with the party directorate in order for these government officials to be advised about persons in their departments whose behavior displeased the party. The ministers, all stanch Fascists, resented this interference, but were powerless to prevent it. A sample of a 1926 loyalty examination of state employees was published in the *Fogli d'ordini* after the individuals involved were cleared. The minister of the interior attended the meeting of the directorate to answer charges brought by Dario Orlandi, local party secretary of Carrara, against the loyalty of certain employees of Federzoni's department. The party had previously appointed one of the members of the directorate to investigate the charges, and at this meeting he reported them to be without foundation. The minister of the interior then thanked the member for his declaration "which eliminated any unjust suspicion" about his associates in the department. The results of the inquiry, he continued, affirmed the "perfect harmony of objectives existing between the party and the government, two forces which on different levels but with identical devotion serve the cause of the regime."[10] What is interesting in the case is not the result but the fact that the secretary of the interior allowed members of his ministry, and in a sense himself, to be tried by the party.

In the years 1927 and 1928 the "Fascistization" of the Foreign Office, the Judiciary, the Ministry of the Interior, and the communal and provincial administrations, was in full swing. The *concorsi* (civil service examinations) gave preference to party members, thereby ensuring that the immense majority of new employees would be, at least outwardly, firm Fascists. In the Foreign Office, 82 of the 450 employees working in the Palazzo Chigi were "retired," and 200 Fascists were added during these two years. As Lasswell and Sereno observed, in 1928 the "diplomatic and consular services were flooded with *ventottisti* . . ."[11] In addition to new appointments and replacements in all top policy-making positions, the rank-and-file bureaucrat was left in uneasy possession of his job, all too aware of the spy network surrounding him.

There is no way of ascertaining how many civil servants at given periods were removed from their positions as a result of party surveillance. At the end of 1932, however, Starace, only recently appointed secretary, made the announcement that during the preceding year about five thousand government officials had been replaced.[12] The years 1932 and 1933 appear to have been a period of particularly severe vigilance by the PNF toward state employees.

The Arpinati case reveals how the PNF kept watch even over former members of the party elite once they had moved from a party position to one in the government. The same phenomenon of the party turning on its own children seems to have occurred in Nazi Germany. Men like Frick (who became minister of the interior) and Guerthner (who headed the Ministry of Justice), both "old and trusted party members," once they had embarked on their official nonparty careers found their status changed and were treated exactly like "other civil servants."[13]

Before the March on Rome, Leandro Arpinati had been the Fascist party leader of Bologna and had served on the party directorate in the early years after the conquest of power. In September 1929 he had been appointed head of the Ministry of the Interior. The specific cause of Arpinati's ouster appears to have been that, in complying with the order to force government employees to take out party membership, Arpinati insisted on giving membership cards to persons Starace mistrusted, Mario Missioroli among them.[14] Starace compiled through the party's information services an alarming report against Arpinati accusing him of friendship with known anti-Fascists and sent it to Arpinati himself, who returned a hostile reply. There ensued a violent encounter between the two in Mussolini's presence.[15] On May 4, 1933, the accused was forcibly dislodged from his government position.[16] On July 23, 1934, the party announced his expulsion from the PNF, asserting that Arpinati "in various circumstances" had "assumed positions contrasting with the directives to be followed by all who have the honor to march in the ranks of the PNF."[17] A week later the expulsion of twelve of his associates, and the withdrawal of the membership cards from eight other persons accused of cooperating with Arpinati in opposing the regime were revealed to the public.[18] Arpinati himself was banished to a penal island to serve a five-year sentence.

As Ciano's diaries reveal, not even members of Parliament were immune to party action. In February 1939, the deputy Martire was overheard speaking disrespectfully about certain officials, including Ciano, to another parliamentarian, Ferretti. The pair, naturally both members of the party, were tried by Starace, who sent Martire to prison. Ferretti's membership card was withdrawn from him (which meant the automatic loss of his seat in Parliament) for not having denounced Martire immediately to the party. As Ugo d'Andrea, the editor of Ciano's diaries, observes in the introduction, Ciano relates this incident as if it were an everyday occurrence.[19]

Irony triumphed, and only a few months later, in December 1939, the tables were turned on Ciano. Not even Mussolini's son-in-law could evade the party's espionage ring. Ciano tells how Starace visited him to show him a report prepared by the spy services of the PNF hinting at evidence of possible dissension between Ciano and Mussolini.[20] In the diary Ciano shrugged the report off as nothing and Starace promised not to mention it to the Duce, but Ciano was left in a state of obvious uneasiness and tension.

The years 1938 and 1939 were the high point of the party's effort to give the bureaucracy at least an externally Fascist appearance. By decree law of September 5, 1938, uniforms were made obligatory for all male employees of the government. Civil servants had their ranks and insignia, all in exact military fashion. In February 1939 matrimony was made a prerequisite for promotion of all employees, thereby aiding the party's heightened campaign to increase population. Both in the outer appearance and the psychological condition of its members, the Fascist bureaucracy became something quite different from the administrative services of the "decadent demo-liberal" regimes.

The party "associations" were among the main instruments employed by the party to control the bureaucracy. But the associations, also utilized by the Nazi party in Germany, were not created simply to make the task of surveillance less difficult. In addition and even primarily they were to foster in their members an active, passionate allegiance to Fascism and its ideology. The associations were to "perfect the political conscience" of their members and to "render the bureaucracy a worthy instrument of the regime."[21] The mass drafting of employees into associations (actually misnamed because they were artificially imposed from above and devoid of the elements of spontaneity and naturalness which characterize genuine associations) in Nazi Germany and Fascist Italy can, then, only partially be explained by the party's desire to watch and check on the accessible members. As Duverger has expressed it, the party in modern dictatorships is concerned both with "verifying the fidelity" of the bureaucracy and, even more important, with "assuring the dynamism" of the bureaucracy's actions.[22]

The five major Fascist associations of public functionaries (Public Employ, Railroad Workers, Postal and Telegraph Employees, State Monopolies, and Teachers) were originally outside party control. The first to be transferred to direct dependence on the party was the Teachers' Association, in September 1926. "No one," asserted the secretary in commenting on the move in the party's *Fogli d'ordini*, "can doubt the significance of this act." The party intended to use the association as an instrument for "enforcing discipline," and under the leadership of the party the Teachers' Association would serve as "a spiritual militia always mobilized for the propagation of the Fascist faith." Through the association the party would conquer the schools, thereby affirming the PNF's "revolutionary vision of life and of history."[23] The other four associations passed to the party from the Confederation of Fascist Corporations on February 5, 1927.[24]

According to their statutes, membership in all the associations was a "voluntary act," presupposing the "full and unconditional adhesion of the member to the Fascist regime." Those enrolled in the associations were required to "observe the special duties imposed by party discipline" and follow a course of "fervid activity" in conjunction with that of the party.[25] In the beginning each association was presided over by a national secretary, but after the party assumed their direction its secretary appointed a fiduciario and an advisory commission of four members to govern each of the five groups at the national level. In turn the national fiduciario of each association appointed, with the guidance of the provincial secretary, the provincial fiduciarii. The latter then chose the local leaders.[26] The closeness of party control over the associations is shown by the provision in the statute of March 7, 1932, forbidding anyone not enrolled in the party to hold office in the associations. Article 12 of the same statute explicitly placed association members under the jurisdiction of the party's Federal Courts of Discipline.[27]

The Fascist association was the government employee's sole representative in discussions of wages, hours, and working conditions. All questions involving the status, promotion, and transfer of individual members had to be handled through the office of the association. On the local and provincial level, many of the associations ran a Dopolavoro for the members, which organized sporting activities, trips, and excursions. Usually these leisure-time sections of the associations had their own recreation centers. Thus the party even imposed regimentation on the functionaries' spare time.[28] In the summers the organization directed camps for the employees' children. And, of course, at the periodic meetings of the local and provincial associations, members were subjected to heavy indoctrination and propaganda. This part of the associations' activity was particularly intense in the teachers' group and will presently be discussed at greater length.

Originally, membership in these civil service organizations had been declared "voluntary" in order that the party could claim that those who joined did so for the love of Fascism. The statute of March 7, 1932, retained the fiction of voluntary membership, "except for members of the party" in the bureaucracy "for whom it is obligatory" (Article

3). But on March 8, 1937, the Grand Council approved the law which required that "all of the employees of the state administration be enrolled in the Fascist associations."[29] This was the signal for total incorporation of the bureaucracy in the party associations, particular targets being a few incorrigibles in the Ministry of the Interior and the Foreign Office.

Actually, of course, the talk about membership being voluntary had always been pure myth, because advancement in position was nearly impossible without such membership.[30] Total membership in the associations (see Table 10) rose from 538,000 in 1927 to 691,531 in 1936, 767,999 in 1938, and 806,129 in 1939. Except for the Teachers' Association[31] this increase is not very considerable, in view of the fact that during and following the Ethiopian War the bureaucracy was augmented with a large number of employees recruited for newly created offices. Apparently the overwhelming majority of government employees had joined the associations at the very beginning, and between 1933 and 1937 nearly everyone had joined.[32]

The party was not satisfied with drafting the bureaucracy into its associations. In addition to this instrument of control it sought from the first to add another, even stronger, check: forced membership in the party itself for all civil servants and teachers. As early as 1927 for

Table 10. Membership in the Fascist Associations (Directly Dependent on the Party)

Association	April 23, 1927	Oct. 25, 1928	Oct. 29, 1936	Oct. 28, 1938	Oct. 28, 1939	Oct. 28, 1942
Public Employ	251,000	232,836	249,926	286,278	294,265	386,865
Railroad Workers	90,000	100,560	127,376	134,046	137,902	158,582
Postal, Telegraph .	41,000	65,600	76,762	80,889	83,184	87,645
State Monopolies .	77,000	83,000	92,517	100,470	120,205	153,421
Teachers	79,000	85,500	144,950*	160,316	170,573	. . .
Total	538,000	567,496	691,531	767,999	806,129	786,513

Sources: 1927 figures, *Foglio d'ordini* no. 29 (April 23, 1927); 1928 figures, *Foglio d'ordini* no. 51 (October 28, 1928); 1936 figures, *Foglio d'ordini* no. 167 (October 29, 1936); 1938 figures, *Regime Fascista*, October 28, 1938, p. 1; 1939 figures, *Foglio d'ordini* no. 244 (October 28, 1939); and 1942 figures, Attilio Tamaro, *Venti anni di storia, 1922–1943*, III, 444. No data are available on the Teachers' Association for that year.

* In the figure for 1936, a breakdown of the various divisions of the Teachers' Association showed elementary teachers, 109,564; secondary school teachers, 29,134; university professors, 2,697; fine arts and librarians, 1,286.

all practical purposes, new recruits for the bureaucracy and the schools were taken almost exclusively from members of the party. By decision of the Council of Ministers on May 27, 1933,[33] party membership was made a legal requirement for participation in any examination for government or educational employment, although employees already in office were not legally compelled to join the party.[34] With the enactment of two additional laws the following year the requirement of May 27 was extended to the judiciary as well.[35]

An Italian scholar who has written an illuminating work on the judiciary under Fascism concluded that the party was able almost at will to influence "all the powers of the state, including the judicial power." Several examples of flagrant and direct interference by the party with the judicial process are given in his work. Judges were subjected to heavy party pressure and any of them who dared decide against the party either lost their positions or were transferred to lesser posts and lost all chance of appointment to the higher benches.[36]

The party did not leave undisturbed senior members of the civil service and the teachers in state educational institutions in its drive to Fascistize the bureaucracy. With the opening of party membership in 1932, pressure was brought upon the entire range of government employees, and on police and army officers as well, to join the party. Those state officials who were obstructionist (like Arpinati in the Interior) were deposed and discredited. The great majority of employees were enrolled in the PNF between 1933 and 1937. In Turin's Association of Employees of the State Monopolies, for example, only thirty of its members had been inscribed in the party at the beginning of 1932, before the opening of the recruiting campaign. In 1933 party membership in the association totaled 1,437, or 84 per cent of the association's membership.[37] And this report was made before the processing of new requests had been entirely completed. As Salvatorelli and Mira have written, by 1937 the number of civil servants who had not asked to join the party could "be counted on one's fingers."[38]

In 1940 party membership was made a legal prerequisite for advancement in one's career.[39] But even before this date the Council of Ministers "in obedience to higher orders" publicly ordered that all responsible officials in the bureaucracy "in making decisions for promotions" had to "give preference to those employees enrolled in the Partito Nazionale Fascista."[40] The 1940 law went one step farther in declaring that all personnel, administrative, judicial, and scholastic, on both the national and local levels, had to possess membership in the PNF in order to be eligible to participate in the examinations for promotion. According to Article 6 of the statute, employees not already belonging to the party had ninety days in which to apply for membership. Persons who made such a request were eligible to take the tests for promotion, but if they passed they were not given the promotion until their application had been approved by the party's offices. Thus, the party completed the construction of its web around and through the Fascist bureaucracy. Through the associations the party controlled the more technical procedures relating to the employees and even attempted to regiment their leisure time by means of the association Dopolavori. In requiring party membership the PNF subjected the functionary to another round of meetings during which he was the victim of the most vigorous indoctrination possible.

Even more important than the continuous indoctrination was the initial party oath sworn to by the civil servants. The moral anguish and guilt felt by many of these persons, particularly those in the teaching profession, is still perceptible in Italy today when one talks with those who were not sincere Fascists but who took the oath rather than face starvation or worse, for themselves and their families. Hannah Arendt has made some brilliant observations on the psychological effect of forced party membership on the individuals concerned: "Universal complicity, that is, organized guilt, helps to hold the system together even if the individuals concerned still feel pangs of conscience. Conscience under these conditions . . . cuts both ways: people who joined the party for essentially economic reasons and without any convictions whatsoever then began to feel guilty of their 'opportunism'; the result was that they became *gleichgeschaltet* in true earnest. There are very few people who have the strength of character to remain 'cynical' enough to keep their personalities intact . . ."[41]

According to Article 20 of the 1932 party statute, "The Fascist who is expelled from the party must be prohibited from participation in public life."[42] This provision, which Salvatorelli terms "without precedent in the modern history of any civilized country,"[43] gave, after the mass draft of civil servants in 1932, full and final power to the party's courts to ruin any member of the bureaucracy whom the PNF's elaborate spy system might find suspicious.

THE PARTY VERSUS THE PREFECTS

The relations between the party and the state at the provincial level were even more strained than on the national plane. Party surveillance over provincial and local government began in an intensive manner immediately after the conquest of power. Indeed, at the very first meeting of the Grand Council (then only a party organ) on December 15, 1922, Mussolini announced his decision to replace with party stalwarts a number of persons who were serving as provincial prefects. Many of the party leaders, including Farinacci, declined to serve as regular prefects,[44] preferring the position of "flying prefect." Officially entitled *alti commissari*, these men moved about the country at will, inspecting the state bureaucracy. The Nazi party also had its flying prefects during the first months after assuming power. The institution in Italy created such confusion that it was abolished a few months after its creation. As its means of control over local and provincial administration the party then used its subordinate secretaries. The conflicts between the government-appointed prefect and the party-selected provincial secretary were numerous and violent. The provincial and local governmental scene in Fascist Italy between 1923 and 1927 was one of chaos and confusion.[45]

On January 5, 1927, at the height of the normalizing phase following the Matteotti crisis, Mussolini published his "Circular to the Prefects," designed to clear up once and for all conflicts between provincial party secretaries and government prefects. The circular plainly gave to the prefect superiority over his companion party official. Mussolini wrote: "The Prefect is the highest authority of the state in the province. He is the direct representative of the central executive power. All citizens, and especially those who have the great privilege and honor of being Fascists, owe respect and obedience to the highest political representative of the Fascist Regime and they must collaborate in a subordinate way with him so as to render his task easier."[46]

Although this circular marked the beginning of a crackdown on certain of the more independent and arrogant party bosses (the most notable was Giampaoli of Milan), it by no means meant the end of party influence on provincial and local government. By the law of December 27, 1928, a representative of the party was made a member of the provincial advisory council to the prefect. In 1934 this number was raised to four active members and two inactive members of each

95

provincial council, all chosen directly by the national party secretary on proposal of the provincial secretary.[47]

So far as eliminating the dualism of authority between provincial secretary and prefect and local secretary and *podestà* (mayor) is concerned, the 1927 "Circular to the Prefects" was "not . . . realized in practice."[48] That Mussolini's directive quickly became *lettera morta* (naturally only with the Duce's consent) is evident from passages in the party's semiofficial manual for communal secretaries.[49] On the subject of collaboration between the local party secretary and the podestà, the author, a former national inspector of the PNF, reprints a directive issued while he was in office, propounding a theory of equal authority for separate spheres. Both officers are responsible to different hierarchies, according to the directive. Each is supreme in his own sphere. As for the podestà, "insofar as he is a member of the party, he is a follower without distinctions or privileges, but is completely dependent on his particular communal secretary for his personal activity as a Fascist." In turn, the party secretary should lend his aid to the podestà whenever he is called upon with regard to matters of local administration. Far from reiterating Mussolini's 1927 order for the secretary to "collaborate in a subordinate way" with the government official, the author of the manual states that in cases of conflict the local secretary should inform his superior on the provincial level, who, in conference with the prefect (obviously as an equal partner), would resolve the matter in favor of one or the other.[50]

In like manner, Antonio Canepa in his volume on the organization of the party concluded that the party and state officials on the provincial level were equal in authority. Commenting on the fact that the party statutes made no specific mention of the problem of the relationship between prefect and provincial secretary, Canepa assured his readers that the reason for the omission was that all conflicts had been long resolved. "But, in the event that a conflict should occur, the common superiors of each official would know immediately how to judge the matter . . . according to justice."[51]

Alongside the state officials at the local and provincial strata were arrayed the party secretaries, each claiming independent power and the right to investigate, supervise, and generally verify the loyalty of the state's representatives. In Fascist Italy each administrative district had two chiefs, one of whom was the party's agent. But, powerful as the Fascist provincial secretaries were, it should be noted that they possessed nothing like the absolute power over provincial government that was exercised by party district leaders in Germany. The Nazi *Gauleiter* was unrivaled in his power over his locale. He appointed the *Bürgermeister* and other important leaders in the communal administration and designated the members of the communal council.[52] As Hitler said in his table-talk, in praise of his Gauleiter: "I have made the Gauleiter true kings, inasmuch as they receive from central headquarters only very schematic instructions . . ." Their decisions are irrevocable "even if they come into conflict with . . . the Ministry of the Interior. Only in this way is it possible to arouse fresh initiative. Otherwise, one permits a stupid bureaucracy to develop and prosper . . ."[53]

THE PARTY INVADES THE SCHOOL SYSTEM

If the party thought it essential for every civil servant to act as if he were not simply a loyal employee but a convinced, militant Fascist, it was even more vital that the teachers in the schools and universities of the state, those who molded the minds of youth, should radiate all the qualities of the Fascist man. In the mid-twenties the PNF began to interfere more and more with the work of the Ministry of National Education in an effort to reach the party's goal of a school which was "not only in form, but above all in spirit . . . profoundly Fascist in all its manifestations."[54] On the top policy-making level the PNF's secretary was a member of the Supreme Council of Education. By a law of 1932 he was empowered to appoint representatives on the Advisory Council for National Education and the Disciplinary Committee for Teachers.[55]

Until 1937 the president of the youth organizations was legally an undersecretary of education, and in this capacity Renato Ricci attended all summit conferences of the Ministry of Education and was able to argue continually the viewpoint of the youth organizations and their officers against the more traditionalist members of the ministry. With the creation of the GIL in 1937, a permanent *Commissione Centrale per il Collegamento tra la Scuola e la GIL* was established, composed of the highest officers of the Ministry of Education and of the party's youth group, for the purpose of settling disagreements between the two institutions over educational policy.

The clashes between the GIL and school officials were legion because there were not enough hours in the school day to allow the youth organizations ample opportunity for their ambitious program and still leave much time for the traditional curriculum. First the ONB and then the GIL "supplemented" the work of the school by staging excursions, offering training schools for youth leaders, conducting visits to museums and monuments, giving political lectures accompanied by propaganda films, piping political broadcasts into the schools—all during school hours.[56]

Occasions like the one announced in a 1939 *Foglio di disposizioni*, when a "day of propaganda for autarky" was held in the Trieste schools, and students and teachers were compelled to collect scrap iron and distribute propaganda leaflets, were very frequent.[57] Many of the GIL demonstrations were scheduled during school hours. In spite of complaints from school authorities, the party secretary would not forbid such meetings, but settled for asking merely that the provincial secretaries "give warning" to the school when such sessions were to occur.[58] Likewise, special GIL camps, which often lasted for as long as two weeks, were repeatedly conducted during the regular term. In response to objections from the government's Ministry of Education, the PNF commander of the GIL went through the motions of suggesting that for "at least two hours per day" campers be permitted to study.[59] Every Saturday afternoon of the schoolboy's time was consumed by compulsory GIL meetings, and many Sundays were used for athletic events, excursions, and, for the older youth, military maneuvers. Not infrequently, special night schools were held under party sponsorship. Summers, of course, were crammed with camps. All these activities taken together constituted a stupendous drain on the student's time. The burden became progressively heavier during the thirties, when it was obvious that the party's ultimate goal was total domination of the schools.[60] The PNF never achieved this objective, but if the sum of the party's interference is taken into account, it came quite close to attaining that end.

The teachers themselves, of course, felt the direct control of the party through their association. The Teachers' Association had three subdivisions, one each for elementary schoolteachers, secondary schoolteachers, and university faculty. The web of the Teachers' Association extended even to private instructors. In 1937 there was some question whether private teachers should not be included in the Corporation

98

of Professions and Artists, but it was decided to leave them under PNF control.[61] As the associations of civil servants handled all requests for promotion, transfer, and wage increases, so the Teachers' Association (AFS) directed these matters for the teachers. [62] The school groups also had their *sezione dopolavoristica,* which organized leisure activities for the members.[63] Membership in the AFS was made compulsory in 1937, and by October 28, 1938, the association had 160,-316 adherents, comprising almost all the elementary, secondary, and university teachers in the country. As with the governmental bureaucracy, heavy pressure was put on school personnel to join the party in 1932, and with the law of 1933 all new teachers were forced to take PNF membership. Since the Grand Council ruling of March 27, 1930, all rectors of the universities and principals of the elementary and secondary schools had to be selected from professors who had been enrolled in the party for at least five years.[64] At least from 1937 promotions were given only to party members. On February 27, 1939, the Ministry of Education went one step further with the announcement that no teachers would be awarded the special commendation in their promotion ratings who had not given to the youth organizations "useful and concrete activity."[65] Not even party membership would suffice to ensure advancement; now one had to be positively and demonstrably a leader in the GIL. All these pressures took their toll, and by the late thirties almost every teacher had been incorporated in the party, in addition to having been forced to participate actively in the AFS. An increasingly large proportion found it expedient to become GIL officers. The figures for the Milanese AFS for 1939 are revealing: out of 6,780 members of the association (which legally included every teacher), 6,430 were PNF members and 2,197 were active in GIL leadership.[66]

One of the chief functions of the associations was the "forming" (*formazione*) of the political beliefs of the members, a task which was not "sufficiently attended to in the teachers' institutes," and the "reinforcement of the revolutionary spirit" of the members in order for them to be more adequate for their task of the "diffusion [*volgarizzazione*] of Fascism's work and doctrine among the . . . masses."[67] In order to supplement the "insufficient" work of the teachers' colleges in the area of indoctrination, the Teachers' Association, in close cooperation with other party organizations, sponsored an endless round of conferences, lectures, summer training schools, and "pilgrimages" to Rome.

On the provincial level, a typical example of this activity was the special course held in Cremona in October 1938, under the aegis of the association and the GIL. The course consisted of six two-hour lectures on "the Fascist theory of physical education and mass demonstrations," the role of the GIL in the education of Italian youth, and the best methods for inculcating the new Fascist reforms in custom among the youth. Attendance at the courses was not required, but it constituted a "preferential title for all promotion examinations, requests for transfers, and demands . . . for temporary positions."[68]

In the summer of 1938 five "National Courses for Principals and Teachers in the Primary and Secondary Schools" were held in various parts of Italy under the direction of the Teachers' Association. The courses lasted from two weeks to one month and covered the following subjects: theory and practice of physical education, techniques of youth organization, the importance of the military in the national life, Fascist politics, and the organization and scope of the GIL. Again, although attendance was not compulsory, it was "seriously taken into account" for promotions and transfers. School directors were for all practical purposes required to frequent the lectures.[69] Every year in all parts of Italy during the summer, special schools resembling these were held, so that it was practically impossible to escape attending one occasionally.[70]

Teachers were sometimes required to give propaganda lectures to their students' parents,[71] in addition, of course, to making certain that no opportunity was missed to inject Fascist principles into the regular subject matter taught in the classrooms. Also, on frequent occasions the party leaders in the association drew up recommendations on educational policy to present to the Ministry of Education. Members of the association were invited to submit ideas on textbook changes, classroom organization, and curriculum revision. Those suggestions best "corresponding to Fascist principles" were passed on to the government authorities.[72]

Through the years the party leadership became ever more vocal in its demands for politicizing the schools. Turati made many speeches in the late twenties advocating modifications in the curriculum and a reduction in hours spent on the more traditional subjects.[73] In the early thirties dissent in party ranks over the slowness of the schools to become completely Fascistized was apparent in the parliamentary orations of Paolo Orano (who later was a leader in the anti-Semitic campaign and was appointed to the faculty of the Center for Political Preparation) against the Ministry of Education and in the newspaper articles of Piero Bolzon, Emilio Settiminelli, and Silvio Maurano in *L'Impero*, leading mouthpiece of the party's veterans.

The objections of these extremists are well summarized in an article by G. A. Fanelli, editor of *Il Secolo Fascista*, another important organ representing the hard core of the PNF.[74] The article was in the form of an open letter to Francesco Ercole, renowned Dante scholar and confirmed Fascist, then minister of education. First, complained the article, the school was giving too little cooperation to the youth organizations, which ought to be "at least tripled" in size. In the second place, the program for indoctrinating the teachers with Fascist principles was inadequate. Simply requiring teachers to be members of the party and the associations would not produce a completely Fascistized school, insisted Fanelli. The final goal must be to make active participation in the party youth organizations obligatory for all elementary and secondary school teachers. At the universities, professors and assistants should be compelled to take vigorous part in the GUF and the university militia. This state of affairs, in turn, could not be achieved until the party had a greater share in the direction and planning of the education of present and future teachers. At the very minimum this meant a compulsory two-year course sponsored by the party for all who taught. And third, continued this editorial attack on the Ministry of Education, the curriculum had to be revised to place less stress on classical and "apolitical" studies and to spend more time on "Fascist culture." The party extremist spokesman would have been content only with a course in Fascist politics obligatory for all children.

Fanelli's demands were partially fulfilled within the decade of the thirties. The youth organizations did approximately triple in size by 1939 and more and more pressure was put on teachers to participate in the leadership of the GIL. In the reform of the curriculum party proposals were also heeded, although not to the degree desired by Fanelli and his followers. Under Cesare Maria De Vecchi, Ercole's successor at the Ministry of Education, a number of changes in courses offered and in required examination material were effected during the

101

years 1936–1937. In the universities a new discipline was introduced for the degree in jurisprudence: "The History and Doctrine of Fascism." These courses were often taught by provincial party leaders turned professor, and the main textbook used was the giant three-volume *Sistema* of Antonio Canepa.[75]

By the law of June 10, 1937,[76] interesting alterations were made in the examinations for the secondary schools. For admission to the fourth *classe ginnasiale*, all students submitted to an oral examination on Fascism and its accomplishments. "Elements of corporative law" became by the statute an additional topic on which students of classics had to be competent before graduation. Even scientific candidates, as part of their test in history, had to display a knowledge of Fascist doctrine. Candidates for teachers' degrees had to hold forth on "Fascist pedagogy" and were quizzed on Fascist economic theory and "Fascist culture." Nor did the technical schools escape revision of the required subjects, although their students were asked less esoteric questions on Fascist government and organizations.

The party's greatest triumph was the 1939 *Carta della Scuola*, the second article of which proclaimed a long-sought party goal: membership in the GIL was made obligatory for every student. Another important requirement of the 1939 school law was contained in Article 5, which made experience in manual labor mandatory for all students. Obviously, the Nazi *Arbeitsdienst* program had strong influence here.[77]

However much they applauded the 1939 law, party leaders were never fully satisfied with the regulations governing the schools. When the minister of education, then Giuseppe Bottai, announced the project for the new law in November of 1938, the extremist nucleus of the party was enthusiastic about the minister's speech calling for an "organic union of party and school throughout the youth organization." This union, Bottai stated, would "finish forever the age of the agnostic school, which was indifferent to political life . . . We decisively wish a Fascist school, a Fascist pedagogy, Fascist teaching to create the Fascist man, by the thousands upon thousands."[78] But a month later two articles appeared in the journal *Regime Fascista* which indicated that the proposed reforms did not go far enough, from the PNF's point of view. [79]

The first article, by "Scolasticus," observed that the *Carta della Scuola* was good as a beginning, but averred that the real problem, "the problem of men," was left untouched by the statute. A complete unification of school and party would not be accomplished until all teachers could receive the same training as did the instructors in the GIL, that is, until the party controlled teacher education and licensing. Then all the schools of the land would function like the party's military academies. Only when "all the school" became "one homogeneous block" would Fascist Italy have a "truly political" school.

The second essay, by "Miracchi," deplored the "distance . . . between the school and the *Casa Balilla*" still remaining even after the enactment of the new statute and applauded the criticisms made by "Scolasticus." All teachers, said the writer, should be trained by the party in subjects like Military Culture, Comparative Critical Politics, and Fascist Mysticism. Such a program would "not merely reform, but would renovate" the teaching profession, which in 1939 was "not prepared, absolutely not prepared, for its complex mission."

The advent of World War II interrupted the more grandiose designs of the party, but there are many Italian educators who will testify that through its activities the PNF went far toward realizing its dream of a school system functioning as "one homogeneous block." Certainly education constitutes one of the governmental areas in which party interference was the greatest and most persistent. Through its youth organizations and associations it exercised a power over education at least equal to that of the government's ministry.

Gaps did exist, of course, in the party's network of controls. An eminent German scholar has made some most acute observations on the limits of the effectiveness of the Nazi party's surveillance over the schools—especially the universities—which are applicable also to the Fascist system. Even with the NSDAP's efficiency, the party often failed to detect teachers who were opposed to the regime, or, if these were detected, to act against them because of red tape, bureaucratic buck-passing, or resistance by personnel in the Ministry of Education. The arrogance of party leaders, said Gerhard Ritter, "caused such exasperation that frequently the ministers formed alliances with the professors in order to push through the ministerial measures against the Party officers."[80] It should be observed, however, that this kind of laxity of control was far more common within the universities than in the lower schools of Italy, and that certain shortcomings in efficiency did not alter the atmosphere of tension and uncertainty pervading the whole educational system. I have talked with persons who were university professors under Fascism and who harbored anti-Fascist sentiments; it is clear from their accounts that not all professors had Ritter's good fortune in escaping counter-measures taken by the party and the regime.

7

Three Uneasy Allies

T H E relations between the party and the governmental bureaucracy were always hostile. Party leaders considered the state their natural enemy, and, in their impatience to build the Third Rome in a day, they conceived of the state administration as an unnecessary impediment placed in the path of the Revolution. A slightly different attitude prevailed toward the army and the secret police, because they were essential to the survival of the Fascist state. The party shared with these organs of force and repression, the army and the Organization of Vigilance for the Repression of Anti-Fascism (OVRA), the function of protecting the regime from overthrow by either internal or foreign enemies. The PNF by itself was not adequately equipped to guarantee the permanence of the regime, and could not allow its leaders to exhaust their energies in cloak and dagger intrigues, however interesting those activities might be. Party leaders were not chosen primarily because of their skill as military strategists or ballistics experts. Since the PNF was principally concerned with the diffusion and perpetuation of Fascist political truth, its elite was selected and its structure fashioned with this end in mind. The party needed the army and the police as auxiliaries.

Totalitarian regimes feed on suspicion, and therefore those who are logically friends are easily converted into opponents. Paradoxically, the more the power of the Fascist party increased, the more its leaders feared the existence of power elsewhere. Ultimately, the long arm of the PNF's control system reached into the affairs of police and army in much the same way it intruded into the governmental domain. Unlike the state, the political police and the military were not viewed as actual hindrances to the realization of the ideology. Any independent center of power was, however, a possible impediment. The party sought to gain control over other forces within the regime in order that there could be no effective opposition to the dictatorship whenever a radically totalitarian course of action was prescribed.

THE PARTY MILITIA AND THE REGULAR ARMY

Hannah Arendt in her frequently cited book on totalitarianism has said that Italian Fascism "in contrast to the true totalitarian movements . . . could use such intensely nationalist instruments as the army, with which [it] identified [itself] . . ."[1] She sees no essential difference between the Fascist dictatorship and that, for example, of Generalissimo Franco, so far as the relations between government and army are concerned. Nationalist dictatorships, she comments, in contrast to truly totalitarian regimes, rest on the power of the professional army.

While this analysis appears to be valid for the Franco regime (Franco himself was a regular army commander before leading the rightists in the civil war, a war in which regular army contingents were his principal support), it is by no means true of Italian Fascism, which never "identified itself" with the army, but instead went to great trouble to maintain its own separate army of volunteers in much the same way that the Nazis retained the SA. Mussolini, who began to rule without the active support of the army, always distrusted the high command of the regular army, most of whom he thought were more loyal to the king than to Fascism.[2] Accordingly, from the very beginning he kept the original party Blackshirts as Fascism's own armed guard and invested them with powers which frequently conflicted with what the regular army regarded as its own sphere.[3]

Mussolini considered the establishment of the *Milizia Volontaria per la Sicurezza Nazionale* (MVSN) alongside the professional army as a very significant event. In 1927 he wrote: "The creation of the Militia is the fundamental, inexorable fact which placed this government on a plane absolutely diverse from that of all preceding governments . . . The armed party leads to the totalitarian regime."[4] The extreme dislike of the regular army's officer corps for this unprecedented party army is manifested in almost every one of the numerous postwar

106

memoirs of former Fascist generals and other high officials. Emilio Canevari, chief aide of General Graziani and the author of the most extensive and helpful of all these volumes on the Italian army, has called the decision to retain the militia after the March on Rome "undoubtedly one of the gravest errors of Fascism: it had the result of alienating . . . the army from the regime . . ." The officer corps regarded the institution of the MVSN as the result of "unjust suspicion" concerning the army's loyalty.[5] Far from "identifying itself" with the army, Fascism always suspected the army and believed it should be watched, countered, and controlled.

Officially, the MVSN came into existence on January 14, 1923,[6] about three months after the conquest of power. Massimo Rocca has described the meeting of the Grand Council at which it was determined to retain the militia as a permanent institution. At this meeting Farinacci advocated the continuance of provincial squads. Cesare Rossi and Italo Balbo opposed both the autonomous MVSN and the squads. It was Starace and Teruzzi who were among the chief architects of the idea of the militia.[7]

In actuality, of course, the law of January 14 created nothing new; it merely recognized the fact that the Blackshirts had never been and were never going to be disarmed; it sanctioned the "armed party" as an enduring hallmark of Fascism. The militia, according to Article 2 of the statute, was "at the service of God and Country," and "under the orders of the *Capo del Governo*." No mention was made of swearing allegiance to the king, as did the regular army. The militia was to act "in cooperation with the armed corps of the Division of Public Security and with the Royal Army to maintain internal public order . . ." The law called for the appointment of all those between the ages of seventeen and fifty "who possess the required moral and intellectual qualities," and who had previously belonged to the militia of the Partito Nazionale Fascista. Additional enlistments were to be made through the local fasci of the PNF, which would pass along recommendations to the provincial secretary, who, together with the provincial commander of the militia, would make the final choice.

By the January 14 law, officers were technically appointed by the minister of the interior, under whom the militia was at first placed as an organ of public order. The decree of March 8, 1923,[8] gave the appointment of the commanding generals to the *Capo del Governo*. The generals in turn appointed the lower officials. In fact the militia was always a component of the party, and all the top party leaders had dominant posts in it.[9]

According to the verbose statute of March 8, 1923, every member of the militia was characterized by a "mystic purity of spirit." He served Fascist Italy "with an indestructible faith and an inflexible will, despising, on a level with all other forms of vileness, that prudence which is born of opportunism, [and] coveting sacrifice . . . [He] senses the fierce beauty of his apostolate, for which he gives all to make the great common Mother strong and secure." Unlike the regular army, the militia does not, proclaimed the statute, place career in the first place; the militiamen are the "spiritual aristocracy" of Fascism.[10]

Very soon the militia developed its own "decalogue" and "prayer." Some sample commandments from the decalogue are these:

"Italy is to be served always and with whatever means; with work, and with blood.

"The enemy of Fascism is your enemy: do not give him any quarter.

"Conscious and total obedience is the legionnaire's virtue.

"Mussolini is always right."[11]

In addition to the regular militia there were subsequently established five special militias. Two of these, the Militia of Communications and the Militia of the Ports, were formed in 1923, only shortly after the enactment of the law creating the regular militia. The Militia of the Streets and the Militia of the Forests were constituted in 1925. The Militia for the Supervision of the Penal Islands was set up in 1927 to give the party a voice in the administration of the camps for political prisoners.[12] Most of these special militias were outgrowths of the prerevolutionary "forces of authority" *(gruppi di competenza)* established by the party for the purpose of taking over various strategic government services in the event of national strikes or sabotage against the party by enemy syndicates. Under Fascism they had the task of policing railroads, waterfronts, boundaries, and trains against enemies of the regime.

The 1923 statutes had presented the militia as an institution which would relieve the army of the prosaic details of internal policing;

Article 7 of the January 14, 1923, law specifically called for the MVSN, in the event of a general mobilization, to be "absorbed by the army." But something quite different occurred in the thirties when MVSN units fought as separate and independent units in the Ethiopian War and in Spain. Actually, the MVSN was allotted its own supply of weapons from the outset and in 1928 participated in the general military maneuvers as an independent army alongside the regular army. General Enrico Bazan, the MVSN's commanding officer, interpreted this to mean that in any future war the militia would act as a distinctive unit, the statute of 1923 notwithstanding. And the official magazine of the militia stated flatly in September 1928 that the question of whether the MVSN would go to war as a separate force had been "permanently decided" in the affirmative.[13] Thus, it became apparent that Article 7 of the 1923 statute had been inserted simply to soften the army's initial objections to the militia's being made a permanent institution and without any intention of its being observed.

From the first the militia was composed only of the party's hard core of veterans from the March on Rome and other carefully selected persons. It is true that in May 1925 the party directorate decided that all members of the party were to be considered as enrolled in the militia,[14] but this order was never put into effect, as may be

Table 11. Membership in the Milizia Volontaria
per la Sicurezza Nazionale

Year	Number
1926	211,000
1927	251,378
1929	300,000
1934	461,502
Full-time members	
Officers	1,312
Men	6,581
Reserve members*	
Officers	36,974
Men	416,635
1938	763,904

Source: 1926, 1927, and 1929 figures from Alessandro Melchiori, *Milizia Fascista*, p. 166; 1934 figures from A. Marpicati, M. Galian, and L. Contu, *La Dottrina del fascismo. Storia, opere ed istituti*, pp. 158–159; 1938 figure from *Regime Fascista*, September 4, 1938.

* These members devoted part time to service and were subject to immediate call to full-time duty.

seen from the official membership statistics of the MVSN (see Table 11). The militia included a total of 211,000 men in 1926, a figure which grew to 300,000 by 1929 and 461,502 by 1934. With the advent of the Ethiopian War its ranks were swelled considerably, and in 1938 there were 763,904 inscribed in the militia. But even at this peak membership level, the militia contained only about one third of the PNF's entire membership, approximately two and one half million in 1938. The militia, like the German SA originally, and later the SS, should be regarded as the elite formation of the party, and it included the most militant of the party's members. Left outside the pale were all the "Fascists of 1932" and later, who had been forced to join the party to keep their jobs in the bureaucracy or elsewhere. An indication of this elite nature of the MVSN is that persons suspended from the party for a serious offense and later readmitted could not be readmitted to the militia.[15]

It is one of the unique features of the institutional arrangements existing in Fascist Italy and Nazi Germany[16] that premilitary training, instead of being entrusted to the regular armed forces, was carried out by the armies of the respective single parties. This is highly significant, considering that in both countries premilitary training came to be required for almost all the youth. In administering the program in the place of the army the party could indoctrinate the youth with its own conceptions of loyalty and interfere with the relations between the youth and the officer corps of the army. Furthermore, the party leaders could observe which of the graduates of the premilitary courses could be counted on to be most cooperative as regular army officers. Party influence could then be used, as it undeniably was used, to further the promotion of such friendly persons. In this manner, within twenty years the PNF could hope to transform the officer corps into its own instrument. The regular army, naturally, bitterly resented this infringement on its own territory of influence.[17]

Exclusive authority to conduct the premilitary program was first given to the militia on August 4, 1924.[18] Not until the end of 1930, however, were all youths reaching their eighteenth birthday compelled to participate in the training, unless they could secure exemptions for reasons of health or vital occupation.[19] From at least March 1, 1933, membership in the party youth organizations and participation in the militia's premilitary training program were obligatory for acceptance at one of the army's military academies or colleges.[20] In December 1934, a statute was passed declaring the "function of the citizen and the soldier" to be "indistinguishable in the Fascist state." This law set up "courses of military culture" in the public schools, with the faculty for the courses selected from the officers of the Fasci Giovanili, the ONB, and the militia.[21] In the spring of 1938 control of premilitary training was shifted from the militia to the GIL. From that date the entire national premilitary program was directed by one of the vice-commanders of the GIL, who had established under him separate divisions for land, naval, and air preparation. The school for training premilitary instructors was also brought under GIL control. On the provincial level, the vice-commander of the GIL ran the program.[22] In practice, the change in the direction of the program did not have great importance, because the personnel administering the courses remained the same militia officers who had been doing the work before. Indeed, all the GIL leaders were officers of the militia.

The courses were divided into two categories: one general, and required of all eighteen-year-olds, and one specialized for students of "physical, intellectual, and professional" excellence, who had proved themselves outstanding in the general course. The specialized courses prepared the student for officers' training. In 1934 there were 15,341 officers of the militia employed in giving the courses and they had instructed a total of four million young men.[23] In the late thirties, at the height of the Fascist militaristic mania, stricter requirements were made regarding exemptions for the courses, and many more youths were enrolled. In 1938 there were 35,000 instructors for the program, more than double the number used in 1934.[24]

As the party directed the training of Italian youth before they went into the army, so it also controlled them upon their retirement, whether temporary or permanent. Both of the large veterans' organizations, the *Associazione Nazionale Combattenti* and the *Associazione Nazionale Mutilati e Invalidi di Guerra,* had been captured by the party shortly after its assumption of power. Their direct dependence on the PNF, in precisely the same manner that the other associations of governmental employees depended on the party, was made official in 1938, when they were legally placed under the PNF's control.[25] As of October 28, 1939, these associations had 802,468 and 200,116 members respectively.

The Italian Fascist Party in Power

The peak of party influence and pressure on the regular army came during the middle and late thirties. Party extremists had been demanding a full-scale Fascistization of the army for some years. In the columns of the extremist periodical *Il Secolo Fascista* the proposal to force all regular army personnel to don black shirts had been advanced in all seriousness. There are countless ex-Fascists and anti-Fascists in postwar Italy who have argued that the party pressure was greatest on the army during the term in office of General Federico Baistrocchi, who from July 1933 until October 1936 was undersecretary to the Ministry of War. Baistrocchi was brought to trial in 1946 as a result of accusations made against him by a number of high officials in the Italian army. The principal accuser was General Quirino Armellini, whose book, *La crisi dell'esercito*,[26] was a sustained polemic against Baistrocchi's conduct in the Ministry of War. As a result of the testimony of these generals in an inquiry, Baistrocchi was indicted on the following counts: (1) working for the Fascistization of the army; (2) inserting the MVSN as an independent unit into the ranks of the regular army; (3) introducing the spirit of Fascist squadrism into questions of a technical and military nature and into the disciplinary regulations of the army; (4) provoking dissension and disorganization in the army by, among other things, promoting men on the basis of their "Fascist merits"; and (5) injecting "affairism, intrigue, and corruption" into the activities of the Ministry of War. Each of these broad charges was subdivided into a number of specific accusations.

After the trial got under way, some curious things began to happen. As they proceeded to testify, one after another of the former Fascist high army officials who had brought the charges — including Armellini himself — "put water in his wine," as the press observed. They arose in court to soften and modify the testimony they had offered in the pre-trial hearings.[27] As a result, Baistrocchi was acquitted on September 21, 1946.[28]

The allegations during the course of the trial have great relevance for this analysis, in spite of the fact that Baistrocchi was acquitted. For it was universally admitted that the various interferences and pressures by the militia and the PNF that were listed in the indictment did actually occur. Baistrocchi and his friends were concerned

112

solely with establishing either that a given "illegality" was not his direct responsibility or that it occurred before or after his tenure of office as minister of war. Some of the accusations against the general for succumbing to party influence were not refuted at all. Rather, it was asserted that Baistrocchi did his best to minimize these pressures and was never a willing instrument of the party leadership — as the prosecution maintained. Consequently, the question of the general's guilt or innocence has no bearing on the primary issue. What matters is the extent to which, between the years 1933 and 1940, the party interfered with the activities, policies, and promotions of the professional armed forces.[29]

As with the bureaucracy, the teaching profession, and the police, the PNF seems to have tried very hard to induce army officers to join the party during the big membership drive of 1932–1933. Similarly, inscription in the party was not legally compulsory until 1940. But Generals Oddone, Ronco, Mazzetti, Dall'Olio, Zoppi, Villasanta, and Tosti di Valminuta accused Baistrocchi of using direct and indirect means to convince officers to join, and of having made such membership an important hurdle for promotions. Baistrocchi was even alleged to have set up a special *Ufficio per il tesseramento* to facilitate the party's recruitment campaign.[30] In his defense, Baistrocchi admitted only to having issued in 1933 a circular informing the officer corps that they "were authorized to enroll themselves" in the party.

Badoglio in his memoirs had attacked Baistrocchi for having "introduced politics into the army" by requiring that the "Fascist merits" of a candidate for promotion be weighted heavily.[31] Other high officials seconded the accusation, stating that Baistrocchi as minister of war showed favoritism in promoting officers recommended by the PNF. Baistrocchi freely confessed that the party did attempt to influence promotions, but stated that he was more successful in resisting than his successors had been. He offered some specific examples of promotions which he insisted were effected by him over the vigorous opposition of the party. He argued that the greatest influx of *uomini politici* into the leadership of the armed forces occurred during the years immediately following 1936.[32]

The trial testimony shows that there was established, beginning in Baistrocchi's secretaryship, an *Ufficio di collegamento* (Liaison Office) between the army and the militia. Baistrocchi admitted its existence, saying that the Liaison Office served to "resolve questions of common interest to the two forces."[33] Armellini accused the MVSN of having worked against the employment of sound military tactics and attributed to the militia leaders much of the responsibility for Italy's shamefully inadequate preparation for World War II. The militia's officers of "squadrist mentality" created a "disharmony between will and power, theory and available means" through their unwillingness to consider objective, strategic maneuvers. Instead the militiamen thought only of grandiose offensives. Again, Baistrocchi admitted that this current was strong in high army councils, but he pleaded that he minimized its effects.[34]

There were a number of other examples of party interference given during the trial which are relevant and specific. The Fascist hymn "Giovinezza" was made an official army anthem in the early thirties. Official army correspondence was ordered written in the "Fascist style." Party propaganda and portraits of the Duce were permitted to be posted on the walls of the barracks. Distribution to the troops of party and militia magazines like *Milizia Fascista* and *Gioventù Fascista* was allowed on army premises. And provincial party secretaries apparently gave propagandistic harangues on more than one occasion to army personnel.[35]

In addition to these innovations aimed at politicizing army life, there followed in the late thirties the order for the army to adopt the *passo romano*, or goose step, in the place of its former, less ridiculous manner of marching. This change occurred in February 1938 after the party's youth organizations and the militia had demonstrated in numerous parades that the goose step was the pre-eminently Fascist mode of marching. This requirement was quickly followed by a forced change in the army's traditional salute. The MVSN divisions incorporated in the regular army had enjoyed since the late twenties the right to use their Roman salute, even to regular army officers superior to them in rank. Now the militia's salute was adopted for the entire army, and the older one was outlawed.[36]

THE MILITIA IN WARTIME

As indicated above, MVSN units, contrary to the original statute of the militia, were used separately from and independently of regular army units in actual military operations. The first instance of such deployment was in September 1923 when the government, not wishing to take regular army troops from Libya where native uprisings were serious, sent three legions of the militia to Corfu, where they remained until May 1924. Immediately thereafter, two MVSN legions were assigned permanently to service in the colonies.[37]

In Ethiopia the militia made its first big showing in actual combat. At a meeting of the national directorate of the PNF on May 21, 1935, Starace announced the mobilization of the first two divisions of militia troops which were to fight with the regular army in Ethiopia. The secretary stated: "This fact is of the highest significance. It is testimony once again of the continuity of the Revolutionary ideal and of the Militia's efficiency that [the MVSN] has been called to defend our intangible interests and our security in East Africa."[38] As Salvatorelli writes, this decision to use the militia "made for difficulties" with the regular army.[39]

For the Ethiopian campaign a total of 224,410 militiamen were mobilized, of which number 154,531 (in addition to 5,377 officers) saw active service at the front.[40] These MVSN troops were grouped in seven divisions and 184 battalions.[41] In addition to the divisions there were special "columns" of militia members which were assigned special tasks. The most famous of these was the *Colonna Celere*, commanded by none other than Starace himself and composed of 160 officers and 7,300 men. Starace, with the rank of lieutenant general in the MVSN, entered the Ethiopian campaign in the spring of 1936 and directed independently the conquest of Gondar, one of the Ethiopian provinces.[42] With this mission accomplished in less than two months, Starace returned to Italy and his job as head of the party. It should be pointed out that in order to prevent complete confusion, ultimate command of both forces was given to regular army officials, although at the very beginning Marshal De Bono, not a regular army man but one of the original Blackshirts, had run the whole campaign. He proved somewhat inept and was quickly replaced by Badoglio.[43]

No sooner had the Ethiopian campaign ended than another contingent of the militia was off to fight on the side of Franco in the Spanish Civil War. Approximately forty thousand Italian troops participated in the enterprise, of which the great majority were members of the militia. This enabled Mussolini to claim that the men were "volunteers" instead of members of the regular army.[44] The entire expedition was under the direction of General Mario Roatta, a regular army officer.

In 1938 it was revealed that some twenty regiments of veterans of the Ethiopian War had been organized, within the regular army, under the direct control of the secretary of the PNF, who appointed the commander of each one. The purpose of these unusual units was to "collaborate with the armed forces and . . . work for the military preparation of the nation."[45] Nonmembers of the PNF in the armed forces could join, but party members wore a distinctive insignia on their uniforms.

During the late thirties the militia grew even larger than it had been during the Ethiopian War (see Table 11).[46] In a speech to the party leaders of Genoa on September 3, 1939, Mussolini called the MVSN the "armed guard of the Revolution," and an "organic part of the regular army." Having proved itself in Africa and Spain, the militia would continue to perform in military operations as a unit distinct from the regular army. Thus, in the 1939 campaign in Albania, the militia fought again. With these precedents, it came as no surprise when, with the outbreak of World War II, Mussolini confirmed that "the MVSN will fight with its legions incorporated in the great mobilized unity which is the army. I am sure that you Militiamen will merit this great honor."[47]

Sometimes the objection is raised that the 1943 *coup d'état* demonstrates the predominance of the army over the party in Italian Fascism. Actually, it only proves Italy's complete demoralization over badly losing a war in which even victory would have spelled subservience to Germany. It is true that, at the instigation of Grandi, Bottai, and Ciano, the Grand Council voted, in that fateful all-night session of July 24–25, by a majority of 19 to 7, in effect to call upon the king to dismiss Mussolini from office and to appoint someone in his place capable of reaching an armistice agreement with the Allies. It is also a matter of historical record that, twelve hours after the adjournment of the Council, Mussolini was taken prisoner by the king, who had the cooperation of the regular army. But all through the crisis the party and militia leadership remained faithful to Mussolini. Most of them went north to join the Germans and to assist Mussolini in establishing his Salò Republic following the Duce's spectacular liberation by a Nazi paratrooper in early September 1943. But for some inexplicable reason, Mussolini at the time made no effort to halt his overthrow by calling on these loyal forces, in spite of the fact that Carlo Scorza, the secretary of the PNF, had warned him in advance of the seriousness of the plot against him.[48]

The coup of July 1943 can only be interpreted in the context of Allied military victories and should never be confused with something like the overthrow of Perón in September 1955. Perón was ousted in peacetime because he had never sufficiently checked the military. It is extremely unlikely that Mussolini and the militia could have been overthrown by a regular army clique in time of peace.

THE PARTY AND THE POLITICAL POLICE

The full-fledged dictatorship of recent times is characterized by a "close net of 'spies upon spies.' "[49] The existence of this net means that even the political police, whose full-time job is to watch everyone else, are in turn watched. Under Fascism the party maintained its separate investigation services, insisted upon having a share in the decisions regarding political criminals and in the administration of the penal islands, and controlled the police in a number of ways.

In totalitarian dictatorships relations between the party and the police are both collaborative and antagonistic. Merle Fainsod has described this situation as it existed in the Soviet Union, and his words could apply to Fascist Italy as well: "The security organs were supposed to assist their opposite numbers in the Party hierarchy by keeping them informed of the political mood of the inhabitants, calling their attention to abuses and irregularities, and locating and rooting out opponents of the regime. But in another respect, the relation was potentially antagonistic. The Party apparatus exercised jurisdiction over . . . [police] employees in their capacity as Party members, while the security officials had as one of their missions checking and reporting on the Party apparatus itself."[50]

The Fascist secret police, or OVRA (*Opera Volontaria per la Repressione Antifascista*, or *Organizzazione di Vigilanza per la Repressione Antifascista*) did not exist until the autumn of 1926, when Arturo Bocchini was appointed chief of the entire police corps. According to the principal source of information on the OVRA, Guido Leto,[51] the Fascist police before the advent to power of Bocchini were in a state of amazing disorganization and inefficiency. Many police headquarters

117

had "antiquated equipment, there did not exist an efficient telephone network, and technical services were in a primeval state." Buildings were insufficient and in bad condition, and training schools for personnel were "inefficient or nonexistent," depending on the locality.[52] Into this situation came Bocchini, arguing that "without an efficient police the dictatorship would not be able to continue to exist."[53]

Bocchini took office as *Capo della polizia* on September 12, 1926. The immediate cause of the displacement of the previous chief, Francesco Crispo-Moncada, appears to have been the ineptness of the police in dealing with the September attempt on Mussolini's life by the anarchist Gino Lucetti. Significantly enough, Bocchini, who before going to Bologna had been prefect of Brescia, the city of Augusto Turati, owed his appointment largely to good relations with the secretary of the PNF.[54]

The prestige of the police was so low at this time that various provincial party bosses had instituted their own police units, most notably at Ferrara and Padua. On November 7, 1926, the Grand Council announced that it was "inviting" all fasci which had formed secret police and compiled "lists of proscription" to "cease such activity immediately."[55] Bocchini turned his attention instantly to modernizing police facilities, improving the training schools, and installing an expensive new communications system. Not until the end of 1927 had Bocchini consolidated his position sufficiently to move on to the creation of an *Ispettorato Speciale di Polizia*, which had as its sole function the uncovering of political enemies of the regime. The inspectorate, originally quite small, was led by Francesco Nudi and had its home base in Milan. Shortly afterwards, another section was established at Bologna under Giuseppe D'Andrea. The secret police quickly mushroomed until it had many centers and a thousand functionaries. Mussolini reportedly suggested in 1928 that the service be called OVRA.[56]

From the very beginning of Bocchini's tenure in office relations between the party and the police were anything but cordial. Leto, Bocchini's chief assistant, continually complains in his memoirs of the "hostile and prejudiced mentality" of party and militia leaders toward the police, an attitude which left their relations "always cold, often hostile, and sometimes very strained."[57] Party leaders throughout the fourteen years of Bocchini's rule never ceased to be possessed of "the mania to play police," and to "put their noses into police affairs . . ."[58]

118

A most interesting technique was employed by the party to control the police, who were in these first years to a great extent under the direction of the PNF. Bocchini's first chief of the political police, Ernesto Gulì, was selected personally by the secretary of the party, Turati. Leto wrote: "The control was very strict: rarely was Bocchini able to receive anyone without Gulì, who had a room adjacent to Bocchini's office and took notice of the arrival of every visitor, being present." At the end of each day, Bocchini's former close associate stated, "Gulì called at the office of the Fascist party to confer with Turati on affairs relating to the police."[59] Gulì also had an important voice in appointments and was responsible for hiring, according to Leto, party hacks in the place of more competent applicants. By the end of the twenties, however, this extraordinarily direct control by the party of the police was ended. Bocchini gradually strengthened his position to become undisputed master in his own house. As with Himmler in the Nazi system, Bocchini was never actually subordinate to the Ministry of the Interior, under which he was legally placed. In the middle and late thirties the chief of the Fascist police came to have frequent and violent conflicts with Guido Buffarini-Guidi, then secretary of the interior.[60]

On the national level the PNF retained its own police, the Special Service of Political Investigation of the Militia. This body was created about a month after Bocchini took office in 1926.[61] A section of it was established in the care of each provincial commander of the militia. The Special Service was authorized to conduct, independently of the regular police authorities, investigations "with reference to crimes against the personality of the state." The Ministry of the Interior, according to the statute, was to be notified "from time to time" of the subject and nature of the investigations in progress.

From its inception the party appears to have controlled the Special Tribunal of the State, which it succeeded in establishing, despite police opposition,[62] on November 25, 1926. The immediate reason for the special court was the near success of the attempted assassination of the Duce on October 28, 1926, by Tito Zaniboni, who had been a leading Socialist member of the Chamber of Deputies before the Fascists drove all opposition parties underground. During the next month the party leaders succeeded in ousting their enemy Federzoni from his position as minister of the interior and in establishing the Special Tribunal, with heavy party representation. The Special Tribunal was composed of a president, chosen from the generals of the army, air force, or party militia; five judges, selected from those officers of the militia who had attained the rank of colonel; one or several vice-presidents, also of the rank of general or admiral. None of the members were required to hold a law degree. Mussolini had the ultimate authority to initiate investigations and he appointed the investigating staff (*guidici istruttori*) of the tribunal.[63] In 1929 a Council of Revision, composed of the president of the Special Tribunal and two members selected from the higher officers of the militia, was set up to review certain very unusual cases. Previously, the decisions of the tribunal had not been subject to review.[64]

The Special Tribunal concerned itself largely with crimes which, from the Fascist viewpoint, merited death sentences or long prison terms. More frequently utilized and perhaps, over all, a more important institution of the terror was the *confino,* or consignment to one of the penal islands. Persons deemed only suspicious by the provincial authorities were spirited away to one of the several penal islands off the coast of southern Italy without even the formality of a trial. Assignment to a penal island or radical restriction of movement on the mainland (for those less offensive) might be inflicted on any persons "who are a danger to public order even though they have not previously incurred police supervision or legal penalties . . ."[65] It often happened that provincial authorities had assigned to *confino* persons previously absolved and cleared by the Special Tribunal for the Defense of the State. Leto, always the apologist for the police, blamed this unusual procedure on "local extremist groups" in the party.[66] However, in the same book he inadvertently demonstrates how the police also had total power to place a man in *confino* instead of permitting the case to come before the Special Tribunal, as would have happened normally.[67]

The informally organized commissions of confine were generally composed of the prefect, the procurator, the *questore,* an officer of the carabinieri, and an official of the party's militia. In cases of disputes appeal was made to a committee presided over by Bocchini and including the advocate general of the Roman Court of Appeals and a general of the militia.

To illustrate the extent of the party's control over the Special Tribunal, the case of Guido Cristini, president of the Tribunal until November 1932, should be mentioned. According to Rossi,[68] Cristini was forced out of office for having been in close touch with Arpinati and perhaps having revealed secret information to that unfortunate minister of the interior at the time when the party was preparing to jettison him. Thus, not even the head of the Supreme Tribunal was immune to party action.

The year 1932 was not a happy one for the police in their conflict with the party. Beginning in the autumn of that year the police, like all other employees in the bureaucracy, were compelled to join the party. This had long been a pet project of the party, but had been successfully thwarted by Bocchini until then. The older members of the police force considered themselves "professional" employees performing specific technical functions, and they fought the drive to impose party membership as an illicit attempt to politicize them.[69] Thus, the police as well as the regular bureaucracy were caught in the net of the party during the 1932–1933 opening of the membership rolls.

Although squadrism was vastly reduced after 1925 by central party control, party gangs, with their immunity to police arrest, continued from time to time to exercise their own police action. Party officials retained the right to beat up and threaten selected victims and to destroy property. The police turned a deaf ear to complaints from abused citizens.

In April 1937 the Fascist government announced that its political police had uncovered at Milan an organization of "Communists, Socialists, and Republicans" intent upon aiding Republican Spain by working against Fascism in Italy. The party used this episode as a pretext for setting loose once more its squads of action to undertake punitive expeditions against various "anti-Franco cells" throughout the country.[70] The year 1937 was marked by savage repression both at home and abroad: in June the internationally famous murders of the leftist anti-Fascist leaders Carlo and Nello Rosselli were revealed to have occurred in France, apparently committed by French sympathizers of Italian Fascism at the instigation of Mussolini's regime. Fascist *agents provocateurs* were also especially active in other European countries during this period, as the dictatorship became progressively more totalitarian.[71]

The period of the later thirties showed an increase in the arbitrary attacks by party personnel on the citizenry. Ciano relates his observation of party terrorism in telling about the clubbing he saw administered by a group of Fascists to a man on Rome's Via Veneto in September 1939. The victim had apparently been overheard using the traditional *lei* instead of the Staracian *voi* in conversation. There is no way to measure the number of such incidents.

In the early years of the Fascist regime the police were little more than instruments of the party and the Ministry of the Interior, to both of which they catered. As the years passed, although the party retained effective control of the Special Tribunal, shared through the militia in the administration of the penal islands, and kept a certain domination over the police through forced party membership and the reports of its own spy service, by and large it is correct to say that, as in the Nazi system, the police eventually attained a position of power independent of both the party and the Ministry of the Interior.

The Nazi case affords an enlightening parallel. By a law of March 29, 1935, the Nazi SS had been officially listed as one of seven components of the NSDAP. But, the Nuremberg prosecution stated, "as the plans of the conspirators progressed," the SS "acquired new functions, new responsibilities, and an increasingly important place in the regime. It developed . . . into a highly complex machine, the most powerful in the Nazi state, spreading its tentacles into every field of Nazi activity."[72] The section of the SS performing the special functions of the political police was the SD (*Sicherheitsdienst*). Both the SS and the SD had originally been party organs and in the early months of the Nazi regime were in some conflict with the Gestapo, the political police of the government. In the spring of 1934 Himmler, the head of the SS, succeeded in obtaining control of the Gestapo as well. He was officially made chief of the German police on June 17, 1936. Himmler was legally under the Ministry of the Interior until the very last years of the regime, but he participated in the cabinet as a full-fledged member and built up his own empire. Authorities on National Socialism like Hannah Arendt report that after Hitler, Himmler was the most powerful figure in the Nazi ruling clique.

Similar as were the positions of Bocchini and Himmler in their respective systems, Bocchini's power was indubitably never as great as Himmler's, if for no other reason than that the scope of the terror in Italy was much less. Fascist Italy did construct an extensive system of concentration camps under police control, and the regime did produce a fear-ridden society because of the arbitrary procedures of police and party in handling suspects. But, with a lack of thoroughness which always irritated the Nazis, the Fascists never carried matters to their "logical implications" in the sphere of terror. In Italy, the police never passed into the hands of a party elite as they did in Germany. Rather, the Italian Fascist police seem to have been less extreme on questions of the terror than the party wished. It is inconceivable that Himmler, if he had lived, could have written a book arguing that the police had actually been conservative in applying the regime's arbitrary rules and that it was the party which was responsible for the major abuses in the system. This is, however, exactly what Leto affirms in his memoirs. One reviewer properly sneered at Leto's book for depicting the OVRA in idealistic terms as a benevolent institution resembling the Red Cross. But it is undeniably true that the police under Fascism had nothing like the power of their German counterpart and were responsible for nothing like the incredible number of scientifically prepared atrocities which the Nuremberg trial records show to have been the work of the Nazi SS.[73]

8

Party and Regime in Perspective

I T USED to be the fashion for political scientists, writing about Fascist Italy, to remark that in Mussolini's dictatorship the single party was rigidly subordinated to the state. In contrast, the party was supposed to be superior to the state in the Soviet Union and equal to the governmental machinery in Nazi Germany. If this neat generalization were valid, Fascist Italy could not be characterized as a totalitarian regime. For, as C. J. Friedrich has brilliantly argued, one of the crucial traits displayed by totalitarian dictatorships is that the party is "either superior to or commingled with the bureaucratic organization."[1]

H. Arthur Steiner was close to the truth when he wrote in 1938 that a study of Mussolini's regime had to begin with "an analysis of the functions of the . . . Party."[2] He correctly believed that the PNF had come to occupy a position at least equal to that of the other organs of the dictatorship, and that in many areas the party actually predominated. However, Steiner went too far in describing the governmental machinery as "meaningless and formal." The power of Buffarini as minister of the interior, of Bocchini in the OVRA, and of Ciano at the Foreign Office was great, as the previous chapters on party-state tensions have attempted to demonstrate. Barrington Moore has written, "There appears to be a sort of symbiosis among party, police, and state administration, in which no one of them can do without the other two."[3] This observation was made solely with the USSR in mind, but it would seem to be a general rule for totalitarian dictatorships.

In order to comprehend fully the power and significance of the party

124

in Italy, it is necessary to compare the PNF's role with that of single parties in other dictatorships. My conclusion is that the Fascist party resembled much more closely the Nazi and Russian Communist parties than it did the parties of the lesser, nontotalitarian dictatorships of the past thirty years.[4] If this is true, it has an important bearing on the problem of whether the Italian Fascist regime may be judged to have been a totalitarian form of dictatorship.

The task of evaluating the Fascist party from a comparative perspective may be rendered less difficult by determining what were the traits which characterized the PNF after it had attained the fullness of its development as the single party of the regime. Then the extent to which other single parties shared these criteria and whether there were any essential traits lacking in the Fascist party can be ascertained. There are ten distinctive characteristics which the Fascist party displayed at the height of its power during the decade 1930–1940. The Partito Nazionale Fascista:

(1) was supported by the regime's official theory as the *permanent* single party (*partito unico*) of the dictatorship;

(2) was, so far as internal structure is concerned, organized from top to bottom in a rigidly hierarchical manner under the immediate control of the dictator, through the secretary, who was the Duce's subordinate;

(3) maintained a "closed" rather than an "open" membership policy, allowing neither free entrance nor free exit;[5]

(4) completely controlled a whole range of associations designed to bring leisure, sport, culture, and joint professional activity within the political sphere and to suppress all spontaneous social groupings;[6]

(5) directed the regime's giant youth organization and the training schools for the elite of the youth;

(6) controlled the Fascist syndicates (in which membership was obligatory) and exercised the dominating influence in the regime's controlled economy, called the "corporative state";

(7) exercised surveillance over the civil service, schoolteachers, and university professors through its spy system, the associations, and, after 1932, enforced party membership;

(8) preserved its own armed militia as a check on the regular army, into whose internal affairs (promotions, policies, etc.) the PNF continually meddled;

(9) carried on continuous propagandistic and indoctrinating activities among its own members and among the masses, diffusing knowledge of the ideology throughout the populace;

(10) and represented through its inner circle a bulwark of ideological intransigence and extremism on questions of high policy.

If the above traits are used as a rough standard of measurement, it is immediately obvious that certain of the single parties which came to power in Europe and elsewhere during recent history failed to exhibit a number of the Fascist party's properties. The most obvious contrast occurs when the party in Kemal Atatürk's Turkish dictatorship is examined. The Kemal regime, which flourished from 1923 until at least 1938, advanced no theory of the single party as a requisite institution and no elite theory of party organization. Indeed, in direct divergence from Mussolini's cynical assertion that a plebiscite could consolidate the dictatorship but never overthrow it, the Turkish single party insisted that its authority was derived from popular election rather than from the mystical quality of its leaders, who had directed, with the support of party veterans, the "Revolution." Recruitment in the Turkish party was open and free, and no large groups were forced to join the party for economic reasons or for advancement in career. Party organization was decentralized, and open factional differences existed. There was no concerted effort to win mass support through the manipulation of modern means of mass communication (still largely nonexistent in Turkey). Likewise, no party youth organization recognized by the state to the exclusion of all other youth groups, composed of the majority of the nation's young people, and aiming at the eventual total incorporation of the youth within its ranks existed in Turkey. The Turkish party apparently interfered very little with the bureaucracy, the army, or the economy: there was no dual state in Turkey.[7] All these facts signify that there is a vast difference among various single parties, and that the mere existence of a one-party system, as in the southern United States, does not automatically brand such a country or area as "totalitarian," or even illiberal. Obviously, the Italian Fascist party was much closer to the single parties of Nazi Germany and the Soviet Union than to the single party of Turkey.[8]

Little material is available on the structure and functions of the dictatorial parties that dominated in Romania, Hungary, and Poland in the 1930s. Somewhat more, although still insufficient, information exists on Portugal, Argentina, Spain, and Vichy France. Under Salazar's

Portuguese dictatorship, between 1931 and 1934, a second faction within the single party was allowed to develop into an independent party, although it disbanded after Salazar refused to be its president. Like the Turkish dictatorship, the Portuguese regime has never advanced a theory of the single party as a permanent institution. Indeed, in December 1954 the Italian press carried several articles indicating that Salazar was preparing to readmit the old Liberal party to public life and move toward a more democratic system.[9]

Events of the summer and early fall of 1955 revealed how weak the party was in Perón's Argentina. Only formed in 1945, two years after Perón came to power as a key figure in one of the perennial Latin American military coups, the Peronista party never succeeded in establishing itself as a strong enough force to check the power of the regular armed forces. In fact, an admiral (Teisaire) held the chairmanship of its Supreme Executive Council. The party was never allowed the chance to develop its own militia. Except for its close ties with the General Confederation of Labor, the Peronista party did not carry on many quasi-governmental activities. It had virtually no control over the bureaucracy (the *Control del Estado* exercised this function) or the schools. The party of Perón was never the single party of the regime, because the Radical party was permitted to survive and to have a small representation in Congress. Structurally, the party presented many differences from the Italian Fascist party.[10]

The role of the Falangist party in Franco Spain is even weaker than that of the Peronista party in Argentina. The Falangists were founded not by Franco but by Primo de Rivera. As a professional soldier, Franco merely utilized the party as an aid in the civil war and his relationship with the Falange has been described as "that of a *mariage de convenance* and not of affection."[11] Especially since the end of World War II the Falange has been declining in strength. "Prestige and power have equally been taken from the blue-shirted men: the Fascist salute, their post in the cabinet, their own organized militia, their control of national press and propaganda."[12] As in Argentina, military men have been assigned to head the party. Catholic Action has attained control of the school system, the censorship machinery, and the foreign office. Only a small minority of the cabinet officials have ever been members of the Falange.

Vichy France appears almost deliberately to have refused to construct a *parti unique*. In the occupied zone there were actually two major Fascist parties competing with each other. Pétain had only the *Legion des Combattants Français* as the main "popular" organ of the regime. This organization, devoid of specific functions, never had great political significance.[13]

Thus far the discussion has centered on single parties which are nontotalitarian, which clearly do not measure up to the standards set by the PNF. It now remains to compare, however briefly, the Italian Fascist party with the two greatest single parties the world has yet seen, the Communist party of the Soviet Union (CPSU) and the National Socialist party of Germany (NSDAP). If these two giant organizations are measured by the ten traits of the Fascist party, it is apparent that they bear a basic resemblance to the PNF. The Fascist, Nazi, and Soviet parties are of one cloth. They do not differ in kind, for each is a totalitarian single party in an advanced stage of maturation. But there do exist between them significant differences of degree.

Of the three, the CPSU shows the most fully developed totalitarian political organization. Under Stalin, the Communist party apparat extended its power until it completely dominated the state bureaucracy. With Khrushchev as its leader, it retains its commanding position today. The Soviet army has been far more effectively controlled by the party than were the armies of the Nazi and Fascist systems, where the political commissar did not take hold. As the author of a recent book on Communist party activities has observed, in the USSR the party leadership "sought to prevent the army from becoming an independent force by controlling its appointments, by atomizing and intimidating the opposition, and, above all, by constant efforts to suffuse the army with the Party's own political outlook."[14]

The CPSU was the only totalitarian party to be largely successful in its drive to supplant the state. In both Nazi Germany and Fascist Italy a dualistic arrangement prevailed, wherein the party was able to exert pressure on the state and to prevent the state from acting against its will while at the same time remaining distinct from the state. But in the Soviet Union the party *became* the state, adding to its organizational table divisions of agriculture, roads, industry, foreign affairs, trade, and the like. The CPSU has for decades minutely supervised the administration of every government ministry. Without the party in the Soviet Union there would be no state.

Party and Regime in Perspective

Professor Merle Fainsod, in a study making use of the archives of
the Smolensk regional party organization captured in World War II,
brings out authoritatively the extensive participation by the Communist party in essentially governmental affairs. Economic matters of
the region took up at least as much time as did the party's own special tasks: "Soviet methods of rule were consciously constructed
around overlapping, duplication, and parallel functions. . . . The
secretariat of the obkom [party regional committee] paralleled the
governmental departments; it intervened constantly to direct, scold,
and prod the administrative organs subject to its supervision."[15]

The Soviet leadership has not been entirely pleased with the substi-
tution of a party for a state bureaucracy. From time to time party
leaders are urged to become less involved in state administrative affairs. For the more the party becomes swamped with technical, administrative operations, the greater is the danger that the zeal and
revolutionary energy of the party may be impaired. The totalitarian
single party inevitably arrives at a paradoxical position, for not to
become involved in the state machinery means to let power slip from
its hands, while over-involvement may result in the neglect of the
party's revolutionary, extremist functions. It may become more interested in bureaucratic means than in ideological ends. The orders of
the Soviet leaders to regional party organizations reflect this tension.[16]

There is, then, a limit to party-state unity beyond which the totalitarian party ceases to fulfill its primary function: the expansion and
preservation of the ideology. It must have power, but not more than
it can use. Although conditions vary from one dictatorship to another,
it may be that the dualistic pattern which emerged in Germany and
Italy is a more "natural" totalitarian arrangement of party and governmental power than is the monistic principle upon which the Communist world has tended to operate.

In comparing the PNF and the Nazi party, certain structural differences should be noted. Because the Nazi system was larger and more
complex, and the party if anything more ubiquitous than the Fascist
party, the NSDAP exhibited greater administrative decentralization.[17]
The PNF never developed the dual ministries which confuse the student of the German dictatorship.[18] Nor did the Fascist party adopt
the technique of the *Personalunion* used by the Nazis and by the So-
viets.[19] The provincial secretaries of the Fascist party, although they

129

exercised a powerful influence in matters of local administration, did not possess (with isolated exceptions like Farinacci of Cremona and, for a time, Giampaoli of Milan) anything like the complete control enjoyed by the German Gauleiter. However, these contrasts can only be suggested here, for a full consideration of the Nazi party is a subject for further study. In terms of Friedrich's definition of the totalitarian single party (see p. 13 above), the two giant organizations display many more similarities than differences.

The age through which mankind has just passed has been most creative in experiments with various forms of dictatorship. One of the lessons which emerges from this experience is that no dictator can get to first base without a strong single party. In fact, the presence of a powerful, predominating party is a rudimentary test of totalitarianism. Those dictatorships in which such a party may be detected display a much higher level of totalitarian dynamism than do regimes in which the party is weak or nonexistent. The party-dominated regimes of Germany, Italy, and the Soviet Union worsened over time, in the sense that they became more terroristic internally and more imperialistic externally. On the other hand, National Front governments like Spain and Portugal, which have been forced to depend for their support on conservative groups like the army, the higher clergy, and the landed aristocracy, have mellowed with time. Spain and Portugal have followed the paths of the traditionalist autocracies rather than the totalitarian regimes. They give the appearance of immobility; they have been concerned with domestic order and stability rather than with world conquest in the name of a new truth. Neither Franco nor Salazar has been able to develop an ideology of his own. The announcements that have been coming out of Spain in recent years promising a restoration of the monarchy are an indication that party extremist groups are not in power there. Spain has not had, nor does it seem destined to have, its Era Starace.[20]

The existence of a complex system of party leadership schools is another important feature distinguishing totalitarian regimes from traditionalist dictatorships. The Italian Fascist, Nazi, and Soviet regimes were interested in doing more than maintaining power and privilege for the original leadership group. They were concerned with creating a political discipleship, which would faithfully translate the aspirations of the ideology into reality and thus continue the never-ending task of winning the world to the new truth. The curriculum of the leadership schools was meticulously planned so that the core of the ideology would be inherited by each new generation. These schools have apparently not been established in any of the National Front dictatorships.

In a justly celebrated book, Herman Finer has argued that the Fascist regime was wholly created and sustained by Mussolini, and that with the passing of this "genius" the regime itself would have collapsed.[21] Actually, it is as fallacious to use the personal dictatorship hypothesis for Italy as it is for Germany. Totalitarian regimes seek to institutionalize power in order that they will not be wholly dependent on the survival of their founder and leader. In Fascist Italy, the party and the youth organizations were the institutions fostered to ensure the regime's perpetuation. Military defeat by a foreign enemy spelled the doom of Italian Fascism. Had World War II not occurred, it is highly probable that the Fascist regime would yet be on the historical scene — with or without Mussolini. The party had trained a new generation of leaders; it was prepared to handle the succession problem, and most probably could have crushed any internal revolt.

Although there can be no certainty in the answers given, it is interesting to speculate about why some dictatorial single parties remained weak and insignificant, while others expanded in power and became more autocratic internally. Aside from the more obvious explanations which would emphasize the personal and ideological differences between the various dictators and their chief lieutenants and the presence or absence of modern means of communication and control in the societies they inherit, one reason hinges on the different circumstances in which power is acquired. The pre-power stage in the development of a single party has an important bearing on its subsequent history. In the Nazi, Fascist, and Soviet dictatorships the party could claim that it made the revolution unaided. Also, these single parties took the reins of government with an extensive political organization and settled loyalties formed during relatively lengthy periods of preparation. In Poland, Argentina, and Portugal, on the other hand, the single party had no existence before the seizure of power and played no role in the making of the "Revolution." Actually, no revolution occurred; rather, a group of right-wing parties already in power formed a National Front coalition and suppressed opposition elements with the support of the police and the army. Likewise, the Spanish regime rode to power on the back of the regular army (with nonmilitary aid from the majority of the Catholic clergy) rather than on that of the party.

WAS FASCIST ITALY TOTALITARIAN?

The development of a single party in Fascist Italy basically similar to the parties in the two most important totalitarian states does not automatically signify that the Italian system was itself totalitarian. But totalitarian parties do not develop in a vacuum. They depend for their growth on favorable conditions in the regime as a whole. Therefore, where there is a totalitarian single party,[22] there is also likely to be an entire totalitarian system.

Few persons who have heretofore written about Fascist Italy agree that Fascist Italy was totalitarian. The Italians themselves, with the rare exceptions of Salvemini and Salvatorelli, have been quick to find affinities between the Fascist regime and mild-mannered despotisms like Salazar's in Portugal. As for non-Italians, three representative citations should suffice to illustrate prevailing scholarly opinion. Sigmund Neumann has observed: "Italian Fascism, in comparison to national socialism, was a mere prelude to revolution . . . It never matured into a full-fledged modern dictatorship."[23] In his recent volume on Italy, the historian H. Stuart Hughes has stated flatly that "Although Mussolini . . . coined the word 'totalitarian' to describe his regime, the Duce's Italy, as compared with subsequent development in the Nazi and Soviet states, scarcely deserved that title."[24] Hannah Arendt has been even more emphatic: Mussolini's regime was "Not totalitarian, but just an ordinary nationalist dictatorship developed logically from a multiparty democracy."[25] Portugal, Spain, and the Poland of Pilsudski are, according to Arendt, other examples of nationalist dictatorships. That her view has been gaining credence in American political science circles is evident from the approving reference to her remarks about Fascist Italy in a recent volume by Professor Walter Berns.[26]

The basic problem of an analysis of this kind is the definition of the word "totalitarianism." Fortunately, a definition has recently been put forward by C. J. Friedrich which clears up much of the confusion normally accompanying the use of this term. As a result of an extensive study of Fascist and Communist dictatorships, Friedrich has extracted four characteristic and unique features of totalitarian systems. These traits have the great advantage of being empirically verifiable with reference to any current or recent dictatorship.[27] They do not appear fully developed at the outset in any totalitarian dictatorship. Rather, they constitute a pattern toward which a totalitarian system steadily evolves. Traditionalist dictatorships, on the other hand, lose their totalitarian momentum, stagnate, and end by falling far short of the mark.

Of the four factors which basically are shared by all totalitarian societies of our time, one, the powerful single party, has already been counted present in the Fascist dictatorship. The others, according to Friedrich, are (1) "an official ideology . . . characteristically focused in terms of chiliastic claims as to the 'perfect' final society of mankind"; (2) a "technologically conditioned near-complete monopoly of control of all means of effective mass communication"; and (3) a "system of terroristic police control . . . directed not only against demonstrable enemies of the regime, but against arbitrarily selected classes of the population [as well] . . ." These are the criteria against which the Fascist system must now be measured.

FASCIST IDEOLOGY

In contrast to the Nazi and Soviet regimes, Italian Fascism came to power with only the most nebulous concepts to distinguish itself from other political forces. Mussolini himself had written only newspaper articles of a transitory nature and had, before the March on Rome, neither the time nor the inclination to compose anything comparable to *Mein Kampf*. There was no venerable oracle resembling Marx which the Fascists regarded as the source of doctrinal truth; the Fascist movement could claim no figure like the Nazi party's Alfred Rosenberg, interested in formulating systematically the new party's ideas.

A striking conflict in the realm of ideology occurred when Giovanni Gentile, a former disciple of Croce and until early 1923 a member of the Liberal party, was converted to Fascism. Gentile decided to fill the Fascist ideological void by constructing his own political theory of Fascism. Because of his reputation in Italian intellectual circles, his two books of the twenties, *Che cosa è il fascismo* (1925) and *Origini e*

133

dottrina del fascismo (1929), came to be regarded by many as the most significant expressions of Fascist ideology. An avowed disciple of Hegel, if not a correct interpreter of him, Gentile developed in these volumes, through the medium of his own brand of historical idealism (called "actual idealism"), the concept of the "ethical state," the actual embodiment of which he curiously found in the dictatorship of Benito Mussolini.

Actually, Gentile's influence on Fascist ideology has been vastly overrated. If ideology in a dictatorship is defined as an idea or combination of related ideas which apparently influences the practical political measures taken by the leaders of the regime and which is promulgated by the party and other organs as the official explanation for these measures,[28] then Gentile cannot be called one of the principal Fascist *idéologues*. The party opposed Gentile from the beginning because it regarded him as a latecomer to the game and suspected him of having loyalties other than to Fascism. The party elite, which had made the Revolution and considered itself the guardian of "revolutionary truth," could hardly permit an outsider, a former Liberal, a man who had come to Fascism after the conquest of power, to formulate the official ideology of the regime.[29] Accordingly, when party leaders learned that Gentile planned to write the article on Fascist ideology for the 1932 *Enciclopedia italiana* they protested strongly and demanded that Mussolini write a definitive tract, even if ten years late, on Fascist ideology. Mussolini, according to the testimony of a former vice-secretary of the PNF,[30] accepted the invitation, took the Gentile draft home, and for three days worked at revising it. The result was the Duce's "La dottrina del fascismo," the official statement of Fascist ideology published in the encyclopedia. It is in the second portion of that article, apparently written completely by Mussolini, that the gist of Fascism's "working ideology" is stated most completely.

The extent of opposition to Gentile by the party's hard core was revealed in 1933 with the publication of a most rare thing in a dictatorship, a genuinely polemical book reflecting dissension within the regime. The volume, which was written by G. A. Fanelli, party veteran and extremist editor of *Il Secolo Fascista*, proclaimed itself in the title to be against the "mystification" of Gentilian actual idealism.[31] Fanelli accused Gentile of having said at the time of his conversion to

Fascism that it was not he who had come to Fascism but Fascism which had come to him, that is, that Fascism chose to accept his ideas rather than the reverse.[32] Gentile, insisted Fanelli, drew his philosophical inspiration from foreigners like Fichte and Hegel rather than from the Fascist Revolution. Fanelli expressed the party's revolutionary prerogative of interpreter and guardian of the faith when he demanded that those "who, coming from other political faiths, did not join . . . the squads ought to . . . stand and listen, like catechumens, to the Word [*il verbo*]" as preached by the men of the Revolution. Instead, Fanelli complained, as soon as Gentile joined Fascism he "began to play the Pope." In doing so Gentile claimed "a dogmatic authority incompatible with a party which does not know any other authority than that of the Duce," who is the source of all authority. Fanelli lashed out at Gentile for having spoken too frequently against the party and cited a number of Gentile's remarks, some out of context, to document the allegation.[33]

Fanelli's book was the most outstanding example of party hostility to Gentile's attempt to found Fascist ideology around the philosophy of actual idealism. Other Fascist writers plainly anti-Gentilian and closely allied with the party elite's position as expressed by Fanelli were Sergio Panunzio, Carlo Costamagna, Alfredo Rocco, and Paolo Orano. According to Bottai, by the end of the Ethiopian War in 1936, Fascist culture had become more and more rigid and arid, with the opponents of Gentile carrying the day within the party. Actual idealism had "always more rigorous criticism conducted against it" which succeeded in "forcing it definitely outside the revolutionary process . . ."[34]

The party was forced to reject Gentile and his cohorts because the Gentilians tended to lapse into use (or misuse) of the intellect instead of staying within the bounds of sterile imitation of the latest thoughts of the dictator.[35] As the party's campaign to deify the Duce gathered momentum in the middle and late thirties, the regime became increasingly intolerant of "intellectuals" who sought, within however prescribed a circle, to think for themselves.[36] According to party extremists the one and only source of Fascist doctrine and ideology was the writings of the Duce. A speech the party secretary made in 1935 to a gathering of university professors illustrates the lengths to which the party went in establishing the infallibility of the leader and the degree to which it rejected all independence of thought. Too many professors, the secretary observed, relied too much on their own minds and as a result wished to explain everything, even "that which comes from the mind of the Duce," thereby "having the enormous presumption of putting themselves on the same level with Him . . ." The difference, insisted the secretary, between the Duce and ordinary mortals was a "distance truly astronomical." "If professors, habituated to reasoning, must reason, they must do it with appropriate caution. When the brain no longer succeeds in understanding it must give way to . . . the heart . . ."[37] As Bottai has written, in the late thirties all of the party's energies were "directed toward crystallizing the power held by the Duce."[38]

It is useful for purposes of analysis to draw a sharp distinction between Italian Fascism's "working ideology" and its "ideology for export." The ideology for export, only tolerated by the regime, spoke of the "ethical state" and a kind of pseudo-democratic corporativism. Foreign scholars who in the twenties and thirties chose to dwell on this aspect of Fascist thought created a biased picture of what the ruling elite really believed and preached to their followers.[39]

The core of Fascism's working ideology, as it may be gleaned from the most significant speeches of Mussolini and his party stalwarts and from the indoctrinating manuals of the party and its youth organizations, was neither simple nationalism nor nineteenth-century state-worship, but a universalistic paganism modeled after the example of ancient imperial Rome.[40] Italian Fascism was not simply a *coup d'état* of a rightist nationalist group — of an Italian Hugenberg rather than an Italian quasi-Hitler. Fascism did not draw its ideological inspiration from the right wing of the Risorgimento.[41]

The Fascist party's catechism for the youth organizations explicitly repudiated any theory explaining Fascism in simple nationalistic terms.[42] It is true that Mussolini had at first, as Hitler was to do after him, told the world that Fascism was not an article for export. But in a speech of October 23, 1930, the Duce denied that he had ever made the statement. Instead, Fascism was the "order of the day in all countries"; soon there would be *una Europa fascista*. As Fascist or semi-Fascist movements sprang up in Hungary, Romania, Austria, Great Britain, Spain, and Switzerland, Rome was revered as the capital of the European Fascist empire, and Mussolini was kept busy receiving delegations from these countries. In a speech on October 25, 1932, commemorating the tenth anniversary of the Fascist Revolution, the Duce described his regime as a "Third Rome." The twentieth century was to be "the century of Italian power . . . the century during which Italy will return for the third time to be director of human civilization." "Within ten years," he shouted, "Europe will be Fascist or Fascistized! . . . The antitheses which agitate contemporary civilization are capable of resolution only in one way: through the doctrines and wisdom of Rome . . ."

In his famous article written for *L'Enciclopedia italiana,* Mussolini called the Fascist regime a "will to power and empire." The Roman tradition, he wrote, "is an idea of force . . . For Fascism the tendency to empire . . . is a manifestation of vitality, while the opposite is a sign of decadence . . ." He went on to show how the call of Rome served as a rationale for tightened internal controls and a system of terror. Empire "demands discipline, coordination of forces, duty and sacrifice: this explains many aspects of the regime's practical action, and the necessary severity against those who would oppose themselves to this . . . fateful impulse of twentieth century Italy."[43]

As the core of Fascist ideology, the obsession with the idea of a Roman empire did indeed "explain many aspects of the regime's practical action." There is little doubt that the Roman madness was the principal motivation behind the Ethiopian War, the first great break in the European security system of the interwar years and the "prelude to World War II" (as Salvemini called it, in *Mussolini diplomatico*). This stretch of desert was hardly economically or strategically worth the risk of flouting the entire League of Nations. Only in the ideological context does the enterprise make sense.[44]

With the initiation of the Ethiopian campaign, the emphasis on Rome in Fascist thought reached such proportions as to exclude all other concepts.[45] In his victory speech of May 9, 1936, Mussolini, to the shouts of thousands of jubilant followers, saluted "after fifteen centuries, the reappearance of the Empire on the fateful hills of Rome." And on April 15, 1939, when announcing the annexation of Albania, party secretary Starace called the "new Albania" another indication of the "attraction which the Rome of Mussolini, perpetuating the traditions of the Rome of the Caesars, exercises over peoples."

The Italian Fascist Party in Power

The Roman idea left its traces everywhere on the internal operations of the Fascist system. The requirement of the Roman salute in place of the handshake, the attempt to use Catholicism as the civil religion of the state, the legislation encouraging population growth, the policy of economic autarky, the inculcation of an intense militarism and love of violence in the youth — all of what Mussolini termed the "aspects of the regime's practical action" become comprehensible when we understand the hold which the idea of a new Roman empire had over the minds of the Fascist ruling elite.

Fascist "monuments" help today's student of Fascism recreate the imperial atmosphere of the Italy of the 1930s. When, in 1938, the party built its *Foro Mussolini* (now called the *Foro Italico*), it outdid even the architects of the exposition grounds in slavishly counterfeiting ancient Rome. Only in size does the imitation succeed. The primary attraction is one of the largest stadiums in Europe. A second amphitheater at the Foro, called the *stadio dei marmi*, is encircled by fifty giant statues representing all forms of athletic prowess (and therefore *virtus*). On all sides of a large building that served as the national party school for youth extend black and white mosaics of athletes and warriors. Fascist slogans cover almost all available space between the figures. The power of repetition was evidently recognized, for over and over the black letters shout: *Duce A Noi, Duce A Noi, DuceDuceDuceDuce.* A symbol of the world itself is in the center of the grounds. An obelisk towers coldly over the entrance; formerly capped with a golden tip, today the legend alone remains undefaced — *Mussolini Dux.* No one who enters here can help but realize that the builders and makers of this monument to decadent aesthetics genuinely believed that Italy could again attain the size and power of ancient Rome. The era of the Third Rome was the Messianic fulfillment of history for Italian Fascism in much the same way that the establishment of the Third Reich was for the Nazis and the classless society is for the Communists.

Heinrich Heine in a famous passage predicted the crumbling of "the taming talisman, the cross," and the eruption of the "savagery of the old warriors." "The old . . . gods will rise from the ancient ruins . . . rub the millennial dust from their eyes" and "shatter the . . . cathedrals." Italian Fascism attempted just such a full-scale revival of the savage elements in the pagan tradition. It is no accident that the distinguished Irish Catholic scholar D. A. Binchy greatly feared the effect Fascism would have on the Church in Italy, which Fascism sought to employ as an *instrumentum regni*.[46] Binchy thereby displayed a more acute understanding of Mussolini's regime and the extent of its destructive potentialities than does Hannah Arendt when she applauds the Church's early decision not to oppose Fascism as an anti-Christian movement.[47]

THE CONTROL OF MASS COMMUNICATIONS

In common with its contemporaries, Nazi Germany and the Soviet Union, Fascist Italy developed a network of party and state agencies devoted exclusively to the control of the channels which distributed information to the public. At the beginning this machinery was only partially effective. Literature was left comparatively free, although Italian writers found it expedient to censor themselves. Non-Fascist writers, with occasional exceptions like Alberto Moravia and Carlo Levi, evaded political topics and retreated into the literary essay. Except for Croce, no non-Fascist scholar could write on recent or contemporary history, and even Croce did not carry his *History of Italy from 1871* beyond 1915. Movies were subject to fairly strict control by the Institute LUCE. The state-owned radio was of course thoroughly Fascistized; a phenomenal amount of time was absorbed by political broadcasts. The theater was somewhat less controlled at first than the cinema, but after 1935 the stage degenerated sharply, producing almost wholly banal and politicized plays.

The Italian press, which Mussolini liked to call "an orchestra played in concert, although on different kinds of instruments," was closely supervised from the outset. Anti-Fascist editors of *La Stampa* and *Corriere della Sera* were forcibly removed; indeed, with Albertini's ouster from the direction of the latter journal early in the history of the regime, liberty of the press was dead. The press was censored and controlled by the Press and Information Office of the *Capo del Governo*. This office was closely supervised by Mussolini and the party leaders.

Monotonous and conformist as were the Italian press, radio, cinema and theater from the very beginning of the dictatorship, not until the middle and late thirties did Fascism proceed to use systematically these mass media for what one scholar has termed the *Gleichschaltung* of the nation.[48] On June 1, 1937, all the various Fascist censorship offices were abolished, and the control of the press (except for party journals), radio, cinema, live productions, periodicals, and books passed to the new Ministry of Popular Culture (known in common parlance as "Minculpop"). No longer was the regime concerned principally with negative censorship. Through the new ministry a positive campaign of indoctrination was embarked upon.[49]

Immediately after the fall of Fascism, an Italian scholar managed to acquire a considerable number of Minculpop's orders to the press, and he published an instructive sampling of them.[50] These *note di servizio* gave detailed commands on the content of certain articles, the space and emphasis to be accorded the pieces, and even the size type to be used in headlines. The directives on the anti-Semitic campaign and the reform of custom are especially interesting, as are those ordering the press to follow the latest twist in Fascist foreign policy.

Supplementing the continuous indoctrination by Minculpop was the more specialized propaganda activity of the Fascist party.[51] Thus, the total impact of propaganda upon the average Italian citizen was impressive. The propaganda machinery of Fascist Italy throws the censorship techniques of traditionalist dictatorships into the shade. Under Napoleon III, for instance, there were practically no positive indoctrinational orders to the press. The regime was concerned solely with negative censorship, and often even stooped to bribing popular editors to cease their attacks on the government.[52] Franco's censorship office is not much more effective; it is staffed with members of Catholic Action rather than with party veterans, as was the case in Germany and Italy. Fascist Italy's propaganda machinery must be ranked with that of Nazi Germany in terms of its over-all effectiveness.[53]

The party and the Ministry of Popular Culture under the Italian Fascist dictatorship were united in a drive to elicit mass ideological conformity. Their efforts reveal the mania for mass support so typical of the three major dictatorships of recent times. And activities in propaganda demonstrate the crucial importance to these modern dictatorships of up-to-date techniques of mass communication as instruments for the manipulation of public opinion. As one writer neatly expressed it: "The Genevan exiles in Elizabeth's first Parliament might [have been] totalitarian by temperament, but they lacked a radio station."[54]

THE TERROR

Most foreign students of Fascism writing during the heyday of the regime made far too little of the importance of the terror as a permanent part in the machinery of the dictatorship. On the other hand, it is true that some undoubted exaggerations were also published on the subject.[55]

In his recent volume on the Special Tribunal for the Defense of the State, Fascist Italy's Star Chamber, Cesare Rossi has placed the total number of persons "tried" during that body's twenty-year existence at 21,000.[56] This figure does not include the persons taken into protective custody and assigned to confinement on one of the penal islands or in isolated areas of southern Italy. As noted earlier, these persons were detained, often permanently without even a mock trial. Many times the victims were persons previously tried and found not guilty by the courts. Nor do the statistics account for the numerous raids by party *squadristi* directed against those Italians whom the party deemed suspect. However, the detention camps on the islands and mainland appear never to have held more than five thousand inmates at any one time, except for the period of the Social Republic (1943–1945), when the terror had a far greater scope. These are small figures compared with Nazi and Soviet operations in this area.

Guido Leto has written of the conditions existing on the penal islands: "Many have asked . . . especially after the terrifying reports which have come out of Germany . . . [how Italian detention camps compared with those of the Nazis]. On this point . . . although excesses undoubtedly occurred, it is opportune to say a word of truth and clarification for our good name and our humanitarian tradition . . ."[57] Leto presented an unquestionably idealized account of life on the islands;[58] the fact remains that not even the most violently anti-Fascist Italians have contended that conditions there, even at their worst, began to approximate either in scope or intensity the scientific cruelty of the Nazis.

But these observations should not obscure the reality of the Fascist terror. Italian Fascism was not "just another despotism" which was "really not so bad after all." The scope of the terror is not the only factor to be considered. Fascist Italy was a fear-ridden society in which a man could be taken from his domicile and at the very least be threatened or beaten because of some vague complaint lodged with the police or the party. There was no way for the average citizen to know the numbers of people in *confino* or how they were treated; the mere existence of the institution was enough to cause universal anxiety. Ignazio Silone captured this atmosphere of terror under Italian Fascism in his *Bread and Wine*: "Minorca: It is well known that the police have their informers in every section of every big factory, in every bank, in every big office. In every block of flats the porter is, by law, a stool pigeon for the police. In every profession, in every club, in every syndicate, the police have their ramifications. Their informers are legion, whether they work for a miserable pittance or whether their only incentive is the hope of the advancement in their careers. This state of affairs spreads suspicion and distrust throughout all classes of the population. On this degradation of man into a frightened animal, who quivers with fear and hates his neighbor in his fear, and watches him, betrays him, sells him, and then lives in fear of discovery, the dictatorship is based. The real organization on which the system is based is the secret manipulation of fear."[59] It is precisely this atmosphere which Signor Leto omits describing, although it is an indispensable background for the reading of his book.

THE BALANCE SHEET

It is clearly on the last of Friedrich's four criteria, the terror, that Fascist Italy fell short of the totalitarian mark. As Arendt has emphasized, the totalitarian terror is not concerned solely with the "suspect" but also with the "potential enemy."[60] The mass imprisonment and destruction of entire occupational or ethnic groups, chosen for ideological reasons, simply did not occur under Fascism.

An exception to this statement might be made with reference to the Italian Social Republic (sometimes called the Republic of Salò), which was established by Mussolini as the government of northern Italy on September 23, 1943, and which existed until the final extermination of the Fascist regime on April 28, 1945, when Italian partisans captured and shot Mussolini, his mistress, Clara Petacci, and a score of his top party and state leaders. During the period of the Social Republic, Mussolini greatly intensified the terror, and gave orders for Jews to be treated as enemies for the duration of the war. However, in many respects, the Social Republic was simply a puppet regime of the Nazis; it may therefore be questioned whether the new

ruthlessness in the employment of the terror against Jews was a development indigenous to Italian Fascism.

This does not mean that the possibilities for the more developed
form of terror were not there. In spite of the fact that his internal
position was never more secure, Mussolini insisted that the terror be
heightened in the late thirties.[61] The party's campaign against the
"bourgeoisie" and the Jews after 1937 demonstrated that the Italian
Fascists at least had the idea of imitating the totalitarians of Russia
and Germany in labeling whole classes of persons as fit victims for
the secret police.[62]

Italian Fascism encountered two barriers which slowed its rate of
totalitarian development. The first of these impediments was the
Italian people. While it cannot be truthfully said that any people is
suited for totalitarianism, it is notorious that the Italians were *not* so
constituted. Mussolini regarded contemptuously the Italians as inferior material for his dictatorial work of art, and, in his personal
comportment, always strained to act the reverse of the stereotyped
Italian. Indeed, it was for the purpose of transforming the Italian
who liked to sing in the streets, talk and gesture extravagantly, and
take a long siesta that the party undertook its reform of custom. The
second hindrance was the relative smallness of Italy's population and
territory. Arendt has correctly observed that smaller countries
"simply [do] not control enough human material" to allow for the
required "great losses in population." Even Nazi Germany did not
reach its zenith in this sphere of terror until the conquests of the war
gave it control over a sufficient number of people.

If for these reasons Fascist Italy was deficient in meeting the fourth
of Friedrich's criteria, there is little doubt that it was fully totalitarian with reference to the other three. A nationalist dictatorship like
Franco Spain, on the other hand, could never claim this record; its
ideology is nebulous or nonexistent, the party is miserably weak, and
the Spanish educational system and propaganda machinery are in the
hands of the Roman Catholic Church. It is true that Italian Fascist
ideology lacked systematic formulation in comparison with Marxism-
Leninism. Yet Fascism did have an ideology in the call of Rome. In
this concept was implied the "political messianism" (as Talmon has
called it) so characteristic of the totalitarian ideologies of our time.
The frequent clashes of Fascism with the ecclesiastical authorities,

especially in youth education, resulted from the regime's attempt to enforce an opposing ethical system on the Italian people.

If correctly viewed, totalitarianism is not so much an accomplished fact as it is a process of becoming. Fascist Italy did not come as close to achieving its totalitarian *telos* as did Nazi Germany or the Soviet Union. But the strange men who ruled Italy never took their eyes off the totalitarian target. Only the hand of time prevented the maturation of yet more monstrous projects, already conceived in the fertile minds of the Fascist leaders.

Italian Fascism was neither a comic opera nor a South American palace revolution. It was a political religion, equipped with the machinery necessary to realize its program. During its twenty-odd years of existence the Italian Fascist dictatorship developed relentlessly toward the totalitarian pattern. The twilight shadows of late Italian Fascism were inexorably deepening into totalitarian night.

Notes, Bibliography, and Index

Notes

Chapter 1. A New Tool for a New Despotism

[1] The point about the uniqueness of the single mass party as a tool for totalitarian rule is brilliantly made by C. J. Friedrich in a volume edited by him: *Totalitarianism* (Cambridge, Mass., 1954), p. 57.

[2] Bernard Crick, an unpublished manuscript.

[3] Arguments for the inclusion of Italy with Germany and the Soviet Union as "totalitarian" will be given in the final chapter, "Party and Regime in Perspective."

[4] *Republic*, 562–576B.

[5] J. L. Talmon, *The Rise of Totalitarian Democracy* (Boston, 1952); N. Berdiaev, *Regno dello spirito e regno di Cesare* (Milan: Communità, 1954), Ch. IV, translated from the Russian by E. Grigorovich.

[6] For an account of the extent to which the new technology captured the imagination of important political theorists, see J. H. Hallowell, *The Decline of Liberalism as an Ideology* (Berkeley and Los Angeles, 1943), and Frank Manuel, *The New World of Henri Saint-Simon* (Cambridge, Mass., 1956). Positivistic, technocratic thought entered the Fascist mind via the works of Marinetti and the futurists.

[7] Strictly speaking, there was no Communist party in Italy until January 1921, when the Socialist party split over the issue of subservience to the Soviet Union. A segment of the party withdrew and formed the Communist party at that time. The remaining Socialist party subsequently split further into "maximalist" (revolutionary) and "reform" Socialists.

[8] Luigi Salvatorelli and Giovanni Mira, *Storia del fascismo* (Rome, 1952), p. 141.

[9] For an account of the alternation of his moods during this period and of the influence of party leaders in persuading him to resolve the crisis, see Paolo Monelli, *Mussolini piccolo borghese* (4th edition, Milan, 1954), pp. 145–153.

[10] *Mussolini's Italy* (New York, 1935), p. 161.

[11] This is Friedrich's definition of a totalitarian single party, given in *Totalitarianism*, pp. 52–53.

[12] In articles in *Popolo d'Italia* of July 2, 1919, and July 3, 1920.

[13] Vincenzo Sinagra, *Profilo storico del Partito Nazionale Fascista* (Rome, 1938), I, 87. On early party history see also Angelo Tasca, *Nascita e avvento del fascismo* (Florence, 1950).

[14] Giuseppe Bottai was a leader of this school. See his memoirs, *Vent'anni e un giorno* (Rome, 1949), especially pp. 40–41. See also the work of the famed Dante scholar who was converted to Fascism's "respectable" wing: Francesco Ercole, *La Rivoluzione fascista* (Palermo, 1935), p. 484. Giovanni Gentile desired a "party of educators" *Origini e dottrina del fascismo* (Rome, 1929), pp. 47–48).

147

[15] See his *Il Partito e i suoi compiti* (Rome, 1928), pp. 8–9.

[16] H. W. Schneider thought the party was on the way out. *Making the Fascist State* (New York, 1928), p. 131.

[17] Inexplicably, Maurice Duverger wrote of the Fascist party as having been in perpetual decline after the seizure of power: *Les partis politiques* (Paris, 1951), p. 103. Perhaps it did decline during Turati's leadership, but under Giuriati and Starace it was clearly in the ascendancy, no matter what interpretation one cares to give to the term "decline."

[18] Galeazzo Ciano, *1937–1938 Diario* (Rocca San Casciano, 1948), p. 276.

[19] Among advocates for the term "order" were Mihaïl Manoïlesco, *Le parti unique* (Paris, 1937), and Duverger, *Les partis politiques*. Duverger utilized Schmalenbach's concept of the *Bund* — an intermediate grouping between the *Gesellschaft* and the *Gemeinschaft*. The church analogy has been made by a great number of writers, among them A. Rossi, *A Communist Party in Action* (New Haven, 1949), and Rudolf Heberle, *Social Movements* (New York, 1951). The army comparison was used by Gottfried Neesse, *Partei und Staat* (Hamburg, 1936), and Alessandro Melchiori, *Milizia fascista* (Rome, 1929).

[20] A stanza of Federico Ratti's "Party Hymn" reads:

> "We are the leaves of an oak
> Born with a new spring
> We will fall before evening comes
> But the oak will remain."

[21] After 1935 it was the custom in many fasci for the party member, after marriage in church, to take his bride to the local party headquarters, there exchanging the golden wedding rings for two iron bands, supplied by the party secretary and unblessed by the priest. The gold rings were placed upon the "Altar of the Country" and went to defray the cost of the Ethiopian War. A. C. Jemolo, *Chiesa e Stato in Italia negli ultimi cento anni* (Turin, 1952), p. 598.

[22] Konrad Heiden, *Der Fuehrer. Hitler's Rise to Power* (New York, 1944), p. 653.

[23] C. J. Friedrich, *Constitutional Government and Democracy* (Boston, 1950), p. 419. This is a modification of Max Weber's definition, found in A. M. Henderson and Talcott Parsons, eds., *Max Weber: The Theory of Social and Economic Organization* (New York, 1947), p. 407.

Chapter 2. The Indispensable Party

[1] Mussolini himself castigated party extremism as a nuisance on occasion during Fascism's normalization period, from 1926–1929. His 1927 "Circular to the Prefects" was intended to curb the party secretaries who wished to go too fast in weeding out lukewarm Fascists in the government and in the populace at large.

[2] For ideological differences between the three totalitarian systems on the position of the state, see especially G. Ambrosini, O. Ranelletti, and C. Schmitt, *Gli stati europei a partito politico unico* (Milan, 1936). The paper by Schmitt, a leading Nazi theorist, is particularly interesting because of its strong emphasis on the superiority of the "movement" (*Bewegung*) over the state, an interpretation which Hitler also stressed in *Mein Kampf* (New York, 1939), pp. 594–595. The Marxist derogation of the state, continued faithfully by Lenin, is too well known to bear recapitulation. An interesting article by V. A. Aspaturian, "The Contemporary Doctrine of the Soviet State and Its Philosophical Foundations," in the *American Political Science Review*, XLVIII (December 1954), 1031–1057, shows that Stalin, on the other hand, developed a much more positive theory of the state. The doctrine of the *stato forte*, a central element in Fascist ideology, is definitively expressed in Mussolini's article in *L'Enciclopedia italiana*, reprinted as *La dottrina del fascismo* (Rome: Treves-Treccani, Tumminelli, 1933). See also Alfredo Rocco, "The Political Doctrine of Fascism," *International Conciliation*, no. 223 (October 1926).

148

[3] "Dinamica del Partito," in *Notiziario del Ufficio Stampa del P. N. F.*, no. 22 (September 22, 1941), supplemento no. 2. See also the works of S. Panunzio and G. A. Fanelli.

[4] *Politics*, 1314a.

[5] Hitler said this of his own party in his *Secret Conversations* (Italian translation, Naples, 1954, p. 146). The statement is equally valid for Mussolini.

[6] *Politics*, 1363b. (Translation of Ernest Barker, London, 1947, p. 286.)

[7] Duverger makes the distinction between *terrorisme interieur* and *terrorisme exterieur*. The first involves control over the ruling class of the regime itself, while the second is directed at opposition and uncooperative elements outside the actual government. The first is more appropriately the task of the party; the second, of the police.

[8] Party surveillance of these other organs of the Fascist state will be more fully discussed in Chapters 6 and 7.

[9] PNF, *Statuto* of 1938, Article 15.

[10] Salvatorelli and Mira, *Storia del fascismo*, p. 293.

[11] Mussolini, *La dottrina del fascismo*. German theorists expressed similar views of the "capillary" nature of the party. Otto Koellreutter wrote: "The party ought to live in the people and with the people and constantly send its roots down into the people." *Deutsches Verfassungsrecht* (Berlin, 1935), p. 150. The Soviet dictatorship in claiming to govern itself by "democratic centralism" is even more emphatic about its democratic character.

[12] Quoted in E. K. Bramstedt, *Dictatorship and Political Police* (New York, 1945), p. 169.

[13] Editorial in *Gioventù Fascista* (March 1, 1935), p. 4.

[14] Mussolini frankly stated in 1929 that he would not abide by the results of the plebiscite if they should turn out contrary to Fascism: "A revolution may be consecrated, but never overthrown, by a plebiscite." Quoted in Salvatorelli and Mira, *Storia del fascismo*, p. 334.

[15] They were called conversations to stress the fact that lively discussion was to go on at the meetings.

[16] According to party statutes, the 1939 courses were attended by 6,894,390 youths, who were taught by 18,880 instructors in 7,241 localities. In *Atti del P. N. F.*, *Foglio di disposizioni* no. 1313, April 20, 1939.

[17] *Foglio di disposizioni* no. 1179, November 2, 1938.

[18] *Atti del P. N. F.*, V (1937), Book 2, p. 18.

[19] Through the *Massaie rurali*. *Foglio di disposizioni* no. 102, March 29, 1938.

[20] *Atti del P. N. F.*, I (1932), pp. 141, 221. It should be remembered that the party organization itself had frequent meetings, and that many citizens were members both of the party and these other organizations, like the Dopolavoro. They were twice-indoctrinated.

[21] For a summary of the propaganda activity of some of the provincial fasci, see *Fogli di disposizioni* nos. 11 and 125, September 3 and October 13, 1942.

[22] Federazione di Milano, *Rapporto* (1941), p. 103.

[23] See the description of the rallies in *Gioventù Fascista*, October 15, 1935, p. 3.

[24] *1937–1938 Diario*, pp. 182, 185, 286, and 307. Ciano narrates Mussolini's instructions to the party leadership to "stir up a strong wave of Francophobia all over the country" as a precondition for Italy's pressing claims to French possessions in the Mediterranean (principally Tunisia and Nice).

[25] *Foglio di disposizioni* no. 1128, August 5, 1938, and no. 1149, September 17, 1938.

[26] *Regime Fascista*, October 19, 1938, p. 2.

[27] *The Rebel* (New York, 1954), p. 153.

[28] Carlo Giglio, *Partito e Impero* (Rome, 1939), p. 10.

[29] The moderates among the ruling elite were Bottai, De Bono, Federzoni, Balbo, Bocchini, and most of the generals of the army. Ciano was at times with them, at other times against them.

[30] See especially Guido Leto, *OVRA* (Bologna, 1952). Leto insists that the Duce himself favored such a move, but that in the end he could not resist the pressures of the party men. Salvatorelli denies that Mussolini ever contemplated relaxing the terroristic aspects of the regime (*Storia del fascismo*, p. 741).

[31] From 1937 to 1939 there was a directive on Fascist "style" in almost every *Foglio di disposizioni*. Those for 1939 are reprinted in Asvero Gravelli, ed., *Vademecum dello stile fascista* (Rome, 1939).

[32] *Foglio di disposizioni* of March 11, 1933, in *Atti del P. N. F.*, II, 197.

[33] *Foglio di disposizioni* no. 706, January 2, 1937.

[34] According to Mussolini's valet, the Duce never failed to use *voi* in place of *lei*, and he vigorously corrected any who might slip and employ the old form (Quinto Navarra, *Memorie del cameriere di Mussolini* (Milan, 1946)).

[35] *Foglio di disposizioni* no. 1200, November 29, 1938. The opposite of the Fascist was the "bourgeois" man, who was "skeptical, compromising, enamoured of the comfortable life, and opportunistic."

[36] Emil Ludwig, *Colloqui con Mussolini* (Verona, 1950), p. 71. This edition indicates Mussolini's corrections of the original page proofs.

[37] Salvatorelli and Mira, *Storia del fascismo*, p. 835.

[38] For the people to have a "racial concept" was "indispensable for the work of the empire" (Mussolini to Ciano, April 20, 1938, in Ciano, *1937–1938 Diario*, p. 161).

[39] Monelli, *Mussolini*, p. 142.

[40] Jemolo, for example, states that the racial campaign was "a certain sign of Italy's enslavement to Nazi politics" (*Chiesa e Stato*, p. 669).

[41] See especially Salvatorelli and Mira, *Storia del fascismo*, p. 836, for a confirmation of this interpretation.

[42] In the discussions within the Grand Council on whether to pass racist legislation, Starace and Farinacci led the forces in favor, while Federzoni, Balbo, and De Bono were against it. Ciano, *1937–1938 Diario*, p. 264. See also the memoirs of Bottai and Leto for a similar picture of the dissensions within the Fascist system.

[43] See *Regime Fascista*, July 15, 1938.

[44] *1937–1938 Diario*, p. 215.

[45] See Eucardio Momigliano, *Storia tragica e grottesca del razzismo fascista* (Verona, 1946), pp. 103ff.

[46] See Chapter 4 for a more extended discussion of these schools.

[47] The enormous concern of the party over creating a political "discipleship" and continuing the regime beyond Mussolini's death casts doubt on Finer's thesis, in *Mussolini's Italy*, that the Fascist regime would necessarily collapse when the Duce died. The regime did collapse, of course, but because of military defeat and not because of internal difficulties of ensuring the succession.

[48] See Ciano, *Diario, 1939–1943*, II, 19, and Leto, *OVRA*, p. 205, for a discussion of the split between the moderates and extremists on whether to enter the war.

Chapter 3. The Flexible Structure

[1] "Some Reflections on the Sociological Character of Political Parties," *American Political Science Review*, XXI (November 1927), 761–772, at p. 772.

[2] For an extended discussion of party organization under the statute of 1921 see Sinagra, *Profilo storico del Partito Nazionale Fascista*, Vol. I.

[3] Heiden, *Der Fuehrer*, p. 291. By May 1926, Hitler's power as leader of the party was absolute.

[4] Revised statute of January 13, 1923. For the period between 1923 and 1925 see especially Antonio Canepa, *L'organizzazione del P. N. F.* (Palermo, 1939), pp. 91ff.

[5] The texts of the statutes of 1926, 1929, and 1932 may be found in the volume issued by the PNF entitled *I "Fogli d'ordini" dal 31 Iuglio IV al 28 Ottobre XIII* (Rome, 1935). The statute of 1938 is reprinted in *Atti del P. N. F.*, VII (1938).

Notes

[6] Giovanni Caneva, "Il Partito e le sue funzioni," in *Critica Fascista*, September 15, 1936.

[7] Statute of 1938, Articles 27, 28, and 29. The Nazi "Uschla," or party court, utilized the same series of penalties from reprimand to expulsion. See R. Pelloux, *Le Parti national-socialiste* (Paris, 1936), p. 76, and Heiden, *Der Fuehrer*, p. 301.

[8] *Atti del P. N. F.*, II (1933), 225.

[9] *Foglio di disposizioni* no. 250, May 21, 1934.

[10] Bottai complains in his memoirs that Mussolini, who also imposed the "change of the guard" on those in government positions, did not desire a true ruling class to assist him, but wanted "men in a series, who were interchangeable" (*Vent'anni e un giorno*, p. 96). This was exactly the party secretary's theory: the party officialdom was to take orders, not to make decisions or give advice.

[11] Statute of 1938, Article 2.

[12] An excellent organizational chart of a typical provincial *federazione* is printed in PNF, Federazione di Genova, *Fascismo genovese*, Anno XV (Genoa, 1937).

[13] For a map of how the city was divided by *rioni* and for photographs of the *case*, see Federazione di Milano, *Il Fascio Primogenito* (Milan, 1938), pp. 20–21, 24–25.

[14] See Niccolo Chiapetti, *Il Fascio di Combattimento e il Gruppo Rionale* (Rome, 1937) for an extended discussion of party organization at this level. Consult also Federazione di Milano, *Rapporto sulla attività federale di un anno* (Milan, 1941), p. 16.

[15] In the NSDAP city organizations the *Zellenleiter* was responsible for an area including several blocks and the *Blockleiter* was in charge of all party members living on a single city block. *Nazi Conspiracy and Aggression* (Washington, D.C., 1946–1948), II, 1–248, gives a detailed view of Nazi party structure.

[16] Massimo Rocca narrates that Marinelli was able through his influence to save Bottai from expulsion in 1924. In that period Marinelli was "even more powerful than Mussolini," according to Rocca. The latter statement may be doubted. (*Come il fascismo divenne una dittatura* (Milan, 1952), pp. 171ff.)

[17] Attilio Tamaro, *Venti anni di storia* (Rome, 1954), II, 456. Mussolini had other reasons for ousting Giuriati than Marinelli's opposition to him. He was disturbed over the extent of the purges conducted by the secretary.

[18] *Ibid.*, pp. 456ff.

[19] Party regulations forbade any provincial secretary from seeing Mussolini or any other high government official without first having arranged the interview through the national office. Only a few leaders were able to escape the limitations of this rule.

[20] Pavolini's special position in the party has been described to me by one of the PNF's former vice-secretaries, Arturo Marpicati.

[21] Hitler's tabletalk, recorded by his party secretary, Martin Bormann, indicates that he did not keep in close touch with party affairs, especially during the war. Neither Hitler nor Mussolini was known within his country primarily as the leader of the *party*, whereas in the Soviet Union the head of the party was, and is today, the most powerful person in the regime.

[22] Each day, beginning at 9:30 A.M., the dictator received these subordinates in the following order: (1) head of the OVRA, (2) foreign affairs minister, (3) minister of popular culture, (4) party secretary, and (5) minister of the interior (Navarra, *Memorie*).

[23] Emilio Canevari, ed., *Graziani mi ha detto* (Rome, 1947), pp. 128–129.

[24] Most of these departments are taken from the list given in Article 8 of the 1929 party statute. Some new divisions were created in the thirties.

[25] Tamaro, *Venti anni*, II, 204.

[26] See Chapters 5, 6, and 7.

[27] The Vidoni Palace Pact, signed by representatives of the Fascist syndicates and the *Confederazione Generale dell'Industria*, recognized Fascist unions exclusively in dealings over wages, hours, and working conditions. The *Carta del Lavoro*, passed on April 3, 1926, outlawed all workers' organizations other than those recognized by the Fascist

state. For a discussion of the Fascist party's conquest of the Italian trade union structure, see Tasca, *Nascita e avvento del fascismo*, pp. 288ff, and Ernesto Rossi, *I Padroni del vapore* (Bari, 1952), p. 76 and *passim*.

[28] *Foglio d'ordini* no. 30, June 4, 1928.

[29] Royal Decree Law no. 1735, December 22, 1931.

[30] See Achille Starace, *L'Opera Nazionale Dopolavoro* (Verona, 1933), for a general description of the OND.

[31] On the German Labor Front and *Kraft durch Freude* see Taylor Cole, "The Evolution of the German Labor Front," *Political Science Quarterly*, LII (December 1937), 532–558, and Alfred Vagts, *Hitler's Second Army* (Washington, D.C., 1943), pp. 155ff.

[32] For the party's position in the Fascist economic institutions, see, among others, Dino Giardini, "Le rôle du parti unique dans l'économie fasciste," *Revue Economique Internationale*, III (September 1935), 436–451; Giuseppe Binello and Carlo Di Castellazzo, *Il Partito nella vita economica italiana* (Turin, 1938); and Comitato Intersindacale Provinciale di Torino, *Il Partito nella vita economica della provincia di Torino* (Turin, 1937).

[33] *Il Partito nella vita economica della provincia di Torino*, pp. 10–21.

[34] Giuseppe Di Nardi, "Le direttive del Partito per l'autarchia," *Civiltà Fascista*, V (December 1938), pp. 1085–1092. On the economically fallacious autarky policy see Rossi, *I Padroni del vapore*, pp. 134–156. C. T. Schmidt, in *The Corporate State in Action* (New York, 1939), pp. 80–81 and 146ff, ably explodes the theory that in economics Fascism was merely the last stage of capitalism; the state controlled the economy and dipped heavily into business profits with high taxes and compulsory contributions.

[35] See the chapter on welfare activities in Chiapetti, *Il Fascio di Combattimento*, pp. 79–111. For a sample EOA budget in a province, see the Turin report, *Un biennio di attività* (Turin, 1935), pp. 34–39.

[36] In his secret papers, Farinacci has described some of the requests for information which he received while he was secretary in Cremona. He has printed his reply to one of the queries from national headquarters on mass reaction to the policy of devaluing the lira ("Dall'archivio segrete di Roberto Farinacci," *La Voce Repubblicana*, January 30, 1947).

Chapter 4. Leaders and Followers

[1] The statutes of 1926, 1929, 1932, and 1938 all explicitly require these criteria to be observed in appointing party officials. The only way of circumventing the rule was to bribe a party official to change the date on one's membership card. Expulsion resulted when these irregularities were detected.

[2] A sketch of Starace's party career was given in the announcement of his appointment as secretary (*Foglio d'ordini* no. 87, December 7, 1931).

[3] Giuriati appears to have been a more honorable type of person than the others who occupied the post of secretary.

[4] H. D. Lasswell and Renzo Sereno, "Governmental and Party Leaders in Fascist Italy," *American Political Science Review*, XXXI (October 1937), 914–932, at p. 926. Of the sixty-six federal secretaries studied by the authors, at least forty-six were found to have been *fascisti della prima ora*.

[5] The partial list of national officers, federal secretaries, and inspectors published in *Foglio di disposizioni* no. 713, January 13, 1937, reveals an overwhelming predominance of older party members.

[6] On the class composition of the PNF leadership cadres, see Lasswell and Sereno, "Governmental and Party Leaders in Fascist Italy," pp. 914ff, especially the chart at p. 915. There are no precise figures on class composition of the party as a whole, but frequently the national secretary would inveigh against the excessively bourgeois character of the adult membership and deplore the fact that the new elite of the youth were also of predominantly middle class origin. For examples, see the *Fogli di disposizioni* of February 20, 1933, in *Atti*, II, 161, and August 3, 1934, in *Atti*, III, 107. For figures

on the Nazi party, see Hans Gerth, "The Nazi Party: Its Leadership and Composition," *American Journal of Sociology*, XLV (January 1940), 527. On the Communists, consult the chart provided in Merle Fainsod, *How Russia Is Ruled* (Cambridge, Mass., 1953), p. 213.

[7] The party leadership schools are discussed in greater detail in Chapter 5.

[8] Federazione di Milano, *Rapporto* (1941), p. 9.

[9] Gottfried Neesse, *Die Nationalsozialistische deutsche Arbeiter-partei* (Stuttgart, 1935), p. 154; Rudolf Semmler, *Goebbels — The Man next to Hitler* (London, 1947), p. 79.

[10] The population of Italy was 39,000,000 in 1922 and 45,650,000 in 1942. See Table 3 for party membership statistics.

[11] *Foglio d'ordini* no. 13, November 7, 1926.

[12] Turati, *Il Partito e i suoi compiti*, p. 136.

[13] The mechanics of this process are discussed in detail in Chapters 6 and 7.

[14] See *Atti del P. N. F.*, II (1933), 31, 338, for the announcement of the campaign. About half the new recruits appear to have been added to the October 28, 1933, figure and the remainder were put on the 1934 statistics. Note that between 1934 and 1936 the party added only about 150,000 new members. If it is assumed that these novices were from the youth organizations, it is apparent that the supply from the youth groups alone could account for only a minor part of the enormous increment between 1933 and 1934.

[15] Chiapetti, *Il Fascio di Combattimento e il Gruppo Rionale Fascista*, p. 56.

[16] Federazione di Torino, *Un biennio di attività*, pp. 17–18; Federazione di Milano, *Il Fascio primogenito*, p. 427.

[17] *Atti del P. N. F.*, II (1933), 88, 230.

[18] Literally and clumsily translated, this means "out of family necessity." Note that PNF corresponds to the initials of the three words in the derogatory phrase. *Fascisti del pane* were "bread Fascists." Both terms implied that the new recruits were Fascists by convenience rather than conviction.

[19] *Atti*, II (1933), 339. For a scathing attack on the new members by an old-guard Fascist, see G. A. Fanelli, "Idee sul Partito," in the party extremist journal *Il Secolo Fascista*, September 30, 1932.

[20] On the Republic of Salò, see Edmondo Cione, *Storia della Repubblica Sociale Italiana* (Rome, 1951).

[21] Sinagra, *Profilo storico*, pp. 180–181.

[22] *Colloqui con Mussolini*, p. 105.

[23] *Un periodo aureo*, pp. 294, 297.

[24] Tamaro, *Venti anni*, II, 191–192.

[25] *Foglio d'ordini* no. 22, October 3, 1927. Under Starace, complete lists of expellees were not given; only the most important cases were aired publicly.

[26] *Foglio d'ordini* no. 35, February 4, 1928.

[27] Cited in Tamaro, *Venti anni*, II, 456. A former vice-secretary of the PNF, Arturo Marpicati, confirmed the occurrence of this vast purge in a personal interview. According to him, Giuriati "completely reviewed and revised the party lists."

[28] This estimate was given to me by Marpicati.

[29] *Foglio di disposizioni* of October 10, 1932, in *Atti*, I, 293.

[30] See pp. 88–89 and p. 121 for treatment of the Arpinati and Cristini cases.

[31] Salvatorelli and Mira, *Storia del fascismo*, p. 415.

[32] *Il Fascio primogenito*, p. 426.

Chapter 5. The Molding of Youth

[1] D. S. Piccoli, *The Youth Movement in Italy* (Rome, 1936), p. 9.

[2] Law no. 2247 (April 3, 1926), and the administrative rules of January 9, 1927, in *Codice della legislazione sul Partito Nazionale Fascista* . . . (Milan, 1939).

The Italian Fascist Party in Power

[3] The transfer was effected in 1936. *Nazi Conspiracy and Aggression*, I, 318.

[4] Decree Law of January 9, 1927. The *Esploratori Cattolici* would have been required to disband in towns of fewer than 20,000 inhabitants; the remaining units would have to add the fasces and the initials ONB to their insignia.

[5] The struggle between Fascism and the Church over the youth problem is chronicled in G. Della Torre, *A. C. e fascismo: conflitto del 1931* (Rome, 1945); D. A. Binchy, *Church and State in Fascist Italy* (New York and London, 1941); and Jemolo, *Chiesa e Stato in Italia negli ultimi cento anni.*

[6] Ignotus, *Stato fascista, Chiesa e Scuola* (Rome, 1929). The publishing house was the Libreria del Littorio.

[7] *Foglio d'ordini* no. 64, January 20, 1930.

[8] Salvatorelli and Mira, *Storia del fascismo*, p. 466. The papacy did resume the battle of ideas in another field, when, in 1938, it denounced the racist policies.

[9] Jemolo, *Chiesa e Stato*, p. 666. See Binchy, *Church and State in Fascist Italy*, for a less apologetic view of a Roman Catholic author.

[10] Hannah Arendt, *The Origins of Totalitarianism* (New York, 1951), p. 258.

[11] The Statute of the Fasci Giovanili is reprinted in *Foglio d'ordini* no. 90, February 16, 1932.

[12] For Ciano's observations on the Starace-Ricci struggle, see *1937–1938 Diario*, pp. 13, 17, 19, and 235.

[13] *Foglio d'ordini* no. 182, September 17, 1937.

[14] Royal Decree Law no. 1839, October 27, 1937.

[15] Supplements nos. 1, 2, and 3 to *Foglio d'ordini* no. 187, October 27, 1937, provide detailed organizational charts of the GIL at all levels.

[16] The statute is published in *Foglio di disposizioni* no. 768, March 15, 1937. For membership figures, see Table 6.

[17] Speech reprinted in *Regime Fascista*, August 23, 1938.

[18] Article 31 of the statute of the Fasci Giovanili.

[19] For a description of a typical *Leva*, see *Foglio d'ordini* no. 34, April 30, 1930.

[20] See Achille Starace, *Fasci Giovanili di Combattimenti* (Verona, 1933).

[21] Reported in *Regime Fascista*, August 23, 1938. See also Angelo Cammarata, *Pedagogia di Mussolini alla scuola dell'Opera Balilla* (Palermo, 1931), p. 36, for another account of a Fascistized Mass.

[22] *Il primo libro del fascismo* (Verona, 1942). This work, first published in 1938, went through many printings.

[23] C. J. Friedrich and Z. K. Brzezinski, *Totalitarian Dictatorship and Autocracy* (Cambridge, Mass., 1956), p. 41.

[24] *Atti del P. N. F.*, VII, Book 1 (1938), contains the published minutes of the Grand Council for 1938.

[25] B. Glovenale, "La GIL," *Critica Fascista*, XV (October 1937), 404.

[26] H. Stuart Hughes, *The United States and Italy* (Cambridge, Mass., 1953), p. 74.

[27] Jugend membership was 7,728,259 in 1939, while GIL membership was a little higher for the same year: 7,891,547. See Tables 8 and 9.

[28] Speech of May 1, 1938.

[29] N. C. Festa, *La Nazione Guerriera. Esercito-Milizia-Partito* (Rome, 1935).

[30] For an account of a typical daily schedule, see Cammarata, *Pedagogia di Mussolini alla scuola dell'Opera Balilla.*

[31] *Foglio di disposizioni* no. 356, February 9, 1935.

[32] *Atti*, VI (1937), Book 2, pp. 23, 24.

[33] Umberto Bernasconi, "I corsi di preparazione politica," *Gioventù Fascista*, June 1, 1935, p. 12.

[34] *Foglio di disposizioni* no. 1281, March 8, 1939.

[35] *Foglio di disposizioni* no. 1327 bis, May 13, 1939.

[36] The Adolf Hitler schools, created in 1937, took students at a much younger age

154

and kept them longer. Students entered at twelve and were graduated at eighteen. *Nazi Conspiracy and Aggression,* I.

[37] The Center's charter is published in *Atti,* VIII (1939), Book 1, pp. 97–102. In May 1941, the school was "temporarily" suspended in order that its students might enlist for active combat.

[38] *Autobiografie di giovani del tempo fascista* (Brescia, 1947).

[39] *Ibid.,* pp. 10, 15. See Carlo Levi's classic, *Cristo si è fermato a Eboli* (Turin, 1947), for unforgettable descriptions of GIL activities in the provinces.

[40] See the Italian translation, *Conversazioni segrete* (Naples, 1954), pp. 553, 559.

Chapter 6. Internecine Struggles

[1] The term is Ernst Fraenkel's. See *The Dual State* (New York and London, 1941), p. xiii. Consult also Sigmund Neumann, *Permanent Revolution* (New York and London, 1942), p. 128.

[2] Franz Neumann, *Behemoth: The Structure and Practice of National Socialism* (London, 1942), p. 373.

[3] See Chapter 3, pp. 40–45, for a discussion of the places at which party organizations encroached on the state bureaucracy.

[4] A good idea of the breadth of policy decisions made by the Council may be gleaned from an examination of the summaries of the meetings, published by the PNF in *Il Gran Consiglio nei primi quindici anni dell'era fascista* (Bologna, 1938).

[5] Law no. 2693 of December 11, 1928.

[6] Lead editorial, *Regime Fascista,* January 1, 1929.

[7] For behind-the-scenes descriptions of some of the more important Council meetings, consult the memoirs of Ciano and Bottai.

[8] Farinacci, speeches of March 22 and June 21, 1925, reprinted in *Un periodo aureo* (Foligno, 1927), pp. 59, 167.

[9] Cited in Tamaro, *Venti anni,* II, 92.

[10] *Foglio d'ordini* no. 8, September 26, 1926.

[11] Lasswell and Sereno, "Governmental and Party Leaders in Fascist Italy," p. 915.

[12] Reported in Salvatorelli and Mira, *Storia del fascismo,* p. 415. A large number of these seem to have involved corruption.

[13] Arendt, *Origins of Totalitarianism,* p. 381.

[14] From a conversation with Arturo Marpicati.

[15] Navarra, *Memorie,* p. 138.

[16] Leto, *OVRA,* pp. 155–156; Salvatorelli and Mira, *Storia del fascismo,* pp. 456–457.

[17] *Foglio di disposizioni* no. 269, July 23, 1934.

[18] *Foglio di disposizioni* no. 273. August 2, 1934.

[19] Ciano, *Diario, 1939–1943,* I, 40–41.

[20] Although there is no proof that such a plot existed, there are a number of people in Italy today who were active in the dissident *Roma Fascista* youth circle at the University of Rome and who insist that Ciano was planning a *coup d'ètat* and that the *Roma Fascista* group was prepared to join him. Although the diaries reveal Ciano's unhappiness about the pro-German orientation of Mussolini, there is absolutely no indication that his attitude was anything other than completely loyal. The incident above is reported in *Diario,* I, 194.

[21] Sebastiano Di Massa, *Burocrazia Fascista* (Rome, 1937), pp. 55–56. For material on the civil servants' associations of Nazi Germany, see *Nazi Conspiracy and Aggression,* I, 314.

[22] Duverger, *Les partis politiques,* p. 288.

[23] *Foglio d'ordini* no. 6, September 11, 1926.

[24] By decision of the Duce, who announced the transfer to the party directorate on this date (*Foglio d'ordini* no. 22, February 5, 1927).

[25] See the preamble to the joint statute on associations of January 26, 1931.

[26] For a good discussion of the associations and other aspects of the party's relations with the bureaucracy see Taylor Cole, "Italy's Fascist Bureaucracy," *American Political Science Review*, XXXII (December 1938), 1143–1158.

[27] For this statute and other material on the associations, see in *Atti*, I (1932), the section containing the circulars of the national *fiduciarii* of the associations.

[28] See the 1933 report of the Association of Public Employ of Turin, which comprised over 11,000 members, representing almost all the employees of state and local government offices in Turin, in Federazione di Torino, *Un biennio di attività* (Turin, 1933), especially pp. 67–68.

[29] In *Atti*, VI (1937), Book 1, p. 55.

[30] One of the questions asked on the promotion ratings was "the degree of allegiance to the regime" of the individual. One of the grounds for discharge was "lack of sympathy with the general political policies of the government." (G. Moccia, *Mannuale dell'aspirante ad impiego nelle pubbliche amministrazioni* (1935), pp. 17ff, cited in Cole, "Italy's Fascist Bureaucracy.") Refusal to join the appropriate association could easily bring the person into question on both of these counts.

[31] The teachers at first resisted total incorporation more than did the civil servants.

[32] Salvatorelli and Mira put the number who had not joined by 1937 at practically zero (*Storia del fascismo*, p. 745).

[33] Royal Decree Law no. 641, June 1, 1933.

[34] In the Berlinzola case, decided on May 26, 1937, the courts interpreted existing regulations to mean that all new employees in the public administration had to be enrolled in the party, but that this was not a condition for persons hired before the 1933 legislation to remain in office. See *Codice penale in Codice della legislazione sul Partito Nazionale Fascista e sulla Milizia Volontaria per la Sicurezza Nazionale* (Milan, 1939), p. 65.

[35] Royal Decree Laws no. 698, April 19, 1934, and no. 1162, July 5, 1934.

[36] Mario Berlinguer, *La crisi della giustizia nel Regime fascista* (Rome, 1944), pp. 48ff. In 1934 party membership was made a prerequisite for all professional people hired by the state in the technical and medical fields (*Foglio di disposizioni* no. 289, September 18, 1934).

[37] Federazione di Torino, *Un biennio di attività*, p. 79.

[38] Salvatorelli and Mira, *Storia del fascismo*, p. 745.

[39] Law no. 1482, September 28, 1940, reprinted in Consiglio dei Ministri, *Obbligo dell'appartenenza al Partito Nazionale Fascista per l'avanzamento in carriera dei dependenti dalle pubbliche amministrazioni* (Rome, 1940).

[40] *Foglio di disposizioni* no. 1034, April 8, 1938, contains the published order.

[41] In Friedrich, ed., *Totalitarianism*, pp. 336–337.

[42] The other grave penalties of the party's disciplinary courts, withdrawal of the tessera and indefinite suspension, required the removal of the guilty person from his position, if a party or government one, until he was readmitted to full status.

[43] Salvatorelli and Mira, *Storia del fascismo*, p. 413.

[44] As of 1934, at least twenty-two of the forty-nine prefects studied by Lasswell and Sereno were found to be party appointees ("Governmental and Party Leaders in Fascist Italy," p. 921).

[45] Until February 4, 1926, the local administrative picture was complicated by the fact that administrative elections of the governing giunta still continued. On this date a law was enacted giving a government-appointed podestà full authority at the communal level.

[46] The complete text in English is reprinted in H. W. Schneider and Shepard B. Clough, *Making Fascists* (Chicago, 1929), pp. 138–139.

[47] Royal Decree number 383, March 3, 1934. See H. Arthur Steiner, "The Italian Law on Communal and Provincial Government," *National Municipal Review*, XXV (September 1936), 520–528.

[48] Steiner, "The Constitutional Position of the *Partito Nazionale Fascista*," *American Political Science Review*, XXXI (April 1937), 236.

⁴⁹ Rinaldo Gramondo, *Il Segretario del Fascio di Combattimento* (Milan, 1938), especially pp. 45–46.

⁵⁰ *Ibid.*

⁵¹ Canepa, *L'organizzazione del P. N. F.*, p. 178.

⁵² However, as Schmitt has observed, the Gauleiter is not, "properly speaking, a member of the administration of the commune. He does not take part in communal administration. But he has the power of influencing that activity through his capacity to appoint and remove. The party chooses the administrators, but does not take part in the actual administration itself." (*Gli stati europei*, p. 46.)

⁵³ *Conversazioni segrete*, p. 570. Goebbels once said of the Gauleiter: "They had only to be given the old *jus primae noctis* . . . and their powers would be greater than those of the most absolute princes of the seventeenth and eighteenth century" (Semmler, *Goebbels*, p. 86). Actually, the power of those princes was slight indeed in comparison with that of a Gauleiter who had a mass party and modern technology at his disposal.

⁵⁴ Speech of Mussolini of September 1935.

⁵⁵ Royal Decree no. 1735, December 22, 1932.

⁵⁶ See Piccoli, *The Youth Movement in Italy*, pp. 15ff.

⁵⁷ *Foglio di disposizioni* no. 1353, June 29, 1939.

⁵⁸ *Foglio di disposizioni* no. 913, November 26, 1937.

⁵⁹ *Foglio di disposizioni* no. 1034, April 8, 1938.

⁶⁰ Two symbols of increasing party interference with the schools during this period were, first, the posting of signs in all school buildings reading, "The handshake is abolished. Salute in the Roman fashion [*romanamente*]"; and, second, the requirement, after 1934, promulgated on Starace's insistence, that all teachers wear the Fascist uniform.

⁶¹ Circular no. 26193/112, December 28, 1937, of the national *fiduciario* of the Teachers' Association, in *Atti*, VII (1938), 287.

⁶² As to transfers, the local and provincial associations kept close watch over teachers who shifted from one location to another, carefully noting for the central office of the AFS the reasons for the shift. See *Atti*, I (1932), 193, for the directive to all *fiduciarii* of the local associations requesting information on all teachers who had changed jobs "for political reasons" (Circular of April 20, 1932).

⁶³ During the years 1931–1933 the Turin Dopolavoro section of the AFS reported the participation of the majority of the members in its programs (*Un biennio di attività*, p. 62).

⁶⁴ *Foglio d'ordini* no. 74, April 10, 1930. It should be noted that, by Decree Law of August 28, 1931, all university professors and assistants were required to take the following oath: "I swear to be faithful to the King, to the Royal Successors, to the Fascist regime, to be loyal . . . to all the laws of the Fascist state, to exercise my office . . . with the end of forming honest and worthy citizens, devoted to the country and to the Fascist regime. I swear that I do not belong nor will belong to associations or parties whose activities conflict with the duties of my office." Of about twelve hundred university teachers, only eleven refused to take the oath. On October 11, 1934, the oath was required also of all members of the national academies, including the *Lincei*. Beginning in 1933 with the forced membership in the party, the university professors were subjected to another swearing ceremony: the party oath to serve Fascism and the Duce "with my life, and if necessary, with my blood." The university professors joined almost unanimously in order to retain their jobs.

⁶⁵ *Corriere della Sera*, February 27, 1939.

⁶⁶ Milan *Rapporto* (1940), p. 134.

⁶⁷ In the 1936 report of the elementary section of the AFS, in *Atti*, V (1936).

⁶⁸ *Regime Fascista*, October 26, 1938.

⁶⁹ Circular 85/S.M., March 15, 1938, of the *fiduciario* of the AFS, secondary school section, announced the holding of the courses.

[70] See, for example, the report of the special courses for primary schoolteachers in Sicily by the AFS in the summer of 1932. "Fascist culture" was the chief subject offered. See *Foglio di disposizioni* of the vice-secretary of the PNF in charge of associations, May 9, 1932, in *Atti*, I (1932), 330. See also for similar activities, Associazione Fascista della Scuola di Bologna, *Educazione fascista* (Bologna, 1939).

[71] As in 1939, when the AFS sponsored a series of propaganda "Conversations" to explain the new *Carta della Scuola*, with particular emphasis on the relation between the school and the GIL (Circular of October 19, 1939, from the national *fiduciario* of the AFS).

[72] See the directive of the *fiduciario* of the university section of the AFS of January 20, 1937, in *Atti*, VII (1938), Book 3, p. 267; and Circular no. 35/S.E., February 16, 1937, *ibid.*, p. 327.

[73] See especially his speech to the 1927 convention of the ONB in Naples, in *Il Partito e i suoi compiti*, pp. 54ff.

[74] G. A. Fanelli, "Questa nemica scuola," *Il Secolo Fascista*, March 1–April 1, 1933.

[75] Antonio Canepa, *Sistema di dottrina del fascismo* (Rome, 1937), 3 vols.

[76] Royal Decree Law no. 876, June 10, 1937.

[77] For an interpretation from the party's viewpoint of the 1939 *Carta della Scuola*, see Erasmo Malfi, *Scuola e G. l. L.* (Rome, 1939).

[78] Reported in *Regime Fascista*, November 23, 1938, p. 1.

[79] One article is by "Scolasticus," the other by Ermano Miracchi. Both are in *Regime Fascista*, December 24, 1938, p. 5.

[80] Gerhard Ritter, "The German Professor in the Third Reich," *Review of Politics*, VII (April 1946), 242–254, at p. 250.

Chapter 7. Three Uneasy Allies

[1] Arendt, *Origins of Totalitarianism*, p. 258.

[2] See Max Ascoli, ed., *The Fall of Mussolini* (New York, 1948), for illuminating references about the army.

[3] His distrust of the king's position with respect to the army came out in the open on March 30, 1938, when he had Costanzo Ciano introduce a law in the Parliament creating the grade of *Primo Maresciallo dell'Impero*. This rank was conferred jointly on Victor Emmanuel III and Benito Mussolini. The king was highly indignant, because under the *Statuto* he alone was commander of the armed forces. This provision was now revoked by law as well as in fact.

[4] See the Duce's introduction to Partito Nazionale Fascista, *Il Gran Consiglio nei primi cinque anni dell'era fascista* (Bologna, 1927).

[5] Emilio Canevari, *La guerra italiana. Retroscena della disfatta* (Rome, 1948), I, 225.

[6] Royal Decree Law no. 31, January 14, 1923.

[7] *Come il fascismo divenne una dittatura* (Milan, 1952), p. 123.

[8] Royal Decree Law no. 831, March 8, 1923.

[9] Starace, for example, held the rank of lieutenant general in the MVSN. In 1939, on leaving the party secretaryship, he became commanding general of the militia. The political secretariat of the PNF's national headquarters kept a liaison office which collaborated intimately with the MVSN.

[10] See Giannetti Berlindo, "Il Partito come forza militare," in PNF (GUF), *I Littoriali della Cultura e dell'Arte dell'Anno XIV* (Naples, 1936), pp. 173–207.

[11] Reprinted in Comando Generale della MVSN, *M.V.S.N. XV Annuale* (Rome, 1938), p. 37. Selections from the prayer: "Oh God, Who lights every flame and stops every heart, renew every day my passion for Italy . . . Make more keen my eye and more secure my foot on the sacred boundaries of the Country, which we will make more grand . . . Oh Lord! Make of Your cross the insignia which precedes the labarum of my legion and save Italy through the Duce always and in the hour of our beautiful death. Amen." (P. 36.)

[12] For the statutes of the special militia, see I.R.E., *Codice sul legislazione del P. N. F.* (1939), pp. 343–487.

[13] Lead editorial by Alessandro Melchiori in *Milizia Fascista,* September 30, 1928.

[14] Reported in Melchiori, *Milizia fascista,* p. 69.

[15] *Foglio di disposizioni* no. 834, July 2, 1937.

[16] In Germany the SA, imitating the Italian pattern, had complete charge of pre-military training instead of the regular army. On the SA see especially Vagts, *Hitler's Second Army,* pp. 20ff. In 1934 the SA had 1,200,000 men. Its place as a control against the army was soon taken over by Himmler and his SS units, however. The *Waffen-SS* were the crack troops of the Nazi army in World War II. For a thorough analysis of the complicated system of controls exercised by the party and the O.O. over the Russian army, see Z. K. Brzezinski, ed., *Political Controls in the Soviet Army* (New York, 1954).

[17] For some particularly caustic comments on the premilitary training problem by a former general, see Quirino Armellini, *La crisi dell'esercito* (Rome, 1945), pp. 61–69.

[18] Royal Decree Law no. 1292, August 4, 1924.

[19] Law no. 1759, December 29, 1930.

[20] Canevari, *La guerra italiana,* I, 445–446.

[21] Law no. 2150, December 31, 1934.

[22] *Foglio d'ordini* no. 198, May 11, 1938.

[23] Marpicati, Gallian, and Contu, *La dottrina del fascismo,* p. 159. These officers of the MVSN employed in the premilitary courses are not included in the list of officers in Table 11.

[24] Comando Generale della MVSN, *M.V.S.N. XVI Annuale* (Rome, 1939), p. 53. It is interesting that along with premilitary training, another task of an equally military nature — anti-aircraft defense — was given to the militia instead of to the air force. Colonel Canevari objected that it was absurd to give to the militia this function, and such was apparently the opinion of the rest of the professional armed services (*La guerra italiana,* I, 225).

[25] Law of November 4, 1938, reported in *Atti,* VIII (1939), Book 1, p. 143.

[26] Badoglio also had many unkind things to say about Baistrocchi. See Pietro Badoglio, *L'Italia nella seconda guerra mondiale* (Milan, 1946).

[27] In addition to Armellini the generals who performed in this manner were Pugnani, Ronco, Ago, Trezzani, Oddone, Secchi, and Broccoli.

[28] For a reprint of the accusations by the prosecution, the defense of Baistrocchi, and excerpts from the statements of withdrawal of charges made by the various generals, see Canevari, *La guerra italiana,* I. 440–455, "Sentenza nel processo contro il Gen. Baistrocchi."

[29] The reader should consult along with Armellini the volume by Carlo Silvestri, *I responsabili della catastrofe* (Milan, 1946), in which the author insisted that Armellini and Badoglio and his followers should share the blame with Baistrocchi for the politicization of the army in the thirties. Silvestri was a leading anti-Fascist. See especially pp. 161–178.

[30] Canevari, *La guerra italiana,* I, 446–447.

[31] Badoglio, *L'Italia nella seconda guerra mondiale,* p. 24.

[32] Canevari, *La guerra italiana,* I, 447–448.

[33] *Ibid.,* p. 450.

[34] *Ibid.*

[35] *Ibid.,* pp. 446, 448. Stefano Jacini, in his *Il regime fascista* (Milan, 1947), pp. 124ff, describes the "effective and humiliating subordination of the military authority to the party," in discipline and indoctrination of the troops. "The barracks became centers of Fascist propaganda," and military preparation "was continuously interrupted by parades, celebrations, songs . . ."

[36] Canevari, *La guerra italiana,* p. 445.

[37] See the discussion in Festa, *La Nazione guerriera,* p. 126.

The Italian Fascist Party in Power

[38] Quoted in *Foglio d'ordini* no. 146, October 28, 1935.

[39] Salvatorelli and Mira, *Storia del fascismo*, p. 715.

[40] MVSN, *Annuale XVI* (1938), pp. 7, 50.

[41] Significantly, all these militia divisions had names recalling a special event in the history of Fascism: "23 Marzo," "28 Ottobre," "21 Aprile," "3 Gennaio," "10 Febbraio," "Tevere," and "Cirene." These were popularly called the "Blackshirt divisions." Within the divisions special efforts were made to organize some battalions especially for volunteer university students who were members of the militia. See Berlindo, "Il Partito come forza militare," p. 186.

[42] Starace wrote his own account of the campaign: *La marcia su Gondar* (Milan, 1936).

[43] For the MVSN's summary of its part in the Ethiopian War see Milizia Comando Generale, *La Milizia per l'Impero* (Rome, 1937), the chapter entitled "Sintesi guerriera," pp. 50–127.

[44] The 40,000 estimate is from Canevari, *La guerra italiana*, I, 482. For descriptions of the activity of Italian troops in Spain see especially MVSN, *Annuale XV* (1937), pp. 84–93, and *Annuale XVI*, pp. 31–50.

[45] *Foglio di disposizioni* no. 1193, November 21, 1938. The statutes of the first ten of these regiments are given here.

[46] See the annual report to the Duce of the commanding general of the militia in *Annuale XVII* (1939), which speaks of an increase in the number of militiamen and their heightened activities.

[47] Speech of February 1, 1940. It is outside the scope of this work to deal with the relations between the army and the militia during World War II. There is no doubt that the party continued to interfere with military policy and appointments, particularly when, as was usually the case, the performance of the Italian army was poor. Ciano relates that in November of 1940 Serena, then PNF secretary, opened a campaign against Badoglio, whom he wished to accuse of treason (the party had never liked Badoglio). *Diario, 1939–1943*, I, 333. The columns of *Regime Fascista* for 1940 were full of abuse against Badoglio. It is also known from Ciano that MVSN officials made inspection tours of the army and reported back to Mussolini, who, to Ciano's distaste, took the reports seriously (*ibid.*, II, 121–122). It should be noted that the Fascist party never even approximated the institution of the Soviet *Zampolit*. Neither did the Nazis until after the July 1944 attempt on Hitler's life. After that, Bormann was given command of a "network of political officers of the commissar type," known as leadership officers (*National Sozialistische Führungs Offiziere*). Their task was to check the political loyalty of the military. During the war the Fascist party, like the Nazi party, had command of civil defense and the home guard.

[48] For the most authoritative account of the July 1943 deposition of Mussolini, see Salvatorelli and Mira, *Storia del fascismo*, pp. 943–948.

[49] Arendt, *Origins of Totalitarianism*, p. 385.

[50] Merle Fainsod, *Smolensk under Soviet Rule* (Cambridge, Mass., 1958), p. 165.

[51] Leto, *OVRA*. Leto was one of Bocchini's principal collaborators until the latter's death in 1940. These memoirs rank with those of Ciano in value to the student of Fascism. For the police during the period 1940–1943, see Carmine Senise, *Quando ero Capo della Polizia* (Rome, 1947), especially the section "Il partito Fascista — Malcostume ed arbitrario esercizio di pubbliche funzioni," pp. 40–44.

[52] Leto, *OVRA*, p. 33.

[53] *Ibid.*, p. 34.

[54] *Ibid.*, pp. 30–31.

[55] *Foglio d'ordini* no. 13, November 7, 1926.

[56] Leto, *OVRA*, p. 52.

[57] *Ibid.*, p. 28. Leaders of the party could never be arrested without the express permission of the secretary. This was one of many points of conflict. (Tamaro, *Venti anni*, III, 228.)

160

[58] Leto, *OVRA*, p. 94.

[59] *Ibid.*, p. 34.

[60] *Ibid.*, pp. 155–165.

[61] Royal Decree Law no. 1903, November 6, 1926. See also the supplementary law no. 633, June 15, 1933, which renewed that unit's powers.

[62] Leto, *OVRA*, p. 39.

[63] The Belgian law periodical *Journal des Tribunaux* of April 26 and May 3, 1931, published all the relevant laws on the Fascist Special Tribunal in a form convenient for reference. The statutes are Law of November 25, 1926; Royal Decrees of December 12, 1926, March 1, 1928, and September 27, 1928; and the Army Penal Code, under which the suspects were tried. Cesare Rossi, in the early years head of the Fascist Press Bureau and later deposed and imprisoned by the Fascists, has written an account of the Tribunal's activities, *Il tribunale speciale* (Milan, 1952).

[64] Royal Decree no. 1759, October 3, 1929.

[65] Emilio Saraceni, *Nuova pratica di polizia amministrativa* (Rome, 1929), cited in Cole, "Italy's Fascist Bureaucracy," *American Political Science Review*, XXXII (December 1938), 1143–1158.

[66] Leto, *OVRA*, p. 63.

[67] *Ibid.*, p. 119.

[68] Rossi, *Il tribunale speciale*, p. 233.

[69] Leto, *OVRA*, p. 131. The party elite referred to the new police recruits contemptuously as "Fascists of the Holy Year." Leto, in his zeal to portray the police as the simple instruments of higher orders without any moral responsibility for their actions, undoubtedly overestimated the degree to which the police regarded themselves as nonpolitical bureaucrats.

[70] Salvatorelli and Mira, *Storia del fascismo*, p. 814.

[71] Leto conveniently omits any mention of this foreign spy service, of which the more brutal activities are described in fictitious detail by Alberto Moravia in *The Conformist*. As one reviewer of Leto's book has remarked, "Where Leto is silent, he lies." See the preface to the second edition.

[72] *Nazi Conspiracy and Aggression*, II, 174. See also Vagts, *Hitler's Second Army*, pp. 39ff.

[73] On the German concentration camps see Eugen Kogon, *The Theory and Practice of Hell* (New York, 1950), Gerald Reitlinger, *The Final Solution* (London, 1953), David Rousset, *Les jours de nôtre mort* (Paris, 1947), and Arendt, *Origins of Totalitarianism*.

Chapter 8. Party and Regime in Perspective

[1] Friedrich, ed., *Totalitarianism*, p. 57.

[2] *Government in Fascist Italy* (New York, 1938), p. 37.

[3] *Terror and Progress USSR* (Cambridge, Mass., 1954).

[4] This judgment is tentative; its full verification awaits more intensive studies of the political parties in the various dictatorships of recent times than have yet been undertaken.

[5] Not only was *entrance* into the party not "formally free." Duverger quotes a character in Sartre's play *Les mains sales*, who asserted, "On ne sort du parti que les pieds devant."

[6] This network of controlled substitutes for the wealth of corporate life was described by Mussolini in a flash of candor as a series of "potent institutions . . . which give Fascism the means of controlling the life of the Nation's people from their sixth to their sixtieth year . . ." (speech of May 26, 1927). See Duverger, pp. 142ff, for a discussion of similar organizations directed by the Communist party.

[7] See Manoïlesco, *Le parti unique*, pp. 195–196, and Duverger, *Les partis politiques*, pp. 307–309.

[8] Thus, Manoïlesco, ignoring the differences in the position assigned to the party in

relation to the state in the theory of the three regimes, correctly insists that the Fascist, Nazi, and Soviet single parties occupied positions in their respective orders more nearly similar than different (*Le parti unique*, p. 123).

[9] The nontotalitarian nature of this clerical, reactionary regime was evident at the very beginning when, in his inaugural address of July 30, 1930, Salazar called for the "strong state, but limited by morality, by the principle of the inviolable rights of man, by guarantee of those individual liberties which have an existence superior to the value of social solidarity." It is inconceivable that Mussolini could ever have uttered such a statement. See Manoïlesco's discussion of Salazar in *Le parti unique*.

[10] On paper, the party organization resembled that of the PNF in its earliest stages, although in practice Perón's power was far broader than the charts imply. The General Congress of the party was elected by metropolitan, provincial, and territorial councils of the party. The Superior Executive Council was also elected by the councils of the provincial party organizations. The Congress nominated candidates for the presidency of the nation. All these actions were subject to the veto of the "Chief of the Movement" — Perón. See *Peronist Doctrine* (Buenos Aires, 1952), p. 58, for an organizational chart of the party. Also G. I. Blanksten, *Perón's Argentina* (Chicago, 1953), pp. 336ff, for a discussion on the party and its relations with the government.

[11] S. F. A. Coles, *Franco of Spain* (London, 1955), p. 73.

[12] E. J. Hughes, *Report from Spain* (New York, 1947), p. 21.

[13] See Paul Farmer, *Vichy. Political Dilemma* (New York, 1955), pp. 240, 247ff. Cf. also Robert Aron, *Histoire de Vichy* (Paris, 1954).

[14] Fainsod, *Smolensk under Soviet Rule*, p. 342.

[15] *Ibid.*, p. 93. The entire Chapter 4 of this work is invaluable for an understanding of the role of the party in relation to the government in the Soviet Union.

[16] In Friedrich and Brzezinski, *Totalitarian Dictatorship and Autocracy*, pp. 31ff.

[17] On the Nazi party organization, consult the extensive and complete chart appended to International Military Tribunal, *Trial of the Major War Criminals* (Nuremberg, 1948), Vol. XXI; see also the description of the various offices in II, 162–168.

[18] When the Nazis first came to power and the influence of the party was perhaps at its zenith, the NSDAP established a party Foreign Office, headed by Rosenberg, a party Ministry of Justice headed by Hied, and a party Ministry of War directed by the ill-fated Röhm. All these offices functioned at the same time as and often in opposition to the corresponding "official" government units. On Rosenberg's early Foreign Office, see Heiden, *Der Fuehrer*, p. 616. It should be noted, however, that the Nazis did not employ the technique of *Personalunion* as extensively as did the Communists. In Germany there were many important government ministries, especially in the economic and technical field, which did not have party "doubles."

[19] See the discussion of the *Personalunion* in Neesse, *Partei und Staat*, pp. 64ff. In the cabinet, the food minister, the propaganda minister, the Reich labor leader, the Reich youth leader, and the chief of police all held identical positions in the *Reichsleitung* of the NSDAP.

[20] Franco first gave an inkling that he planned to restore the monarchy in a speech of July 17, 1945, dealing with the succession problem. Since then he has granted permission for the crown prince to be educated in Spain. In January and February 1955, *La Stampa* of Turin carried reports of bitter Falangist-monarchist struggles within Spain over a renewal of speculation about the restoration. The New York *Times* as recently as 1957 has reported reforms contemplated for the future which would further limit the power of the Falange.

[21] This is the thesis of *Mussolini's Italy*.

[22] That is, a party manifesting the same ten traits exhibited by the PNF and shared by the NSDAP and the CPSU.

[23] In Taylor Cole, ed., *European Political Systems* (New York, 1953), p. 322.

[24] H. Stuart Hughes, *The United States and Italy*, p. 322.

[25] Arendt, *Origins of Totalitarianism*, p. 256. These views are somewhat more fully

expounded in her article "Parteien und Bewegungen," in *Die Wandlung*, VI (June 1949), 459–473, especially 464–466.

[26] *Freedom, Virtue, and the First Amendment* (Baton Rouge, La., 1957), p. 165.

[27] "The Unique Character of Totalitarian Society," in *Totalitarianism*, pp. 47–60, at pp. 52–53. A slightly revised version of this essay may be found in Friedrich and Brzezinski, *Totalitarian Dictatorship and Autocracy*, pp. 1–13. Friedrich actually lists first five, and then six, traits, but only four are regarded by him as being in the "unique" category. The other two are weapons monopoly and the controlled economy. Dr. Arendt, whose conclusions on Italian Fascism I am challenging, seems to regard Friedrich's definition as a good one (see *Totalitarianism*, p. 75).

[28] This definition follows closely that given by Friedrich and Brzezinski (p. 74). A totalitarian ideology is a reasonably coherent body of literate ideas "concerning practical means of how totally to . . . reconstruct a society by force . . ., based upon an all-inclusive . . . criticism of what is wrong with an existing or antecedent society." Ideologies are "essentially action-related systems of ideas."

[29] Gentile did not formally join the party until June 2, 1923 (Salvatorelli and Mira, p. 191).

[30] Arturo Marpicati, vice-secretary of the PNF from 1932 to 1936, in a personal interview.

[31] G. A. Fanelli, *Contra Gentiles mistificazioni dell'idealismo attuale nella Rivoluzione fascista* (Rome, 1933).

[32] *Ibid.*, p. 5.

[33] *Ibid.*, pp. 77–79 and 90–97.

[34] *Vent'anni*, p. 64. For an extended discussion of the opposition to Gentile in Fascist circles see "Gentile e gli antigentiliani," in Tamaro, *Venti anni di storia*, III, 79–81.

[35] Gentile called Mussolini a "man chosen by God, tireless and infallible, an instrument adopted by Providence to create a new civilization" — *Origini e dottrina*, p. 54. But Gentile and the corporativists did not repeat these paeans often enough to please the party and they did not cite Mussolini's speeches for every opinion offered.

[36] The same thing seems to have happened under the Nazi system. Rosenberg took "the most jealous care to prevent Oswald Spengler, Moeller van den Bruck or Othmar Spann from gaining any hold on the Party with their ideas and from influencing the Party's work." Carl Paetel, "The Reign of the Black Order," in M. Baumont, J. H. E. Fried, and E. Vermeil, eds., *The Third Reich* (New York, 1955), p. 643.

[37] Quoted in Salvatorelli and Mira, *Storia del fascismo*, p. 751. It is in the light of statements like these and the attacks on Gentile that the party's preoccupation with "style" may be explained. In a sense it is fair to say that the party, by replacing substantive ideas with changing norms of style, intended to destroy the capacity to think altogether. The perfect Fascist was he who immediately and automatically obeyed the directives of the party, without stopping to examine the contents of those orders. Here Fascism's often noted emphasis on action for its own sake is particularly relevant. That the Nazis had similar conceptions is evident from Rosenberg's description of life as the "style of a column on the march, and it is of little importance towards what destination and for what ends this column is marching." (Cited in Albert Camus, *The Rebel* (New York, 1954), p. 151.)

[38] Bottai, *Vent'anni*, p. 118.

[39] Hannah Arendt seems to have made the error of interpreting Fascist ideology from the standpoint of the ideology for export when she describes corporativism as "an attempt to solve the antagonism between state and society . . . with a new integrated social organization . . ." (*Origins of Totalitarianism*, p. 258). As Salvemini, Louis R. Franck, and, most recently and most tendentiously, Ernesto Rossi have shown, corporativism was simply a fancy name for the surveillance of the workers and a rigid system of party-dictated controls over production, prices, and trade. Bottai, who along with Ugo Spirito was a leading "corporativist," has described the *fallimento del corporativismo* in his memoirs, *Vent'anni e un giorno*. The scores of books and articles

written by social scientists in the thirties on this "new integrated social organization" obscured these basic facts.

[40] G. A. Borgese, in *Goliath, The March of Fascism* (New York, 1938), properly stresses the call of Rome.

[41] Gentile, on the other hand, preferred to find his intellectual roots in the "near and uncancellable tradition of our Risorgimento." He deplored, in a little work called *La tradizione italiana* (Florence, 1936), Fascism's "Roman rhetoric," asserting that "Rome is not the particular tradition of the Italians, but of the Europe which it created."

[42] "Q. Is Fascism exclusively an Italian phenomenon?

"A. Fascism, as far as its ideas, doctrines, and realizations are concerned, is universal . . . it is the sustainer and creator of a new civilization." (*Il primo libro del fascista* (Rome, 1942 edition, p. 44).)

[43] *La dottrina del fascismo*, Part II, paragraph 13.

[44] Friedrich and Brzezinski, in *Totalitarian Dictatorship and Autocracy*, distinguish between nineteenth-century imperialism and the imperialism of twentieth-century totalitarian dictatorships. The former was "an outgrowth of the industrial economy," while the latter is related to "the will to conquer the world which animates the totalitarian systems," and is "intimately linked with ideological pre-occupations."

[45] A flood of articles on Rome and Fascism appeared at this time in Mussolini's personally edited periodical *Gerarchia*. See especially Pietro De Francisci, "Continuità di Roma," XV (January 1935), pp. 6–17; Arnaldo Cervesato, "Fondazione e imagine di Roma," XV (April 1935), pp. 302–306; and Nino Guglielmi, "Roma, il fascismo, e l'impero," XV (September 1935), pp. 755–759. One of the most influential early statements of a Fascist theorist was made by Alfredo Rocco, minister of justice under Mussolini. This speech, given at Perugia in 1925, is translated as "The Political Doctrine of Fascism," in *International Conciliation*, no. 223 (October 1926). This essay had the express approval of the Duce, who wrote: "You have presented in a masterly way the doctrine of Fascism. For Fascism has a doctrine, or, if you will, a philosophy of life with regard to all the questions which beset the human mind today." (Note the *total* quality of Fascist ideology.)

[46] *Church and State in Fascist Italy.*

[47] The Church "sagely recognized that Fascism was neither anti-Christian nor totalitarian . . ." Arendt, *Origins of Totalitarianism*, p. 258.

[48] See Salvatorelli and Mira, *Storia del fascismo*, pp. 752–754, for a discussion of the effectiveness of the Ministry of Popular Culture.

[49] The Ministry of Popular Culture was managed by party extremists and had the closest ties with the PNF national leadership. The first head of the new ministry was Alessandro Pavolini, formerly secretary of the Florence fascio.

[50] Francesco, Flora, ed., *Stampa dell'era fascista. Le note di servizio* (Rome, 1945). Observe how closely these press directives compare with those issued by the Communist party organization in the Soviet Union. For a sample Communist communiqué, giving extremely detailed instructions on the content of a newspaper article on a proposed subject, see Fainsod, *Smolensk under Soviet Rule*, p. 367.

[51] See pp. 22–24 above.

[52] Bramstedt, *Dictatorship and Political Police*, pp. 40–41.

[53] For a discussion of the Nazi Ministry of Public Enlightenment, see Derrick Sington and Arthur Weidenfeld, *The Goebbels Experiment* (London, 1942).

[54] Bernard Crick, in *Confluence* (December 1954), p. 453.

[55] H. Hessell Tiltman wrote that "Not even in Soviet Russia has personal liberty suffered a more complete eclipse than it has in Italy . . ." (*The Terror in Europe* (London, 1931), p. 330).

[56] C. Rossi, *Il tribunale speciale*, p. 7.

[57] Leto, *OVRA*, pp. 61–64.

[58] At least two accounts of the conditions on the penal islands written by non-Fascists have appeared and they paint a much harsher picture than does Leto. Stefano

164

Jacini, a respected leader of today's Christian Democratic party, has spoken of the use of torture to extract information, isolation with bread and water for up to three months, wretched sanitary conditions, violence and sadism among certain guards, and so on (*Il regime fascista*, pp. 170ff). Massimo Salvadori, in *Resistenza ed azione* (Bari, 1951) tells of his own experience in *confino* on the island of Ponza.

[59] I. Silone, *Bread and Wine* (London, 1936), pp. 260–261.

[60] Arendt, *Origins of Totalitarianism*, p. 401.

[61] Ciano, *1937–1938 Diario*, p. 207. Mussolini intended a "third wave" of terror and the introduction of concentration camps on the German model.

[62] For a discussion of the Salò Republic, see Salvatorelli and Mira, *Storia del fascismo*, pp. 969–972, where there is special reference to its social program. Some persons interpret the "radical" articles of Fascism's last political program as an effort to return to the "socialist" origins of Fascism's infant days. See Cione, *Storia della Repubblica Sociale Italiana*, for an account written by a professor at the University of Naples and a leader of the Neo-Fascist party (MSI) in contemporary Italy, which professes to draw its inspiration from this last phase of the Fascist regime's history.

Bibliography

Basic Party Publications and Documents

THE first item in the bibliography, *Atti del P. N. F.*, is the principal single source of material on the Fascist party. This series, compiled during Starace's secretaryship, constitutes sixteen large volumes containing the minutes of the Grand Council of Fascism, the national directorate of the PNF, and the national council of the PNF. Also included are the *Fogli d'ordini* and *Fogli di disposizioni* of the secretary of the PNF and circulars of the national secretary of the GUF, the general command of the GIL, the administrative secretary of the party, and the *fiduciarii* of the various party associations.

Of all these records the *Fogli d'ordini* and *Fogli di disposizioni*, containing lists of instructions to provincial party organizations, are incomparably the most important. The orders are given in terse, military fashion; Mussolini wrote in the first *Foglio d'ordini*: "our organization is a true and proper army . . ." The *Fogli* of the years 1941 to 1943 are not as plentiful as the earlier ones. They are preserved in unbound form in Rome's National Central Library.

PARTY ORDERS AND DIRECTIVES FROM NATIONAL HEADQUARTERS

Partito Nazionale Fascista. *Atti del P. N. F.* 16 vols. Bologna: Resto del Carlino, 1931–1940.
———. *I "Fogli d'ordini" dal 31 Iuglio IV al 28 Ottobre XIII*. Rome: Istituto Poligrafico dello Stato, 1935.
———. *Fogli di disposizioni. Fogli d'ordini*. Bologna: Resto del Carlino, 1941–1943.
———. *Il Gran Consiglio nei primi quindici anni dell'era fascista*. Bologna: Resto del Carlino, 1938.
———. [Uffico Stampa.] *Notiziario Settiminale*. Rome, 1941–42.

DIRECTIVES AND REPORTS OF PROVINCIAL PARTY ORGANIZATIONS
(PUBLISHED IN EACH CASE BY THE PROVINCIAL PARTY PRESS)

Federazione dei fasci di combattimento di Alessandria. *Atti, anno XIX*. Alessandria, 1941.
Federazione . . . di Catania. *Tre anni di vita fascista, 1934–1937*. Catania, 1937.
Federazione . . . di Genova. *Fascismo genovese Anno XV*. Genoa, 1937.
Federazione . . . di Lucca. *Realizzazioni del fascismo di Lucchesia negli anni XVIII–XIX*. Florence, 1941.
Federazione . . . di Milano. *Il Fascio primogenito, 1933–1937*. Milan, 1938.
———. *Rapporto sulla attività federale di un anno*. Milan, 1941.
Federazione . . . di Napoli. *Fascismo napoletano, Anno XV*. Naples, 1938.
Federazione . . . di Padova. *Tre anni di marcia del fascismo padovano*. Padua, 1940.

166

Federazione . . . di Torino. *Un biennio di attività della Federazione dei Fasci di Combattimento di Torino.* Turin, 1935.

———. [Comando dei Fasci Giovanili.] *Attività svolta dal 1° ottobre XII al 1° ottobre XIII.* Turin, 1935.

———. *Fogli d'ordini.* Turin, 1926–1943.

———. *Fogli di disposizioni.* Turin, 1937–1943. (This and the preceding item may be found unbound in the *Archivi Civici* of Turin.)

ORDERS OF THE PARTY MILITIA

Milizia Volontaria per la Sicurezza Nazionale. [Comando Generale.] *Fogli d'ordini 1931–1935.* 5 vols. Rome: Istituto Poligrafico dello Stato, 1931–1935.

STATUTES

Codice della legislazione sul Partito Nazionale Fascista e sulla Milizia Volontaria per la Sicurezza Nazionale. Milan: Istituto Redattoriale Editoriale, 1939.

Consiglio dei Ministri. *Obbligo dell'appartenenza al Partito Nazionale Fascista per l'avanzamento in carriera dei dipendenti dalle pubbliche amministrazioni.* Rome: Libreria dello Stato, 1940.

Gazzetta Ufficiale del Regno. With supplements. Rome: Istituto Poligrafico dello Stato, 1925–1939.

RELATED DOCUMENTS ON THE NSDAP

International Military Tribunal. *Trial of the Major War Criminals.* Nuremberg, 1948. (See especially Vols. II and XXI on Nazi party organization.)

Nazi Conspiracy and Aggression. 8 vols. and 2 supplementary vols., A and B. Washington, D.C.: United States Government Printing Office, 1946–1948.

Memoirs

Armellini, Quirino. *La crisi dell'esercito.* Rome: Priscilla, 1945.

Autobiografie di giovani del tempo fascista. Brescia: Morcelliana, 1947.

Badoglio, Pietro. *L'Italia nella seconda guerra mondiale.* Milan: Mondadori, 1946.

Bottai, Giuseppe. *Vent'anni e un giorno.* Rome: Garzanti, 1949.

Canevari, Emilio, editor. *Graziani mi ha detto.* Rome: Magi-Spinetti, 1947.

———. *La guerra italiana. Retroscena della disfatta.* 2 vols. Rome: Tosi, 1948.

Caviglia, Enrico. *Diario (1925–1945).* Rome: Casini, 1952.

Ciano, Galeazzo. *1937–1938 Diario.* Rocca San Casciano, 1948.

———. *Diario, 1939–1943.* 2 vols. Milan: Rizzoli, 6th edition, 1950.

"Dall'archivio segrete di Roberto Farinacci," *La Voce Repubblicana.* January 5, 7, 9, 11, 14, 16, 21, 23, 24, 28, 30, and February 2, 5, 7, 9, 13, 1947.

De Begnac, Yvon. *Palazzo Venezia.* Rome: La Rocca, 1951.

Gasparotto, Luigi. *Diario di un deputato.* Milan: Dall'Oglio, 1945.

Hitler, Adolf. *Conversazioni segrete.* Translated from the German. Naples: Richter, 1954.

Leto, Guido. *OVRA. Fascismo–anti-Fascismo.* Bologna: Cappelli, 2nd edition, 1952.

Navarra, Quinto. *Memorie del cameriere di Mussolini.* Milan: Longanesi, 1946.

Pini, Giorgio. *Filo diretto con Palazzo Venezia.* Bologna: Cappelli, 1950.

Rocca, Massimo. *Come il fascismo divenne una dittatura.* Milan: ELI, 1952.

Salvadori, Massimo. *Resistenza ed azione. Ricordi di un liberale.* Bari: Laterza, 1951.

Senise, Carmine. *Quando ero Capo della Polizia, 1940–1943.* Rome: Ruffolo, 2nd edition, 1947.

Tamaro, Attilio. *Venti anni di storia, 1922–1943.* 3 vols. Rome: Tiber, 1954. (These volumes reproduce key sections of the unpublished memoirs and papers of Turati, Giuriati, Federzoni, and De Vecchi.)

167

The Italian Fascist Party in Power
Books

Ambrosini, G. *Il Partito fascista e lo Stato*. Rome: Istituto Nazionale Fascista di Cultura, 1934.

———, O. Ranelletti, and C. Schmitt. *Gli stati europei a partito politico unico*. Milan, 1936.

Arendt, Hannah. *The Origins of Totalitarianism*. New York: Harcourt, Brace, 1951.

Aron, Robert. *Histoire de Vichy*. Paris: Fayard, 1954.

Ascoli, Max, editor. *The Fall of Mussolini*. New York: Farrar, Straus, 1948.

Associazione Fascista della Scuola di Bologna. *Educazione Fascista*. Bologna: L'assalto, 1939.

Ballarati, Giancarlo. *Il Partito nazionalsocialista*. Rome: INCF, 1937.

Baumont, M., J. H. E. Fried, and E. Vermeil, editors. *The Third Reich*. New York: UNESCO, 1955.

Bella, Paride. *Cultura fascista per la scuola media*. Messina, 1929.

Berlinguer, Mario. *La crisi della giustizia nel Regime fascista*. Rome: Migliaresi, 1944.

Biancini, Bruno, compiler. *Dizionario mussoliniano*. Milan, 2nd edition, revised, 1940.

Binchy, D. A. *Church and State in Fascist Italy*. New York and London: Oxford, 1941.

Binello, Giuseppe, and Carlo Di Castellazzo. *Il Partito nella vita economica italiana. La politica fascista degli approvvigionamenti e dei prezzi*. Turin: Giappichelli, 1938.

Blanksten, George I. *Perón's Argentina*. Chicago: University of Chicago Press, 1953.

Bonomi, Ivanoe. *Dal socialismo al fascismo*. Rome: Garzanti, 1946.

Borgese, G. A. *Goliath, The March of Fascism*. New York: Viking Press, 1938.

Bortolotto, Guido. *Dottrina del fascismo*. Milan: Hoepli, 1939.

———. *Fascismo e nazionalsocialismo*. Bologna: Zanichelli, 1933.

———. *Lo stato e la dottrina corporativa*. Bologna: Zanichelli, 1930.

Bottai, Giuseppe. *Pagine di Critica Fascista, 1915–1926*. Florence: Le Monnier, 1941.

Bramstedt, E. K. *Dictatorship and Political Police*. New York: Oxford, 1945.

Brzezinski, Zbigniew. *The Permanent Purge*. Cambridge, Mass.: Harvard, 1956.

———, editor. *Political Controls in the Soviet Army*. New York, 1954.

Bullock, Alan. *Hitler. A Study in Tyranny*. London: Odhams, 1952.

Cammarata, Angelo. *La scuola del fascismo. Appunti di pedagogia militante per gli educatori*. Palermo: Trimarchi, 1938.

———. *Pedagogia di Mussolini alla scuola dell'Opera Balilla*. Palermo: Trimarchi, 2nd edition, revised, 1931.

Camus, Albert. *The Rebel*. New York: Knopf, 1954.

Canepa, Antonio. *L'organizzazione del P. N. F.* Palermo: Ciuni, 1939.

———. *Sistema di dottrina del fascismo*. 3 vols. Rome: Formiggini, 1937.

Canevari, Emilio. *Considerazioni politico-militari sopra due anni di guerra*. Rome: INCF, 1942.

Carbonaro, Salvatore. *Il Partito Nazionale Fascista e la sua struttura giuridica*. Florence: C. Cya, 1939.

Caristia, C. *Istituzioni di diritto pubblico*. Catania, 1932.

Chandler, A. R. *Rosenberg's Nazi Myth*. Ithaca, N. Y.: Cornell, 1945.

Chiapetti, Niccolo. *Il Fascio di Combattimento e il Gruppo Rionale fascista*. Rome: Signorelli, 1937.

Childs, H. L., editor. *The Nazi Primer*. New York and London: Harper, 1938.

Chimienti, Pietro. *L'organizzazione nazionale fascista nel diritto pubblico italiano*. Turin: Bocca, 1928.

———. *Manuale di diritto costituzionale fascista*. Turin: UTET, 1933.

Cione, Edmondo. *Storia della Repubblica Sociale Italiana*. Rome: Latinità, 1951.

Circolo giuridico di Milano. *Gli stati europei a partito politico unico*. Milan: Panorama, 1936. (Papers by Oreste Ranelletti, Carl Schmitt, and Gaspare Ambrosini.)

Cobban, Alfred. *Dictatorship. Its Theory and Practice*. New York: Scribner's, 1939.

Cole, Taylor, editor. *European Political Systems*. New York: Knopf, 1953. (Chapter on Italy by Renzo Sereno, on Germany by Sigmund Neumann.)

Coles, S. F. A. *Franco of Spain*. London: Neville, Spearman, 1955.
Colitto, F. *Beni del soppresso partito fascista*. Rome, 1949.
Comitato Intersindacale Provinciale di Torino. *Il Partito nella vita economica della provincia di Torino*. Turin: PNF, 1937.
Consiglio di Stato. *Il Consiglio di Stato nel quinquennio 1936–1940. Relazione al Duce del fascismo Capo del Governo*. 2 vols. Rome: Istituto Poligrafico dello Stato, 1942.
Corradini, Enrico. *Il nazionalismo italiano*. Milan: Treves, 1914.
Corsini, Vincenzo. *Il Capo del Governo nello Stato fascista*. Bologna: Zanichelli, 1935.
Costamagna, Carlo. *Elementi di diritto pubblico fascista*. Turin: UTET, 1934.
———. *Storia e dottrina del fascismo*. Turin: UTET, 1938.
Curcio, Carlo. *Il Partito Nazionale Fascista*. Rome: ICE, 1943.
Della Torre, G. *A. C. e fascismo: conflitto del 1931*. Rome: Veritas, 1945.
Di Massa, Sebastiano. *Burocrazia fascista*. Rome: L'ordine Corporativo, 1937.
Di Zinno, Girolamo. *Lo schiavismo dell'Opera Balilla visto da vicino*. Viareggio, 1953.
Duverger, Maurice. *Les partis politiques*. Paris: Armand Colin, 1951.
Einaudi, Luigi. *Il buongoverno*. Bari: Laterza, 1954.
Ercole, Francesco. *La Rivoluzione fascista*. Palermo: Ciuni, 1935.
Fainsod, Merle. *How Russia Is Ruled*. Cambridge, Mass.: Harvard, 1953.
———. *Smolensk under Soviet Rule*. Cambridge, Mass.: Harvard, 1958. (Study based on the Smolensk party Archive.)
Fanelli, G. A. *Contra Gentiles mistificazioni dell'idealismo attuale nella Rivoluzione fascista*. Rome: "Il Secolo Fascista," 1933.
———. *Idee e polemiche per la scuola Fascista*. Rome: Cremonese, 1941.
———. *Saggi sul corporativismo fascista*. Rome: "Il Secolo Fascista," 1936.
Fantini, O. *Il Partito fascista*. Rome: Editrice Italiana Attualità, 1931.
Farinacci, Roberto. *Un periodo aureo del Partito Nazionale Fascista*. Foligno: Campitelli, 1927. Edited by Renzo Bacchetta. (Speeches of Farinacci during the period of his leadership of the party.)
———. *Squadrismo. Dal mio diario della vigilia, 1919–1922*. Rome: Ardita, 3rd edition, 1934.
Farmer, Paul. *Vichy. Political Dilemma*. New York: Columbia, 1955.
Fascist Confederation of Industrialists. *The Fascist Era*. Rome, 1939.
Ferrari, Santo. *L'Italia fascista. Nozioni di dottrina fascista ad uso delle scuole medie e professionali*. Turin: Libreria italiana, 4th edition, 1942.
Ferrarino, Luigi. *La Crisi della scuola e la Riforma Bottai*. Pisa: Vallerini, 1940.
Festa, N. C. *La Nazione guerriera. Esercito-Milizia-Partito*. Rome, 1935.
Finer, Herman. *Mussolini's Italy*. London: Gollancz, 1935.
Flora, Francesco, editor. *Stampa dell'era fascista. Le note di servizio*. Rome: Mondadori, 1945. (Collection of orders of "Minculpop.")
Fossani, I. *Esercito e Milizia*. Mantua: Paladino, 1923.
Fraenkel, Ernst. *The Dual State*. New York and London: Oxford, 1941.
Franck, Louis R. *Les étapes de l'économie fasciste italienne*. Paris: Libraire sociale et économique, 1939.
Friedrich, C. J. *Constitutional Government and Democracy*. Boston: Ginn, revised edition, 1950.
———, editor. *Totalitarianism*. Cambridge, Mass.: Harvard, 1954.
Friedrich, C. J., and Z. K. Brzezinski. *Totalitarian Dictatorship and Autocracy*. Cambridge, Mass.: Harvard, 1956.
Garosci, Aldo. *Storia dei fuorusciti*. Bari: Laterza, 1953.
Gentile, Giovanni. *Che cosa è il fascismo*. Florence: Vallecchi, 1925.
———. *Fascismo e cultura*. Milan: Treves, 1928.
———. *Genesi e struttura della società*. Florence: Sansoni, 1936.
———. *Origini e dottrina del fascismo*. Rome: INCF, 1929.
Gerth, Hans, and C. Wright Mills. *Character and Social Structure*. New York: Harcourt, Brace, 1953.

169

The Italian Fascist Party in Power

————, editors. *From Max Weber: Essays in Sociology.* New York: Oxford, 1946.

Giglio, Carlo. *Partito e Impero.* Rome: Palazzo Brancaccio, 1939.

Gramondo, Rinaldo. *Il Segretario del Fascio di Combattimento.* Milan: OLM, 1938.

Gratton, Giulio. *Origine ed evoluzione dei partiti politici.* Trieste: Zigliotti, 1946.

Gravelli, Asvero. *I canti della rivoluzione.* Rome: Nuova Europa, 1934.

————, ed. *Vademecum dello stile fascista.* Rome: Nuova Europa, 1939.

Graziani, Rodolfo. *Processo Graziani.* 3 vols. Rome: Ruffolo, 1948.

Gropallo, Enrico. *Il Partito unico.* Rome: Diritto del lavoro, 1935.

Gruliow, Leo, editor. *Current Soviet Policies; the Documentary Record of the 19th Communist Party Congress and the Reorganization after Stalin's Death.* New York: Praeger, 1953.

Haider, Carmen. *Capital and Labor under Fascism.* New York: Columbia, 1930.

Hallowell, John H. *The Decline of Liberalism as an Ideology.* Berkeley and Los Angeles: University of California, 1943.

Heberle, Rudolf. *Social Movements.* New York: Appleton-Century-Crofts, 1951.

Heiden, Konrad. *Der Fuehrer. Hitler's Rise to Power.* Boston: Houghton, Mifflin, 1944.

Henderson, A. M., and Talcott Parsons, editors. *Max Weber: The Theory of Social and Economic Organization.* New York: Oxford, 1947.

Hitler, Adolf. *Die Reden Hitlers am Parteitag der Freiheit 1935.* Munich: Eher Nachf., 1935.

————. *Mein Kampf.* New York: Reynal and Hitchcock, 1939.

Hughes, E. J. *Report from Spain.* New York: Holt, 1947.

Hughes, H. Stuart. *The United States and Italy.* Cambridge, Mass.: Harvard, 1953.

Hussard, V. *Du parti à l'état.* Paris, 1935.

Ignotus. *Stato fascista, Chiesa e Scuola.* Rome: Libreria del Littorio, 1929.

Jacini, Stefano. *Il Regime fascista.* Milan: Garzanti, 1947.

Jemolo, A. C. *Chiesa e Stato in Italia negli ultimi cento anni.* Turin: Einaudi, 3rd edition, 1952.

Koellreutter, Otto. *Deutsches Verfassungsrecht.* Berlin: Junker und Dünnhaupt, 1935.

————. *Volk und Staat in der Weltanschauung des Nationalsozialismus.* Berlin: Junker und Dünnhaupt, 1935.

Kogon, Eugen. *The Theory and Practice of Hell.* New York: Farrar, Straus, 1950.

Landini, Pietro. *La dottrina del fascismo.* Florence: La Nuova Italia, 1936.

————. *La nuova coscienza nazionale.* Rome: ano. tipo-editoriale, 1933.

————. *Lo stato imperiale fascista.* Pistoia: Tariffi, 1937.

Leites, Nathan. *A Study of Bolshevism.* Glencoe, Ill.: Free Press, 1953.

Levi, Carlo. *Cristo si è fermato a Eboli.* Turin: Einaudi, 5th edition, 1947.

Lochner, Louis, editor. *The Goebbels Diaries.* New York: Doubleday, 1948.

Ludwig, Emil, *Colloqui con Mussolini.* Verona: Mondadori, 1950.

Luizzi, B. *Il Partito Nazionale Fascista nel diritto pubblico italiano.* Rome, 1930.

Magno, Gino. *Il Partito Nazionale Fascista per l'ordinamento corporativo.* Alessandria: Grasso, 1935.

Malfi, Erasmo. *Scuola e G. I. L.* Rome: Palazzotti, 1939.

Manoïlesco, Mihaïl. *Le parti unique.* Paris: Les oeuvres français, 1937.

Manuel, Frank. *The New World of Henri Saint-Simon.* Cambridge, Mass.: Harvard, 1956.

Marinetti, F. T. *Futurismo e fascismo.* Foligno: Campitelli, 1924.

Marpicati, Arturo. *Il Partito fascista: origine, sviluppo, funzioni.* Milan: Mondadori, 1935.

————, M. Gallian, and L. Contu. *La dottrina del fascismo. Storia, opere, ed istituti.* Milan: Hoepli, 1935.

Melchiori, Alessandro. *Il P. N. F. nei suoi nuovi ordinamenti.* Rome: Quaderni di "Milizia Fascista," 1933.

————. *Milizia fascista.* Rome: Luzzati, 1929.

Meletti, Vincenzo. *Civiltà fascista.* Florence: La Nuova Italia, 1941.

170

———. *Il Libro fascista del Balilla*. Florence: La Nuova Italia, 1936.
Mende, Raul A. *Justicialism: The Peronist Doctrine and Reality*. Buenos Aires: López Péru, 1952.
Mezzasoma, F. *Essenza dei G. U. F.* Genoa: GUF, 1937.
Miceli, V. *Il Partito fascista e la sua funzione in Italia*. Milan: Arti Grafiche, 1934.
Michels, Roberto. *Political Parties. A Sociological Study of the Oligarchical Tendencies of Modern Democracy*. Glencoe, Ill.: Free Press, 1949.
Milizia, Comando Generale. *M.V.S.N. XV, XVI, XVIII,* and *XIX Annuale*. Rome, 1937–1940.
———. *La Milizia per l'Impero*. Rome, 1937.
Momigliano, Eucardio. *Storia tragica e grottesca del razzismo fascista*. Verona: Mondadori, 1946.
Monelli, Paolo. *Mussolini piccolo borghese*. Milan: Garzanti, 4th edition, 1954.
Montemaggiori, Amerigo. *Dizionario della dottrina fascista*. Turin: Paravia, 1934.
Moore, Barrington. *Terror and Progress USSR*. Cambridge, Mass.: Harvard, 1954.
Mussolini, Benito. *La dottrina del fascismo*. Rome: Treves-Trecanni-Tumminelli, 1933.
———. *Scritti e discorsi di Benito Mussolini*. 12 vols. Milan: Hoepli, 1934.
———. *Opera Omnia di Benito Mussolini*. Florence: La Fenice, in press.
Neesse, Gottfried. *Die Nationalsozialistische deutsche Arbeiter-partei*. Stuttgart: Kohlhammer, 1935.
———. *Partei und Staat*. Hamburg: Hanseatische Verlag, 1936.
Neumann, Franz. *Behemoth: The Structure and Practice of National Socialism*. London: Gollancz, 1942.
Neumann, Sigmund. *Permanent Revolution*. New York and London: Harper, 1942.
Pantaleo, Paolo. *Il fascismo cremonese*. Cremona: PNF, 1931.
Panunzio, Sergio. *Teoria generale dello Stato fascista*. Padua: Cedam, 1939.
Partito Nazionale Fascista. *Dizionario di politica*. 4 vols. Rome: IEI, 1940.
———. *Exhibition of the Fascist Revolution*. Bergamo: Arti grafiche, 1933.
———. *Il primo libro del fascismo*. Verona: Mondadori, 1942.
———. *Testi per i corsi di preparazione politica: Il Partito*. Rome: Libreria dello Stato, 1936.
———. [Ufficio Propaganda.] *Agenda annuario anno XX*. Rome: PNF, 1941.
———. [Ufficio Stampa.] *Venti anni*. Rome, 1942.
Pellizzi, Camillo. *Una rivoluzione mancata*. Milan: Longanesi, 1949.
Pelloux, R. *Le Parti national-socialiste et ses rapports avec l'Etat*. Paris: Hartmann, 1936.
Peronist Doctrine. Buenos Aires, 1952.
Piccoli, D. S. *The Youth Movement in Italy*. Rome: Novissima, 1936.
Pini, G., and D. Susmel. *Mussolini. L'uomo e l'opera. Dalla Dittatura all'Impero (1925–1938)*. Vol. III. Florence: La Fenice, 1955.
Plamenatz, John. *German Marxism and Russian Communism*. London: Longmans, 1954.
Pratesi, Luigi. *Corso per Balilla e Piccole Italiane*. Rome, 1941.
———. *L'Italia imperiale. Corso di cultura per la nuova gioventù italiana*. Livorno: Giusti, 1937.
Pre, Roland. *L'organization des rapports économiques et sociaux dans les pays a régime corporatif*. Paris: Libraire Technique et Economique, 1936.
Prélot, Marcel. *L'Empire fasciste*. Paris: Recueil Sirey, 1936.
Raspa, Edmondo. *Educazione ballilistica*. Catania: "La Stampa," 1937.
Reitlinger, Gerald. *The Final Solution*. London: Vallentine, Mitchell, 1953.
Riccio, G. *Storia del partito*. Turin: Vercelli, 1938.
Romano, Santi. *Corso di diritto costituzionale*. Padua: Cedam, 1933.
Rosenberg, Alfred. *Blut und Ehre. Gestaltung der Idee*. 2 vols. Munich: Zentralverlag der NSDAP, F. Eher, 1938.
———. *Der Mythus des 20. Jahrhunderts*. Munich: Hoheneichen, 1935.

171

The Italian Fascist Party in Power

Rossi, A. *A Communist Party in Action*. New Haven: Yale, 1949.
Rossi, Cesare. *Il tribunale speciale*. Milan: Ceschina, 1952.
Rossi, Ernesto. *I padroni del vapore*. Bari: Laterza, 1952.
Rousset, David. *Les jours de nôtre mort*. Paris: Editions du Pavois, 1947.
Salvatorelli, Luigi, and Giovanni Mira. *Storia del fascismo. L'italia dal 1919 al 1945*. Rome: Novissima, 1952.
Salvemini, Gaetano. *Mussolini diplomatico*. Bari: Laterza, 1952.
———. *Sotto la scure del fascismo*. Turin: De Silva, 1948.
Schmidt, Carl T. *The Corporate State in Action*. New York: Oxford, 1939.
Schneider, H. W. *Making the Fascist State*. New York: Oxford, 1928.
——— and Shepard B. Clough. *Making Fascists*. Chicago: University of Chicago Press, 1929.
Sears, Bixio. *Disegno storico della pratica amministrativa del P. N. F.* Ferrara, 1941.
Semmler, Rudolf. *Goebbels — The Man next to Hitler*. London: Westhouse, 1947.
Silone, Ignazio. *Bread and Wine*. London: Methuen, 1936.
———. *The School for Dictators*. New York: Harper, 1938.
Silvestri, Carlo. *I responsabili della catastrofe*. Milan: CEBES, 1946.
———. *Matteotti, Mussolini e il dramma italiano*. Rome: Ruffolo, 1947.
Sinagra, Vincenzo. *Profilo storico del Partito Nazionale Fascista*, Vol. I. Rome, 1938.
Sington, Derrick, and Arthur Weidenfeld. *The Goebbels Experiment*. London: Murray, 1942.
Spaventa, Renato. *Burocrazia, ordinamenti amministrativi e fascismo*. Milan: Treves, 1928.
Spencer, H. R. *The Government and Politics of Italy*. Yonkers, N. Y., 1932.
Spirito, Ugo. *Capitalismo e corporativismo*. Florence: Sansoni, 3rd edition, revised, 1934.
Starace, Achille. *Fasci Giovanili di Combattimenti*. Verona: Mondadori, 1933.
———. *Gioventù Italiana del Littorio*. Milan: Mondadori, 1939.
———. *La marcia su Gondar*. Milan: Mondadori, 1936.
———. *L'Opera Nazionale Dopolavoro*. Verona: Mondadori, 1933.
Steiner, H. Arthur. *Government in Fascist Italy*. New York: McGraw-Hill, 1938.
Susmel, D. *Carteggio Arnaldo-Benito Mussolini*. Florence: La Fenice, 1954.
Talmon, J. L. *The Rise of Totalitarian Democracy*. Boston: Beacon, 1952.
Tamaro, Attilio. *Venti anni di storia, 1922–1943*. 3 vols. Rome: Tiber, 1954.
Tasca, Angelo. *Nascita e avvento del fascismo. L'Italia dal 1918 al 1922*. Florence: La Nuova Italia, 1950.
Teruzzi, Attilio. *La Milizia*. Milan: Mondadori, 1933.
Tiltman, H. Hessell. *The Terror in Europe*. London: Jarrolds, 1931.
Tönnies, Ferdinand. *Fundamental Concepts of Sociology*. New York: American Book Company, 1940.
Treves, Giuseppino. *Regolamento intersindacale dei rapporti del lavoro*. Turin: Giappichelli, 1931.
Turati, Augusto. *Il Partito e i suoi compiti*. Rome: Libreria del Littorio, 1928.
———. *La dottrina fascista*. Rome: Libreria del Littorio, 1923.
———. *Ragioni, ideali di vita fascista*. Rome: Berlutti, 1926.
———. *Un anno di vita del partito*. Milan: Libreria d'Italia, 1929.
———. *Una rivoluzione e un capo*. Rome: Libreria del Littorio, 1927.
Vagts, Alfred. *Hitler's Second Army*. Washington, D.C.: Infantry Journal, 1943.
Vettori, Vittorio, editor. *Giovanni Gentile*. Florence: La Fenice, 1954.
Villani, Luigi. *Storia diplomatica del conflitto italo-etiopico*. Bologna: Zanichelli, 1942.
Wheeler-Bennett, J. W. *The Nemesis of Power*. New York: St. Martin's, 1954.
Zammarchi, Angelo. *Il libro della IV classe elementare*. Rome: Libreria dello Stato, 1941.
Zangara, Vincenzo. *Il partito e lo stato*. Catania: Studio Edit. Moderno, 1935.
———. *Il partito unico e il nuovo stato rappresentativo in Italia e in Germania*. Bologna: Zanichelli, 1938.
Zincone, Vittorio, editor. *Hitler e Mussolini: lettere e documenti*. Milan: Rizzoli, 1946.

Articles and Essays

Critica Fascista, edited by Bottai, was the periodical of the "corporativist left" and contains a number of articles of a polemical nature which reveal a great deal about the internal situation in Fascist Italy. Directly opposed to this journal was *Il Secolo Fascista*, edited by G. A. Fanelli. This was one of the organs of the "old guard." *Gerarchia*, personally supervised by Mussolini, is more official and therefore duller. *Civiltà Fascista* (until 1934 called *Educazione Fascista*) was edited by Gentile and is more scholarly than any of the above.

The party youth organizations published the following periodicals: *Gioventù Fascista*, *Passo Romano-Vincere*, *Libro e Moschetto*, *Il Balilla*, *Bolletino della GIL*, and *La Piccola Italiana*.

Agresti, A. "Il Partito come organo di controllo nell'ordinamento sindacale-corporativo," *Lo Stato Corporativo*, IV (1937), 2–3.

Allegretti, Franco. "Il Partito e la Corporazione nello Stato Fascista," *I Littoriali della Cultura e dell'Arte dell'Anno XIV*. Rome, 1936. Pp. 25–27.

Arendt, Hannah. "Ideology and Terror: A Novel Form of Government," *Review of Politics*, XV (July 1953), 303–329.

———. "Parteien und Bewegungen," *Die Wandlung*, VI (June 1949), 459–473.

Aspaturian, V. A. "The Contemporary Doctrine of the Soviet State and Its Philosophical Foundations," *American Political Science Review*, XLVIII (December 1954), 1031–1057.

Berlindo, Giannetti. "Il Partito come forza militare," *I Littoriali . . . dell'Anno XIV*, 1936, pp. 173–207.

Bernasconi, Umberto. "I corsi di preparazione politica," *Gioventù Fascista*, June 1, 1935, p. 12.

Bertoni, R. "Funzioni ed avvenire del Partito unitario," *Gerarchia*, XIV (January 1934), 41–44.

Boerner, A. V. "The Position of the NSDAP in the . . . German State," *American Political Science Review*, XXXII (December 1938), 1059–1082.

Bottai, Giuseppe. "Partito e ordinamento corporativo," *Critica Fascista*, XIV (October 15, 1936), 369–370.

Caneva, Giovanni. "Comitati intersindacali e consigli provinciale dell'economia," *Critica Fascista*, XIV (June 1, 1936), 226–228.

———. "Il Partito e le sue funzioni," *Critica Fascista*, XIV (September 15, 1936), 343.

Carbonaro, S. "La missione educativa del Partito," *Rassegna Corporativo*, 1937, no. 2.

Casini, G. "Il Partito e le corporazioni," *Critica Fascista*, XI (June 1933), 201–203.

Cavallucci, Guido. "Il corporativismo di Spirito," *Il Secolo Fascista*, October 1, 1933, pp. 367–368.

Cervesato, Arnaldo. "Fondazione e imagine di Roma," *Gerarchia*, XV (April 1935), 302–306.

Cole, Taylor. "The Evolution of the German Labor Front," *Political Science Quarterly*, LII (December 1937), 532–558.

———. "Italy's Fascist Bureaucracy," *American Political Science Review*, XXXII (December 1938), 1143–1158.

Colucci, A. "Stato e Partito," *Rassegna Nazionale* (March 1937).

De Francisci, Pietro. "Continuità di Roma," *Gerarchia*, XV (January 1935), 6–17.

De Mattei, R. "Verso il Partito unico," *Civiltà Fascista*, III (January 1936).

Di Bitello, R. "L'evoluzione della funzioni ed attribuzioni del Segretario del PNF," *Atti dei Corsi di Preparazione Politica dell'Urbe*. Rome, 1937.

Di Nardi, Giuseppe. "Le direttive del Partito per l'autarchia," *Civiltà Fascista*, V (December 1938), 1085–1092.

Duffield, Marcus. "Mussolini's American Empire," *Harper's Magazine*, CLIX (November 1929), 661–672.

Fainsod, Merle. "Controls and Tensions in the Soviet System," *American Political Science Review*, XLIV (June 1950), 266–283.

——. "Postwar Role of the Communist Party," *Annals of the American Academy of Political and Social Science*, CCLXIII (May 1949), 20–32.

Fanelli, G. A. "Idee sul Partito," *Il Secolo Fascista*, September 30, 1932.

——. "Il Partito, Signori, il Partito," *Il Secolo Fascista*, October 1, 1933.

——. "Questa nemica scuola," *Il Secolo Fascista*, March 1–April 1, 1933.

Fiorioli della Lena, G. "I partiti nel Partito," *Critica Fascista*, VIII (October 1930), 383–385.

Foderaro, S. "Posizione costitutzionale della M.V.S.N.," *Rivista di Diritto Pubblico*, XXX (1938), 312–328.

Freri, O. "L'avvenire della M.V.S.N.," *Gerarchia*, VIII (April 1930), 293–302.

Gerth, Hans. "The Nazi Party: Its Leadership and Composition," *American Journal of Sociology*, XLV (January 1940), 517–541.

Giardini, Dino. "Le rôle du parti unique dans l'économie fasciste," *Revue Economique Internationale*, III (September 1935), 436–451.

Giovenale, B. "La GIL," *Critica Fascista*, XV (October 1937), 404–405.

Giurco, E. "Il Partito unico," *Lo Stato*, VIII (1937), 162–167, 501–504.

Guglielmi, Nino. "Roma, il fascismo e l'impero," *Gerarchia*, XV (September 1935), 755–759.

Hayes, C. J. H. "The Novelty of Totalitarianism in the History of Western Civilization," *Proceedings of the American Philosophical Association*, LXXXII (1940, no. 1), 91–102.

Iannarelli, R. "Stato corporativo e Partito," *Critica Fascista*, VIII (August 1930), 307–309.

Jemolo, A. C. "Natura giuridica del PNF," *Rivista di Diritto Pubblico* XXI (Part 1, 1929), 544–555.

Lasswell, H. D., and Renzo Sereno, "Governmental and Party Leaders in Fascist Italy," *American Political Science Review*, XXXI (October 1937), 914–932.

Lessona, A. "Partito e Stato," *Gerarchia*, X (February 1930), 92–94.

Levi, Lionello R. "L'organizzazione corporativa locale," *Critica Fascista* (May 15, 1936), pp. 222–224.

Longhi, S. "Il Partito fascista organo dello Stato," *Rassegna Penale*, VII (1929), 701–702.

Malvagna, S. "Partito Nazionale Fascista," *Dizionario Politica*, III, 381–392.

Marroni, C. "L'organizzazione dei giovani nel Partito," *Critica Fascista*, VIII (June 1930), 215.

Melchiori, Alessandro. Leading editorial in *Milizia Fascista*, September 30, 1928.

Michels, Roberto. "Some Reflections on the Sociological Character of Political Parties," *American Political Science Review*, XXI (November 1927), 761–772.

Ranelletti, O. "Il Partito Nazionale Fascista nello Stato italiano," *Rivista di diritto pubblico*, XXVIII (Part 1, 1936), 15–33, and 203.

Ritter, Gerhard. "The German Professor in the Third Reich," *Review of Politics*, VIII (April 1946), 242–254.

Rocco, Alfredo. "The Political Doctrine of Fascism," *International Conciliation*, no. 223 (October 1926).

Salemi, G. "L'organizzazione nazionale del Partito fascista e i suoi rapporti con lo Stato," *Rivista di Diritto Pubblico*, XXVIII (Part 1, 1936), 309–330.

Scaligero, Massimo. "Il Centro nazionale di preparazione politica per i giovani," *Regime Fascista*, August 14, 1938, p. 1.

Steiner, H. Arthur. "The Constitutional Position of the *Partito Nazionale Fascista*," *American Political Science Review*, XXXI (April 1937), 227–243.

——. "The Italian Law on Communal and Provincial Government," *National Municipal Review*, XXV (September 1936), 520–528.

Stratta, Giuseppe. "Il Partito e la sua funzione," *Critica Fascista*, XIV (August 1, 1936), 291–293.

Bibliography

Vecchiarelli, Armando. "Comitati Intersindacale e Consigli Provinciali dell'Economia Corporativa," *I Littoriali* . . . *dell'Anno XIV*, 1936, pp. 71–89.

Verna, F. "Il P. N. F., 'associazione privata'?" *Rivista Penale*, III (Part 1, 1932), 603–609.

Newspapers

The most important Fascist newspaper was the *Popolo d'Italia*, founded by Mussolini in 1915 after his break with the Socialists over intervention. It was published in Milan. After the March on Rome, the paper was first edited by Mussolini's brother, Arnaldo, and then by Giorgio Pini.

The views of the party hard core are found most faithfully represented in *Regime Fascista* (before 1925 named *Cremona Nuova*), published in Cremona and edited by Farinacci. Another extremist newspaper was *L'Impero* of Rome, edited by Luigi Setiminelli. Both of these journals had a wide national following, and they gave a large amount of space to reporting activities of the party.

Il Lavoro Fascista, published in Genoa and edited by Luigi Fontanelli, was the daily of the "corporativist left" in much the same way that *Critica Fascista* served as their periodical. Much of Fascism's seamier side may be gleaned from this journal, for it was left comparatively free of censorship.

The most important and most useful of the weeklies of the provincial fasci of the PNF are *L'Assalto* (Bologna), *Il Bargello* (Florence), *Stile Fascista* (Fiume), *Il Popolo di Lombardia* (Milan), *Il Popolo di Sicilia* (Palermo), *Vincere* (Cagliari), *Il Popolo delle Alpi* (Turin), *Italia Nuova* (Venice), *La Voce di Bergamo* (Bergamo), *Il Popolo di Trieste* (Trieste). Party federations published a total of sixty-seven such weeklies; these journals concentrated exclusively on party activities in their respective provinces.

Index

Albania, conquest of, 12, 30
Alti commissari (party officials), 95
Anti-Semitism: as Fascist policy, 12; campaign of *1938*, 23–24, 27–29; purge of Jews in PNF, 60
Apparat, of PNF, 32–33, 37, 46, 48
Arbeitsdienst program, influence on Fascism, 102
Arendt, Hannah: on Church and State, 67; on party oaths, 94; on army under Fascism, 106; view of Fascism challenged, 132–144 *passim*; on Church under Fascism, 139, 164n47; on "potential enemy," 142; on Fascist corporativism, 163n39
Argentina, single party in, 127, 162n10
Aristotle, and tyranny, 4, 19, 20
Armellini, General Quirino, on army and PNF, 112, 113
Army, Fascist: premilitary training, 110–111; party control of veterans, 111; relations with PNF, 112–114, 160n47; officers forced to join PNF, 113. *See also* MVSN
Arpinati, Leandro: as provincial party chief, 47; relieved of office, 88–89
Associations, Fascist, 41–42, 90–92, 111. *See also* Bureaucracy; Education
Atatürk, Kemal, and Turkish party, 126
Autarky, Fascist economic policy, 43–44
Aventine Secession, 11
Azione Cattolica (AC), *see* Catholic Action

Badoglio, General Pietro: critical of PNF, 113; replaces De Bono, 115
Baistrocchi, General Federico, trial of, 112–114
Balbo, Italo: opposes anti-Semitism, 28; mentioned, 8, 15
Balilla, see ONB

Bastianini, Giuseppe, 33
Bazan, General Enrico, on MVSN, 109
Berdiaev, Nicholas, 5
Berlinzola case, 156n34
Berns, Walter, on Fascist Italy, 132
Bianchi, Michele, as secretary, 33
Binchy, D. A., on Church and State, 139
Bocchini, Arturo (head of OVRA): organizes secret police, 117–118; compared to Himmler, 119, 122; power of, 124
Bolzon, Piero, attacks Ministry of Education, 101
Bonomi, Ivanoe, 6
Bormann, Martin, 84
Bottai, Giuseppe (minister of corporations, minister of education): as moderate, 15, 18; announces *Carta della Scuola,* 102; on role of PNF, 136; on "change of guard," 151n10; mentioned, 8
Brzezinski, Z. K., on youth groups, 71
Buffarini-Guidi, Guido (minister of interior): conflicts with Bocchini, 119; power of, 124
Bureaucracy: government employees' "associations," 41, 90–92; employees forced to join PNF, 54, 93–94; clashes with PNF, 84–94; Foreign Office purged, 88

Camus, Albert, on single party, 24
Canepa, Antonio: on prefects, 96; writes Fascist text, 102
Canevari, Emilio, on MVSN, 107
Carta del Lavoro, see Charter of Labor
Carta della Scuola: provisions of, 72; announced, 102
Catechism, Fascist, for youth organizations, 70, 136

Ludwig, Emil, conversations with Mussolini, 57

Machiavelli, Niccolò, 4
Manoïlesco, Mihaïl, on totalitarian parties, 161–162n8
March on Rome, 6, 10. *See also* Rome
Marinelli, Giovanni (administrative secretary), power of, 33, 38, 151n16
Marinetti, F. T., 147n6
Matteotti, Giacomo, murdered, 10
Maurano, Silvio, attacks Ministry of Education, 101
Messianism, political, 5
Michels, Roberto: on PNF, 32; on party leadership schools, 79
Military, *see* Army, Fascist
Militia, *see* MVSN
Milizia Volontaria per la Sicurezza Nazionale, see MVSN
Ministry of Popular Culture (Minculpop): Pavolini as chief, 39; described, 140; control of press, 164n50
Mira, Giovanni, on bureaucracy, 93
Missiroli, Mario, 89
Moderates, Fascist: leading figures among, 15, 149n29; oppose anti-Semitism, 28; oppose entry into war, 30
Molotov, V. I., 5
Montesquieu, Charles de Secondat de, on despotism, 20
Moore, Barrington, on party and state, 124
Moravia, Alberto, 139
Mussolini, Benito: views on party, 3, 18–19, 20, 39; early career, 7; "intransigent" speech, 11; relations with PNF, 18–19, 36, 39, 95, 96; and racism, 27, 150n38; totalitarian temperament, 31; *Capo del Partito*, 36; talks with Ludwig, 57; disbands Catholic youth groups, 65; "Circular to the Prefects," 95, 96; on MVSN, 106–107; overthrown and imprisoned, 116–117; rescued by Nazis, 116; attempts on life of, 118, 119; influenced by Gentile, 134; predicts Fascist Europe, 137; shot, 142; attitude toward plebiscites, 149n14; First Marshal of the Empire, 158n3; mentioned, 5, 10
Muti, Ettore (secretary of PNF), opens membership lists, 56
MVSN (*Milizia Volontaria per la Sicurezza Nazionale*): established, 106, 107; development, 107–110; decalogue, 108; relations with army, 109; membership statistics,

109; compared with SA, 110; used in war, 114–117; prayer, 158n11

Napoleon III, censorship under, 140
Nationalsozialistische deutsche Arbeiterpartei, see NSDAP
Nazism: ideology, 5, 148n2; influence on Fascism, 27, 30. *See also* NSDAP
Neo-Fascism: strength in south, 75; ideological origins, 165n62
Neumann, Franz, on bureaucracy, 84
Neumann, Sigmund, on Fascism, 132
Nitti, Francesco, 6
Non abbiamo bisogno (encyclical): attacks "statolatry," 65; opposed by PNF, 66
NSDAP (*Nationalsozialistische deutsche Arbeiterpartei*): structure, 33, 37, 129–130; old guard, 49; recruitment policy, 51. *See also* Nazism
Nudi, Francesco, 118

Oath, Fascist: required of all party members, 94; required of professors, 157n64
ONB (*Opera Nazionale Balilla*): founded, 63; membership statistics, 72
OND (*Opera Nazionale Dopolavoro*): founded, 41; compared with *Kraft durch Freude*, 41; activities, 42; membership statistics, 43
Opera Nazionale Maternità ed Infanzia, 44
Opera Volontaria per la Repressione Antifascista, see OVRA
Orano, Paolo: attacks Ministry of Education, 101; as Fascist theorist, 135; mentioned, 80
Organization of Vigilance for the Repression of Anti-Fascism, *see* OVRA
Orlandi, Dario, 87
Orwell, George, on inner party, 33
OVRA (*Opera Volontaria per la Repressione Antifascista*): protector of regime, 105; organized, 117–118. *See also* Police, secret; Terror

Panunzio, Sergio, 135
Parties, political: definition, 17; uniqueness of totalitarian, 17. *See also* CPSU; NSDAP; PNF
Partito Nazionale Fascista, see PNF
Pavolini, Alessandro (minister of popular culture), power of, 39
Penal islands, 120, 164–165n58
Perón, Juan: ousted, 117; and party-army relations, 127
Personalunion, Nazi administrative technique of, 129, 162n18

and authority, 119–121; PNF control of, 121

Speer, Albert, 84

Squads of action: leaders of, 8; early activities of, 9; and anti-Semitism, 29; and use of terror, 47

SS (*Schutzstaffel*): as part of Nazi inner circle, 53; compared with OVRA, 122

Stalin, J. V., 5, 39, 128

Stampa, La, 139

Starace, Achille: importance as secretary, 15–16; and anti-Semitism, 24, 28; and reform of custom, 26; method of inspection, 35; dictatorial, 38; as provincial party chief, 47; archetype of militant, 48; conducts purges, 60; feuds with Ricci, 68; expands party training schools, 78; purges Arpinati, 89; leads MVSN, 115; mentioned, 5, 8

Steiner, H. Arthur, on PNF, 124

Sturmabteilung, see SA

Style, Fascist, nature of, 163n37

Syndicates, controlled by PNF, 42

Talmon, J. L., 5

Teachers, *see* Education

Technology, and totalitarianism, 5

Terror, Fascist: *confino* as instrument of, 120; extent of, 122–123, 141; penal islands, 164–165n58; exaggerated view of, 164n55. *See also* OVRA; Police, secret; Squads of action

Teruzzi, Attilio (chief of MVSN), 87

Tiltman, H. Hessell, 164n55

Totalitarianism: uniqueness of, 4; genesis, 4–6; differing interpretations, 132; in Italy, 132–134; defined, 133; ideology, 163n28. *See also* PNF; Terror

Turati, Augusto (secretary of PNF): antimoderate, 15; as provincial party chief, 47; on new members, 53; limits use of purge, 58; disgraced, 59–60; appoints Guli head of police, 119; mentioned, 8

Turkey, 126

Tyranny, pre-totalitarian: nature of, 4; and terror, 19

Ufficio Propaganda del Partito, 45

"Uschla," Nazi party court, 151n7

Vichy France, and single party, 127–128

Victor Emmanuel III: as weak ruler, 7; calls Mussolini to be premier, 10

Vidoni Palace Pact, 151n27

Weber, Max, on totalitarian parties, 50

World War I, and rise of Fascism, 6

World War II, Fascist decision to enter, 30

Youth organizations, *see* Catholic youth organizations; Fascist youth organizations

Zaniboni, Tito, attempts to assassinate Mussolini, 119

Date Due

APR 1 6 1960		
APR 1 6 1960		
JUN 1 1964		
NOV 1 2 1964		
	PRINTED	IN U. S. A.